AJ KAYNATMA >> HIS TRAUMATIC BRAIN INJURY

AJ Kaynatma >> his Traumatic Brain Injury

AJ Kaynatma

[FYI: The "DOUBLE >" (>>) in the TITLE means (MATHEMATICALLY) "MUCH GREATER-than".]

Cover Design by Darja Filipovic.
Interior layout and design by www.writingnights.org
Book preparation by Chad Robertson

Readers should be aware that internet sites offered as citations and/or
sources for further information may have changed or disappeared between
the time this publication is made available, and when it is read.

24   23   22   21   20   19   18   17   8   7   6   5   4   3   2   1

DEDICATION

The brilliant ideas & humorous concepts of this book sprang forth from the [few] peers who braved the all too common MISunderstanding, that my brain injury is not some communicable disease. You will NOT catch TBI from just talking to me. It's NOT like cooties!

Y'all only wish some of my incredible brain-power could rub off on you.

EPIGRAPH

*One's best successes come after their greatest disappoint-
ments.*

—HENRY WARD BEECHER

CONTENTS

VOLUME 1 – THE MENTAL CRESTS AND TROUGHS OF A TURKISH KNIGHT WITH A TB: LIFE'S CHOCK FULL OF EXTREMA

VOLUME 2 – PHYSICALLY DEALING WITH THE INEVITABLE DROP OF A TBI

VOLUME 3 – THE PSYCHOLOGICAL REALMS OF A TBI VICTIM

FOREWORD

AJ was an anomaly, in all the best ways, before his accident at age 23. Nine years later, he is a still an anomaly but in very different ways. AJ's brain is unique, so his TBI is unique.

The reader should know something about AJ as a child and a young man, pre-accident. His personality was slightly different then. He had **MANY** reasons to brag but he never did. He was confident in himself but he didn't boast about it; he just did what he needed to do, and was almost always successful. He was competitive because he was obsessed with numbers, and still is. He was very self-motivated, driven to succeed in all he did. He was also a social animal: he would organize a bunch of people to play kickball, to have a party, to go to a sports event, to play trivia at a local bar, to do anything! He was very active. He mentions in his memoirs many of his accomplishments, academic and athletic; these are generally accurate. But again, pre-accident AJ would never brag about them. Also, he was funny and prone to practical jokes.

According to AJ's siblings------

His sister, Jeyda, 8 years younger, said AJ was "always" an *older brother*-type. Always teaching her relevant life lessons like campfire songs he learned in Boy Scouts. You know, along the lines of, "Hi. My name is Joe, and I work in a button factory. I've got a wife and a dog and a family..." It has a certain rhythm to it. He often impacted brotherly words of wisdom such as " You can pick your friends. You can pick your nose. But you can't pick your friend's nose." He much preferred being goofy to any brotherly mentorship. He begrudgingly checked over her math superstars extra credit assignments, for example, but was the first to stick out his tongue from across the dinner table when no one else was looking.

His younger brother, Bertan, recalls a few choice stories. OR, chose a few stories. He said,

AJ liked toilet humor (and still does). Once when I was driving someone else's car in the rain, AJ was in the back and a friend was in the front passenger seat. I was having trouble seeing out of the rear window. Somewhat anxiously I asked "Is there a rear wiper?" In return, a right hand was proffered from the back seat, coming through the center console, with AJ helpfully explaining, "I have my rear wiper right here," as if the hand he used to wipe his ass would be any use at the time. He always said this stuff with a grin on his face, not smarmy-like.

AJ was addicted to sports, and even as kids, bad weather or lack of equipment and/or? appropriate playing space, never stopped him. Once, when we were quite young, maybe 6 and 8, we decided to play some baseball, in the house. All we had was a baseball bat, but neither a ball nor appropriate playing space; it didn't stop AJ. (I followed his lead.) We had to stay inside, and the closest thing to a ball happened to be a balloon, and the closest thing to an outfield fence turned out to be our nearly floor to ceiling living room window. We soon discovered that, no matter how hard you hit a balloon, it doesn't travel far. This only encourages our inexperienced minds to hit it harder. I took a swung, and then handed it to AJ. In his defense, I believe his grip had not caught up with his arm strength, so as a result, he swung the bat, hit the balloon, and sent the bat flying out of his hands. It crashed straight through the enormous living room window and out into the front yard, leaving a cannonball-shaped hole in its wake. Not knowing what to do, I ran through the house in a panic, perhaps looking for a place to hide. At least it wasn't my fault.

A good example of AJ's antics is when he trapped his flatulence in a car full of people and locked all the windows. OR, I remember AJ's trapping . . . .

I always remember when we played neighborhood football; AJ was the sweatiest guy, and the hardest to tackle.

AJ is the king of nicknames. For me: Bert (from Bert and Ernie), Bertrum Grover Weeks (the movie, "Sandlot"), Bear, Bertrominator, Bartholomew, and just recently,

Berry Berry Boisenberry. (He's still got it!) As pledgemaster of the fraternity at his university, AJ nicknamed approximately 25 pledges for the year, 2006-07.

Post-accident: he is really funny, witty, language savvy. Boastful, it appears, but he explains that behavior as a need to prove himself. Still self-motivated and determined to succeed. Still stubborn. Often demanding and easily frustrated, as he copes with a growing ability to understand his own situation.

For context, AJ was previously known to quote a lot of movies, to recite sports stats, to excel in mental math and to use very correct grammar and good vocabulary. He can still do all of those things, but might forget a conversation you had with him an hour ago.

AJ doesn't remember the accident or the first two years afterwards. Memory protects us from trauma that way. He stayed at three different hospitals before he went to the long term rehab facility, 200 miles from home, where he lived for three years. We rented a trailer home outside the nearby town that whole time. AJ's best friend from childhood, Grant, and his girlfriend, L. stayed there, alternating weeks, for the first year, while I communicated with family and friends across the globe about AJ's challenges and achievements through an online blog. AJ's support system included his brother Bertan, who was in college; sister Jeyda, who was in high school, and my best friends, Grant's parents. Everyone took turns visiting on the weekends. Someone was always there with AJ.

When AJ got to the long term facility at the end of October 2008, he literally couldn't open his mouth because the spasticity clamped it shut. He was barely able to respond to yes/no questions with a thumbs up. He could sit in a wheelchair, with supports, but only for a short time. They used a Hoyer lift to transfer him from chair to and from his bed. He had a feeding tube from the beginning. AJ struggled through three kinds of grueling therapy (physical therapy, occupational therapy, and speech therapy) every day, five days a week, for three years. He never refused to do what a therapist wanted him to do, even though he could barely move ANY of his OWN BODY by himself. He, the two time black belt "Karate kid," could not roll over. I had to leave his therapy sessions many times because my heart broke to see his struggle. Yet, he never indicated he wanted to stop trying.

Almost three and a half years post-accident, AJ moved into his own house, closer to family and friends. This was possible because of a lawsuit settlement with the tire company.

(The cause of the accident was a defective, 9 year old tire that shredded on the highway.) He has caregivers 24/7, and two nurses for tube feeding. He's in a wheelchair most of the time, but he's working hard to walk at a special gym, with minimal assistance. AJ uses a spelling board to express himself. This is a homemade template of the QWERTY keyboard. He points to every letter of every word to spell out his thoughts, using complete sentences. AJ is now making progress using oral speech but he is still very hard to understand..

An observer can see the physical damage. The cognitive damage, however, is a mystery. It's easy to notice that he still has **WAY**-above average intelligence in several areas (especially math and vocabulary), an outrageous sense of humor and a very quick wit. BUT, there are significant deficits in his memory, processing abilities, perception, and judgment that are not so apparent. Neither is his limited emotional capacity. In fact, these are very hidden issues. These "hidden issues" are the direct result of his unique brain injury.

Please IMAGINE the reality of the aforementioned deficits. It is ESSENTIAL to keep these in mind when you're reading his book. His memory deficits are both long and short term so there are some inaccuracies in his story. His perception is often skewed or different from reality. For example, he mentioned in his book that "the government thought he was dead for two years." He perceived that his rights were "taken away" for that time. In fact, a full time guardian was appointed to MANAGE his rights: (the right to make medical decisions, the right to manage his finances, etc.) because he was completely unresponsive for a long time.

It's important to know something about his girlfriend, the love of his life. They dated for 8 months before the accident. She stayed with him for almost four years AFTER the accident. She didn't just visit him, she STAYED with him. In the beginning, she often slept overnight at the hospital; later, she spent every other week at the long term rehab facility, 3 hours away; and finally, she lived with him in his new home for over a year. Eventually she had to break away. You will read how AJ perceived her departure.

I have read a few books about TBI survivors, but those were written by fully recovered individuals, friends, or relatives of someone with a TBI, or perhaps ghostwriters. AJ has NOT RECOVERED from the diffuse axonal brain injury that he suffered 9 years ago. His brain is operating at MUCH LESS than its prior, exceptional capacity. Yet, he has written these memoirs. (Beware!)

His "voice", as he will explain, is evident in the WAY he writes. He cannot use his own, actual voice to emphasize what he wants to emphasize, so he uses a LOT of capital letters. He has several other idiosyncratic means to punctuate his writing, and some other peculiarities sprinkled in. But, it's all him! Bear with it— you will be fascinated!

This is HIS story, as HE perceived it.

— Martha Kaynatma (MOM)
11/16

PREFACE

Humor is a funny thing. What makes one joke side-splitting and another makes you pity the joke-teller? Even moreso, what makes some people inherently funnier than others to the point in which two people can tell the same joke or story, and one has people rolling and the other gets crickets?

Humor is one of those things where if you have to read a book on *'how to be funny'*, you're probably doing it wrong. It's sort of like art or music, in which you develop your own unique sense of style ... over-TIME ... and come to recognize it in others and in yourself.

As long as I've known AJ Kaynatma, he's always been someone whose humor I've recognized--it's hard to miss when it's loud, obnoxious, and in your face. But, I jest.

Now, this is not to say AJ was a standup comedian--that's his uncle Nick. He's just always had a way about him,

Whether it's a strategically deployed movie-quote, a festive or suggestive wardrobe-item, or a citation of no lesser an authority than Barney the Purple Dinosaur in his high school valedictory speech: AJ just makes you laugh.

At least he's always made me laugh. I can't speak for the other 7 billion or so potential readers out there.

— Matt Mawhinney (BUDDY)
10/16

ACKNOWLEDGEMENTS

I've gotta thank everyone who helped partially recover the amazement of what my #1 asset—my brain—once was. This includes doctors, surgeons, therapists, family members & friends. I also need constant encouragement, a positive atmosphere & reigniting flames of memories.

I need to thank my martial arts dojo for—over the course of 15+ years—instilling in me the kind of self confidence & tenacity to just know that I can overcome anything.

I'd like to thank all my Physical Therapy instructors since my accident. They've been instrumental in my partial-recovery of my most severely damaged [visible] body parts from my accident—my arms & my legs.

I need to thank every single one of my employees (nurses & caregivers)—past & present—who've assisted me in participating in all my current activities.

INTRODUCTION

First, I've gotta thank a friend from high school – one Carly S. – who mentioned the IDEA of converting my thoughts and tales into a more widespread text than simply word of mouth. Additionally, she served as my (early) Chief Editor while busily modeling. So, hats off to her, as I seem to just inspire multitasking!

Next, I wanna cite Mr. Thomas Hardy's *The Return of the Native* for his "Turkish knight" reference. I am half-Turkish and half-Minnesotan.

Thirdly, I've gotta thank a longtime associate/peer but newfound friend – Siena K. – for reigniting my passion for writing and people (specifically, women). The fact that she works in publishing is merely an opportune bonus.

The title's wave like words describe the countless UPs and DOWNs of my eventful life. Since I'm very MATHematically oriented, I could've coordinated the title with the various extrema – e.g. MAXima and MINima – of my ~31.73+ years aboard Earth. But, I went with the wave imagery, 'cuz I thought it'd be more relatable for people. I've gotta cater to the masses. I've gotta give the people what they want!

Before y'all commence your examination, I'll preemptively clear the air by noting that much of my *eventful* past – and present – was, and is, quite distinguished.

So, please don't misinterpret my laudable tales as bragging.

This is how autobiographies (by optimists) *work*.

I've omitted most names out of respect. (Except my thank you's – I've gotta give credit where credit is due!) I also CAPITALIZE many words in my tales, only as a point of EMPHASIS and not (as my own mother repeatedly confuses) as an indication of anger. You've gotta read the context clues, but I'll be sure to drop hints of my tone.

Since I don't speak often, I'm unfamiliar with one's natural speaking intonation. I think that the editing might've taken slightly longer than the actual writing.

My work is kind of a tell-all. I lack the feelings of shame or embarrassment. So, I'll just tell it like it is. That's my half-ass warning to any overprotective parents.

I've been ALONE *in my mind* for ~31.73 years. Now, hopefully my writing can *recruit* some *followers of my thoughts.*

(Easier said than done.)

In this text, most of my writing focuses on and around my phenomenal neural activities. 'Cuz I DO have a *Traumatic Brain Injury* that supposedly dramatically diminished my already amazing and phenomenal mental strength.

But, I am an anomaly in that most of my injuries are more physical than mental! That's just fuckin' strange! *WEIRDness* is synonymous with Altan Javit Kaynatma. So, I will be highlighting that aspect of my life.

'Tis not a bragging platform! Just as an aspiring and inspiring AUTObiographer, I've kinda gotta emphasize the PROs, while I minimize the CONs. You cannot fault me for having a laundry list of virtues and talents!

(Don't hate me, because I'm beautiful – mentally, cognitively and intuitively.)

Something to really consider while reading:

I, Altan Javit Kaynatma, am a maniacal mystery wrapped in a ridiculous riddle, firmly ensconced in a fabled enigma, all drenched in avid dialectics.

Alliteration aside. Please don't regard my feats and setbacks as customary. I am ATYPICAL. (AUDIBLE sigh) Despite my years of trying to teach my countless unique styles of deductive reasoning. Ultimately, my work can only be imitated but never duplicated.

Most importantly, I'll request a pardon for my own spotty/unreliable memory. My *Traumatic Brain Injury* has significantly diminished my memory. Ergo, I've forgotten many of the details.

: (

Thus, my story is only semi-chronological.

But, the gist of it is here.

Also, as my writing is rather like a stream of consciousness, some ideas may be repeated. That's usually not deliberate. If so, please accept these as merely points of EMPHASIS.

Furthermore, please keep in mind while reading:

"Sometimes it is the very people whom no one imagines anything of who do the things no one can imagine."
– THE IMITATION GAME

Warning: Do not underestimate me, just 'cuz I have a severe neurologic disorder. SPOILER alert: You're bound to be sorely disappointed.

"The book to read is not the one that 'thinks for you' but the one which 'makes you think'."
– HARPER LEE

Aaah, 'tis the glory of independent thought!

In all three volumes, I note society's tendencies. PLEASE realize that I only do this as a harsh critic and not as a mindful supporter. I am merely specifying the IGNORANCE I'm trying to destroy.

"All human activity lies within the the artist's SCOPE."
– GEOFFREY CHAUCER

(Remember that, as you read.)

Another *note* to remember:

:) → HAPPY face

: (→ SAD face

I find much humor in genitalia and intimacy. It's just one of my numerous sophomoric quirks. So, please don't get offended when I joke about bein' a pussy/wuss or havin' *minuscule ballz*. I simply mean *NOT brave*.

I deliberately misuse the grammar in some situations, 'cuz people just don't talk like that!

Mainly, please note that the goal of this retelling of my adventures is threefold:

1) INFORM you of the trials and tribulations of one person who currently suffers from a *Traumatic Brain Injury* (that's me, Altan Javit Kaynatma)

2) INSPIRE you to overcome anything y'all set your minds to

3) ENTERTAIN via humor and drama (mostly laughs)

PROLOGUE

WAY DOWN SOUTH IN **F**LORIDA, there was this fella I wanna tell ya about. Goes by the name of Altan Javit Kaynatma. At least, that was the handle his loving parents gave him, but he never had much use for it himself. See, this here Kaynatma, he called himself "A.J."[1]

Now, many people might unknowingly assume A.J. does not like his full Turkish name.

---

[1] INTRO was based upon the very beginning of *The Big Lebowski*, 'cuz I am The DUDE. *The Big Lebowski* is, by FAR, my favorite film.

Here's WHY:

– The line "the Dude abides" is a reference to Ecclesiastes 1:4 in the Bible: "One generation passes away, and another generation comes: but the earth abides forever." What a unique and brief way to summarize the moral lessons of the Bible to the agnostic such as myself.

- If I HAD TO select a *way of LIFE*, I'd be a DUDE. Sometimes you roll strikes, and sometimes you roll gutters in the game of life.
- The word "Dude" is referenced 161 times in the film. (Yeah, I counted, post-injury... which *exemplifies* just how MUCH free time I now have – TOO MUCH!)
- That's devotion to such a vague and non-descriptive nickname!
- I like the creepy but interesting foreboding fact that Donny's one non-strike in the entire 117-minute film occurs just before his heart attack, as if the shock *played a part* in (SPOILER ALERT!) his death.

But, he just reasoned (correctly) that most Americans are culturally ignorant and stubborn. But, then there was a lot about A.J. that remained oddly quizzical. Even before his life changing catastrophe, he'd been a *paradoxical playuh*.

But, I certainly wouldn't describe all his feats and accomplishments as oddly self-beneficial. He does surround himself with morally straight and mentally stable people. O' course, I wouldn't make the ridiculously blatant mistake of muttering, "I know how you feel" to him! I can only imagine how much that confused, FAUX empathy infuriates him!

O' course, I've never been so dependent on the sympathy of others. But, I'll tell you what, after talking to my FUTURE-self and reflecting upon this here story I'm about to unfold, well, I guess I've heard something every bit as stupefying as you'd expect from any one of 'dem nonsense spewin' dolts. But, I can die with a smile of pride on my face, knowing all I will have overcome.

Now this here story I'm about to unfold mostly took place between 2007 and 2016, just about the time of my early 20s to early 30s. I only mention that to help y'all imagine what a typical testosterone charged, mathematically starved, socially dependent male athlete/prodigy WANTS and does in that time.

Further reflections indicate that sometimes there's a MAN (I won't say a HERO, 'cause that's rather subjective and stilted), but sometimes there's a man and, well, he's the man for his time and place. He fits right in there. And, that was me.

And, even if I WAS a crippled man, and A.J. was most certainly THAT – quite possibly the smartest T.B.I. victim in all of the STATE of FLORIDA, which would place him high in the runnin' for smartest countrywide. Sometimes there's a man... sometimes, there's a man. Well, I lost my train of thought here. But, aw, HELL. I've introduced me ENOUGH.

All in all, PLEASE bear with me.

ENJOY!

THE MENTAL CRESTS AND TROUGHS OF
a Turkish Knight with a TBI:
Life's Full of Extrema.
A.J. KAYNATMA
MATHLETE

1.
Planting the Seeds
for Imminent Growth

BEFORE I CAN GET INTO my tumultuous tales of tensing triumph, I have to somewhat detail my background of impressive mental feats. Seeing this, y'all will witness both the monumental mental heights from which I fell and the psychological strength on which I currently depend. I used to rely on logic and reasoning far more than I do now. But then, I deduced that logical reasoning can be a form of psychology.

(THAT's a discussion topic for 'Volume III' of my T.B.I. series.)

With that said, we'll commence!

Well, being the firstborn of two brilliant folks certainly began my genetic life rather well! I am a Biomedical Engineer. So, I kinda know a little something (JUUUST a smidgeon. Whoa! Did I not just horribly date myself as way older than the actual ~31.73+ years – as of December 31, 2016 – OLD I am?!) about what I'm blabbering. Maybe.

Yes, I do have a *Traumatic Brain Injury*. (More on that as it surfaces semi-chronologically) But, as you'll see from your imminent reading, I have a propensity for overcoming obstacles.

I abhor restrictions! (except mathematical 'limits'! But, that's 'Calculus' jargon. And, now, I have a massive erection!) Strangely, as outsiders' doubt against me increases, my own mental drive also increases and approaches 100%.

In other words, as the limit of external doubt approaches 100%, so too do my internal flames of movement *ignite*. Then again, 'tis essential to possess that burning desire to always prove doubters wrong! I've got that in my back pocket.

(Ah, ah, AAAHHH! In the words of the comical group The Lonely Island, "I jizzed in my pants!")

(About the math and not NOT the flaming sexuality!)

(Relax! I'm just referring to my tremendous affinity for *numerometry*.)

(Plus, it is just a quote from the comical musical parody group The Lonely Island.)

Numbers relax yet stimulate me. My NeuroPsychoTherapist a licensed professional concluded after many various tests the oddity that I AM:

- ... Mathematics calms yet excites me.
- ... i.e. When's "twelve" *odd* but "thirteen" *even*?
- ... When you count the # of syllables.
- ... ZZZZZZZZZZZZ

My main turn ON is a possession of a mellifluous mix of tremendous intelligence, pants soaking humor and groin tickling beauty in a female. So, y'all can only imagine how arousing for my mind and my crotch my (multiple) mathematics courses (with older girls) were for ME in high school! (TEXTBOOK *Catholic school girl* fantasy!)

Ya see, I've always used my wowing wit as my primary romantic allure, as I lack ginormous muscles bulging from my biceps.

'Tis rhyme time:

NO RULES.
allows for mental VESTIBULES
to file random trivia, which will inherently draw massive ridicules.
Such neural categorizing causes excellence in schools.
Don't question my reasoning, 'cuz I'm as stubborn as five mules.
I may only stare at her HIND.
But, my best pickup jokes come from my MIND.
IF she appreciates my smarts and HUMOR,
over my heart I've SIGNED.

Then, I'll peel off her clothes like an orange RIND.
Although from my accident my posture MANGLES,
I still desire a woman of many curves and great ANGLES.
We'll discuss my appendage that DANGLES.
She took off my shirt, 'cuz she complained, "It TANGLES."

My father was a mathematical genius from the distant Eurasian nation of "Turkiye" (Turkey). Approximately 5% of the country is located geographically in Europe. While ~95% falls in Asia, hence the descriptive name. It's weird, 'cuz he never really sat down to teach me any numerical puppetry. I just share his penchant for algebraic shenanigans. ('Twas a bit of mathematical wizardry by OSMOSIS.)

E.g.

#1: Pick ANY number. (x)

#2: Multiply it by 3. ($3x$)

#3: Add 45 to product. ($3x + 45$)

#4: Double the sum. [$2(3x + 45)$]

#5: Divide product by 6. [$2(3x + 45)/6$]

#6: Subtract quotient from ORIGINAL #. [x $2(3x + 45)/6$]

Answer: +/ 15

(The variable x represents MY AGE. So, it theoretically *approaches* **infinity**.)

The SUM of the first nine prime numbers ($2 + 3 + 5 + 7 + 11 + 13 + 17 + 19 + 23$) = 'Cien' (SPANISH) = 'Un centinaio di' (ITALIAN) = 'Yüz' (TURKISH) = 'Hyaku' (JAPANESE) = 'One hundred' (ENGLISH) = my goal/usual grade on ANY 'Calculus' and/or 'Statistics' test = 100

Question: What monetary piece is reduced by 50% in value, when half is actually added?

Answer: A DOLLAR to a *HALF* dollar.

Question: How do you tell one bathroom full of statisticians from another?

Answer: Check the "p" value.

(I'm snickering, 'cuz you just said, "PEE"!)

(I have the maturity of a six-year-old.)

Question: If the length of each side of a square is increased by ten percent, then the area of the square is increased by what percent?

Answer: 21%

$(10 > +1 > 11; (10^2 =) 100 > (11^2 =) 121; 21/100 > 21\%)$

A *normal person* (NOT I!) can calculate the first seven digits of pi by counting the # of letters in each word in this sentence:

"How I wish I could calculate pi!"

(= 3.141592)

A number is divisible by 9, IF the sum of the digits is divisible by 9.

I'm always searching for patterns:

$1 \times 9 + 2 = 11$

$12 \times 9 + 3 = 111$

$123 \times 9 + 4 = 1111$

$1234 \times 9 + 5 = 11111$

$12345 \times 9 + 6 = 111111$

$123456 \times 9 + 7 = 1111111$

$1234567 \times 9 + 8 = 11111111$

$12345678 \times 9 + 9 = 111111111$

$9 \times 1,089 = $ its REVERSE $= 9,801$

(Thus, 'tis numerically PALINDROMIC.)

The best, most ideal # is 73. Why?!

Ya see, 73 is the 21st prime number. Its REVERSE 37 is the 12th and ITS mirror 21 is the product of 7 and 3.

In binary form, 73 is a palindrome '1001001', which backwards is '1001001'. Of those 7 binary digits representing 73, there are 3 ones. Also, "37+12 = 49" (7^2), and "'73' + 21 = 94 = (47 x 2)" OR "47 + 2 x 1" is equal to seven squared.

(Legitimately, that observation was made by Dr. Sheldon Cooper of "The Big Bang Theory.")

The following deductions were all ME:

quantity of (7 + 3) multiplied by 7 plus 3 is 73.

Furthermore, the difference of 7 and 3, when raised to the power of 3, summed to the square of 3 equals 73.

(I might have too much spare time. Maybe. But, at least my mind's not drifting into thoughts of sorrow and despair.)

So, I got bored one day while working the cash register as a 12-year-old for fun at one of my dad's restaurants. (I calculated each and every bill mentally!) You can *make change for a dollar* one, two, five, 12, 293 different ways.

('Twas a slooow day.)

Relax! I chose to help out only on Sundays, as kind of a work study program. 'Twas not child labor! 'Twas merely a fully cogent and decisive son helping his father. Plus, I always contributed my time Sunday mornings, so I'd be home in time to watch NFL football!

Yes, my Bioengineering background confirms that "mathematical wizardry by osmosis" IS an actual *medical condition*. (Cough cough!) Aaah, YES! My comedic background. (My uncle's a professional comedian in Denver, CO.[1] He supports my propensity for sarcasm.)

Since I'd visit my dad's side of my family every other summer in Turkey, I developed a subconscious urge to just instantly convert (seldom used) American measurements into their (much more common) metric equivalents.

E.g. Speed limit = 60 miles per hour > ~96.56064 kilometers/hour

> 1 mile = ~1.6 kilometers (1 kilometer = ~0.6 miles)

1 foot = 0.3048 meters (> 1 meter = ~3.1 feet)

1 pound = 0.45359237 kilograms (> 1 kilo = ~2.2 pounds)

(Yes, I do all these conversions mentally and semi-instantly.)

The record for "fastest goal" in World Cup history is 10.8 seconds by Hakan Şükür of Turkey in the 2002 bronze medal game against South Korea, a 3-2 Turkish win.

I also learned my dad's unbelievable eye/palate for cooking sans recipe by simply watching his scampering around the stove and oven and fridge.

Funny tangent: rather than using a quick toaster, my dad would grill bread to heat it up. So, since nearly every Turkish (his heritage/nationality) meal includes *'ekmek'* (phonetically > *'ehk mehk'* = 'bread'), my favorite Turkish snack became 'TOST' a grilled Turkish sandwich with meat and alotta cheese on buttery bread. By eating many different types of plates, I created my BASE line for eclectic taste. Now, I kinda hafta follow the directions of a great recipe, when I'm cookin' for others. Ya see, I used to cook by taste. I could just sample a bite and deduce, "HHHMMM, that needs a LIL' black pepper and some cheese and perhaps a dash of oregano and some parsley! But, no salt!"

---

[1] My FUNNY uncle is "Nick Janecky" in Denver, Colorado. LOOK him UP.

(Many lay people think that parsley is merely an artistic add on to better its presentation. However, to a trained tongue, the taste is there.)

Always the health nut, I've never liked salt. ('Tis NOT that I dislike the taste. I just don't like the unhealthy aspects attached to its consumption. 'Tis for the same reason that I did not (used to) eat burgers from 'McDonalds' or mayonnaise on anything! And, now I'm in tip-top physical, non-neurological shape.)

('Tis a victory for my psyche!)

As a quasi "chef", I understand that sometimes a miniscule amount of salt is necessary to combine with other ingredients/spices to optimize the flavor. But, I've never added it purely as a supplement with pepper. Excess NaCl (Sodium Chloride/Table Salt) causes hypertension, because it holds excess fluids in the body, which increases the workload of the heart.

Furthermore, I developed my father's cultural tongue (I operate on the metric system. Sooo, MY tongue rotates counter clockwise. strangely, when I rotate my tongue as an exercise in speech therapy, my tongue just feels a lot more comfortable spinning to my left, or counter clockwise. Are my European genes (50% x ~5% = ~2.5% = ~1/40th) that embedded in my physical makeup that I subconsciously/psychologically *swipe left?!*) with a foreign feel.

Somewhat related tangent: In Europe including Turkey, cars drive on the left side of the road.

(Wowzee! My sister just informed me that Turkish drivers actually operate their motor vehicles on the right side! *New* sh*t has come to light! I guess that it is just England and Australia that are *back ass wards*.)

I can "hold my own" with semi-speaking OR understanding Turkish, Spanish, Japanese, Latin, pig Latin and English obviously. My mother was a Speech/Language Pathologist and a high school valedictorian. Again, she didn't formally teach me proper grammar, diction or verbiage. I just possess her ear for it. Yes, as her offspring, I indirectly learned many habits and tendencies. But, 'twas never in a classroom setting, with desks and attendance check and time out.

(Although, in a bit of a role reversal, she did give me apples. But, that's likely just 'cuz I've long been a health nut.)

(Was "tongue" just a double entendre or a pun?!)

An ongoing theme in/for much of my (academic) learning was my self-teaching. To my various teachers except of *Martial Arts*[2] and of high school 'Calculus', I'm sorry/not sorry for being 1, 2, 3, seven steps ahead of you! So, academically, *Martial Arts* wise and overall, I'm kind of a big deal. (In mathematical jargon, I'd be the independent variable. While in *Martial Arts* and highly advanced math (for me), I'd be FAR more dependent.)

unfortunately, my T.B.I. caused/forced me to forget much of my foreign vocabulary. Strangely, I still know how to conjugate verbs. Is that my mom's half of my genes?! (the more feminine 23 chromosomes)

(Pause! I hafta make my bangs more prominent and push out my chest.)

So, right from when I could multiply double-digit numbers by each other in my head (sooo, ~age 8), I started to have higher expectations of my capabilities to quantify anything. These expectations were totally and completely self-imposed! My parents were very supportive, proud of and complimentary of all I did. 'Tis not that I needed all that praise! (I've always thought very highly of myself!) I am neither cocky nor arrogant. 'Tis definitely not the case! I'm just extremely confident. I know my capabilities and limits. Plus, 'tis good for my psyche (now especially) to get alotta positive support for my decisions! I'd walk with a bit of a swagger pre-accident. Now, I just smile ear to ear, when I am right, and you're not quite.

Thankfully, 22 months, one week, two days and ~12.5 hours after my *introduction to the world*, the 'rents gave me a brother.

(Ya see, even as newborns, we showed: My brother's a morning person. While I am more of a night owl.)

Back to me! So, I'm ~50% Turkish, ~half Minnesotan and, I'm ~14/206[3] (= ~7/103 in lowest/proper terms = ~6.80%) titanium dioxide (TiO_2), 'cuz of my multiple surgeries and medical implant.[4]

---

[2] My vast Martial Arts know how is completely inferior to the kinetic proficiency of my instructor(s).

[3] (Five Surgeries leave) 14 implants divided by 206 Bones in the human body > DO the math. Wait! I already did the quantification.

[4] Left shoulder surgery left a "plate" and nine screws in there. Left hip surgery left a "rod" there to stabilize it. Approximately six years before my car accident, a botched right ulnar (forearm) surgery left me unable to fully extend ~43% of my right fingers

As those anatomic numbers sum to more than a whole (1), it's fairly apparent that I am 'Iron Man'.

(Interpret that, as you may, ladies!) (I'm hard as a rock in my left shoulder and in my crotch.)

SOME people think I say inappropriate things.

But, I prefer to think of it as radical honesty. Also, loosen the elastic band of your underpants. Y'all interpret my words too literally and apply 'em too frequently! I often speak in metaphors, and I'd rather not hafta constantly write "figuratively" or "meta-phorically." But, if I hafta to clarify my point, then so be it. Thus, if you must: judge me by what I do, rather than by what I say.

(DAMNIT! I immediately regret stating that, 'cuz I frequently understand my situa-tion better than I act on it!)

(Unlike during my high school heydays of brilliance, my brain and thoughts now seem to operate on a different *plane* than that of my muscles and nerves.)

In other words, from 9th to 12th grade, my brain to muscle *messages* were so *well-connected* that I distinguished myself with countless academic achievements, a com-mendable four-year wrestling career, a constant sociability and an exemplary valediction.

Sooo, ideally, you my readers will read my thoughts on paper, take time to reflect on 'em, relate to my points/concepts, then (hopefully) apply 'em to your learning(s).

('Tis the Story of my life: trial > error > learn > apply > future success.) As confident as I am, *the Law of large Numbers* (statistics) says that I can't **always** be in the right. Ya see, even the mental studs (I bow) are not gonna always be correct. (ME: "Oh, WHOOPS!") I'm very stubborn, when I think I'm right. Flukes and accidents happen, mainly 'cuz of the moral inconsistencies of the human mind and the UNpredictable var-iance of nature.

'KUDOS' to my fantastic genes! But, 'tis a popular saying that "Stars are made not born", which advocates the **nurture** theory as more influential than nature in child-rais-ing. (I fervently support such a theory.)

To continue my prodigy-esque tales, I did win my elementary school spelling Bee de-signed for 5th graders, when I was only in the 4th grade. This accomplishment first in-stilled some confidence in myself that I was more than just a *Human calculator*. Upon

_____

(~2.15 fingers)

exclaiming my linguistic triumph to my mom, she immediately began belting out her dramatic interpretation of the song, "Something There" from *Beauty and the Beast*.

(She knows my affinity for Disney classics!)

Her: "There might be something there that wasn't there before!"

Consequently, I entered a countywide Spelling Bee in 4th grade, in which I performed relatively poorly. 'Twas my first actual major disappointment of very few in academia. (It was actually great for my life view, 'cuz I first experienced one of Life's many letdowns. now, I had the opportunity to gauge my reaction.) As promising and stupendous as my academic career was, 'tis essential to realize that life, in general, tends to balance out. In a way, life kinda abides by Sir Isaac Newton's Third Law of Motion:

"For every action, there is an equal and opposite reaction."

Nobody's gonna always be successful. Even the legendary baseball great, "Joltin'" Joe DiMaggio had to eventually see his record 56-game hitting-streak end. But, it's not the triumphs but how one reacts to the MISFORTUNE(S) that is the TRUE measure of success.

I.e. I've always been a defensive fighter, when I sparred in Karate class. I took far greater pride and pleasure from a successful *Block and counter* move than from any straight-on attack.

So, it seems as though Mr. Newton was an indirect advocate of karma. Granted, there's no real documented scientific evidence of such a psychologic phenomenon, and I've always been a man of facts and proof as opposed to belief and faith. I am, however, big on feelings and inklings. Thus, I am frantically at a loss as to what I could have possibly done so, so, sooooo absolutely frickin' amazing to offset how terribly catastrophic my post-accident life has been!

I'm semi/quasi/kinda superstitious. I'll start a good luck charm, realize its stupidity and randomness ~38% through, then switch to a more physics-supported tactic. (approximately 38% of the word *superstitious* is super. coincidence? I think not!)

If I am *sitting atop my **dung depository*** without any success yet, I'll try to imagine just how I'll word the event on my blog. Nothin' doin'. Sooo, I'll try opening my clenched left fist in order to remove tension and relax the anus. sure enough, biophysics prevails over psychology, as I feel, hear and semi-smell my *excretory success*.

Contrary to popular belief, *nasal identification* is not all or nothing. when people get a *waft* of something, they have an idea or guess of the *smell-source* that cannot be confirmed, 'til it's seen. So, the complete *nasal identification cycle* begins at the nose (physical) where it's *detected*, travels to the brain (mental) where it's guessed to have a *ballpark figure* of what it is. Next, the psyche determines if the smell is a like or a dis*like*. finally, the process ends with a visual confirmation (physical) of the *smell's source*.

(My nasal and taste nerves are just starting to return ... kinda. so, I get very excited when I can smell *crap* in the bathroom, or taste mustard and/or ketchup in speech therapy.)

CONTINUING with my (jokingly) blasphemic questioning of Mr. Newton's character, I raise this issue: Since gravity is rather absolute/unchanging, is George Lucas the creator of the *Star Wars* saga(s) implying that Newton was an evil "Sith lord?!"

> *"ONLY a Sith deals in absolutes."*
> ## – Obi Wan Kenobi,
> ### Star Wars Episode III:
> ### Revenge of the Sith

Always valiantly trying to right my karma, a couple years ago, in ~2013, post-injuries, I founded/established my own (free) "math tutoring" service. I only had two long-term clients (amongst a smattering of short-term students) during the ~1.25 years or so of the service's existence. But, both were extremely grateful, which made me feel accomplished and proud!

(SAID "math service" is still available! Just, with my mom's now-being retired, I kinda lack an advertising outlet.)

RATHER than always goin' by the book, I've long-preferred to be different. I.e. Since I destroyed every math class available at my middle school, in eighth grade, my middle school (mafia voice:) "gave me an OFFER I couldn't *rih-fuze*." The school provided an *activity bus* every weekday morning to take only me to the local high school for my 'honors Geometry' class as a twelve-year-old! (I laugh loudly and unashamedly.) Take that, public high schools! A preteen aced your 'honors geometry' class all year! I like to joke now that "I needed a 'special bus' for my mental needs."

The irony of my past jokes in lieu of my current neural disorder kinda stings emotionally. OUCH! additionally, this bussing taught me about responsibility, prioritizing and socializing in uncomfortable situations. My being a 12-year-old prepubescent boy in a crowded classroom of ~20 gorgeous 16-year-old ladies was rather awkward. 'Twas certainly not unwelcome! Just weird.

When writing this just now, I am first realizing that my uber competitiveness might directly result from my having a smart and athletic, similarly-aged brother. unbeknownst to him and others, I'd often compare my performances/outcomes to his and peers'. SHAME on me! (you are your own and only judge.)

This "compare and contrast" analysis was especially easy, when we played on the same youth soccer team for two seasons! (I shrug.) I was ~eight and ~nine, and he was ~six and ~seven. We were just kids! (sinister laugh) The key word here is "were". (I still tend to be rather sophomoric.)

Nonetheless, I believe that it is this childish behavior that helps me keep it real. I feel I can better relate to my young students, 'cuz I teach a kids' Martial Arts class. Thank goodness for my childish attitude and uplifting ability to laugh anything off! I shan't lie: There have been times, when my damn T.B.I. has gotten sooo disheartening, frustrating and morale-destroying that unfortunately "SUICIDE" did cross my mind.

: (

But, I internally cried[5] and thankfully pondered the words of legendary author, Ernest Hemingway:

"The world is a FINE place and WORTH fighting FOR."

In lieu of plotting all my terrible life occurrences contrasted with the good morals of most people on an *XY axis*, I'll just agree with the second part.

(Sooo, psychology won another round. whew!)

BUT, I was (PAST tense!) all talk mainly to try to convince my ex-girlfriend to see the errors of her (still inexplicable) ways! NOW, I've slowed my roll, become more accepting

---

[5] My T.B.I. PREVENTS me from *producing FLUIDS*. : (It SUCKS! Sooo, I LIKE to JOKE that I SOLD my TEAR ducts on eBay to pay my LEGAL fees.

of my faults, better highlighting my virtues and enjoying the overall progress I've made.

My OBSESSION with NUMBERS more than LIKELY caused my UBER competitiveness. I don't TRY to be a JERK! It's JUST HOW my mind FUNCTIONS! EVERYTHING to ME is NUMERICAL! I can't FIGHT what I AM! Although, HHHMMM, wouldn't it be WILD to start a FIGHT Club?!

SSSHHH! I MAY or may NOT be "TYLER DURDEN."

(In the movie *Fight Club*, Tyler Durden created the secretive brawl group. Damnit, A.J.! The joke loses its humor, if/when you hafta explain it!)

Besides, I don't openly voice my calculations. (Although, I'm not gonna fib: Showin' off my mathematical wizardry is rather redeeming.) I prefer to keep the scores to myself, and gauge your reaction.

(E.g. Point Sparring in Karate class, Scrabble playing in Speech Therapy, Cribbage playing with friends.)

Speaking of "KIDS", 29 days prior to my eighth birthday, a sister sprang forth *into this world*. I, a sibling, am also very proud of the overwhelming intelligence of all three of the Kaynatma Janecky[6] offspring! My sister was valedictorian of the very same (public) high school to which I bussed for 'honors Geometry'. My brother's studying for his doctorate, while he teaches 'Marketing' in Turkey!

Ergo, regarding my criminal charge of excessive Intelligence, it pains me to admit that I'm guilty by Association. (actually, since I am the oldest, wouldn't my younger siblings learn from me?!)

(SSSSSHHHHH! I like to think and say, "Being the firstborn, I 'sucked out'/accumulated all the excess wisdom from my 'rents." But, begrudgingly, I'll admit that Tweedle DEE and Tweedle DUM got some smarts, I guess.)

(AHHH, reverse hyperbole about the brilliance of the Kaynatma Krew is cleverly sarcastic!)

Am I addicted 'A' (Spanish for 'to') Alliteration, or what?!

(AUDIBLE sigh)

It's not as if I had to study a lot and worry about grades. With my commendable knack for logic, I'd just kinda see a problem, mentally visualize the solution, then apply my hypothesis. (Approximately 86.72% of the time, I just happened to be correct.) At home

---

[6] My father's and mother's last names, respectively.

my parents trusted my judgment and my insight. (GREAT call, 'rents!)

(That remark was very genuine and not sarcastic!)

Even now, post-injuries, I'll occasionally/frequently *balance my mother's checkbook* mentally.

'Twas this relaxed yet very supportive home atmosphere that stimulated my/all our learning appetite(s)[7]. However, not only did said relaxed domestic environment cultivate my prolific academic growth, but it further stimulated my character evolution. Rather than my family's forcing their desired personality on me and my being a mere conseqence of the surroundings, I chose to adapt to my ever changing environment: my different athletic ventures, my brother's various musical escapades, my sister's annoyingly immature friends, etc.

(Remember my ease and comfort with adapting for later, when I constantly hafta use alternative plans for all of my tasks post-accident.)

---

[7] "Appetite" is IRONIC diction/word CHOICE. CURRENTLY, I canNOT TASTE. But, I CERTAINLY DESIRE to! I TRY!

2
EARLY DISTRACTIONS

TO NOT BE A TOTAL/COMPLETE **NERD/DWEEB**[1], I began my Martial Arts training at the tender age of ~7.42 (in September of 1992). I started in 'Okinawan Shorei ryu Karate'. (I've capitalized *Karate*, since I began, since I first wrote it on my calendar as a child. So, excuse the muscle memory. Force of habit) But, my studies have since spread to also/additionally include 'Shuri ryu Karate' and Jujitsu. My eight years of competitive wrestling in high school and college triggered, then repeatedly fueled, my love of Jujitsu, which is ground grappling. In Jujitsu, you the Defender maneuvers his own and his opponent's body weight as a form of self-defense. Since my legs were *taken from* me, I've developed a better understanding and appreciation of the *Jujitsu arts*.

As of October of 2016, I have earned two black belts (in Karate) in two very similar yet way different styles and a high brown belt in Jujitsu. I've taught[2] Kids' classes in both Karate and Jujitsu (on and off) for ~14 years (minus ~five years away for "rehab" so, ~nine active years). I really enjoy molding kids' interpretations of right and wrong. For the most part, kids respond well to instruction, 'cuz they have yet to form their own concepts of bio physics, which is kinda my thing. (This damn dirt won't come off my shoulder!) PLUS, I'll admit that my maturity level is rather sophomoric and childish. So, I can often relate to the little beasts!

---

[1] I am not a "dork", 'cuz that's slang for "dick" and/or "whale penis."
[2] The best way to learn is to teach!

(I chuckle. That's "the pot calling the kettle black!")

***

… Here's a slight tangent: during my 'Shodan' ('Black belt') test, I dislocated my right shoulder while performing some slightly subpar (for me) sparring. I don't know if any of y'all have experienced "poppin' your shoulder out." But, it hurts like a MO' FO! (The shoulder is actually the body's most stable yet most flexible joint.)

Now, post-injuries, I have an even higher, dare I say Unbelievable, pain tolerance. O' course, now, it's mostly because of my many faulty/deadened nerves. But, pre-injuries, I just had big BALLZ/alotta bravery.

Nevertheless, I always like to finish what I choose to start! So, eventually, I successfully completed my painstakingly LLLOOONNNGGG physical exam.[3] Fellow *'Shodans'* now tease me for "standing so cockeyed and clearly favoring my left side" at the conclusion of my "test" (~2.5 hours later). Professor rewarded my resilience by awarding me with not one, as I expected, but two black belts!

***

An ongoing theme/emphasis in my and my dojo's lessons is "discipline and respect" to/for friends and family. Approximately every other weekend, I try to design/create/devise at least one new Karate wrestling Jujitsu technique to co-teach.[4] DESPITE my temporary physical limits, I still visualize logical, doable self-defense techniques for every man.

(As I am by no means anything remotely close to "every man" physically and/or mentally, I kinda hafta use my professional understanding of biophysics to visualize in my mind how the body would react to certain "stimuli.")

---

[3] I had already passed the written portion of my exam.

[4] I have two *'Sempai's* ('Sehm PIYs' PHONETICALLY) ('Assistant Instructors in Japanese), who really HELP.

(SLIGHT TANGENT: I researched biotech companies on a Thursday in mid September of '16, BOUGHT some shares and by MONDAY the share price had increased by ~55.26%. By EARLY January of '17, it had ONLY INCREASED by ~263%! Do I KNOW the INDUSTRY or WHAT?! Thank YOU, Penn studies!)

Ya see, I MAJORED in *Bioengineering* during my 4-year COLLEGE studies at the University of Pennsylvania. Since, the majority of the curriculum FOCUSED around medical applications, I sometimes refer to my studies as "bio-*MEDICAL*-Engineering."

Occasionally, I will view an adults class mainly to compare teaching styles and topics. (But, ALSO 'cuz I'm tryin' to remain social with my friends and colleagues) My dojo has really become a "second home" for me. Despite my ~4+ years (?) away for rehab, I'm still pleasantly surprised, when I roll in for class, and it's like a scene from the classic show *Cheers*:

"Where EVERYBODY knows [MY] name!"

The fact that all the students are kids aged between ~5 and ~14 prompts a necessary thanks to my professor for singing my praises to the young neophytes!

A good teacher shows you how and where to look, not what to see.

As confused, lost and seemingly unknowing as my/the kids/students seem to be, I always like to guide 'em to discover their errors themselves. 'Tis an even greater and better feeling of accomplishment, when a teacher (like me) watches a student (Karate kid) understand and correct his/her own mistake(s)! I've gotta give a big thanks to my *Martial Arts* professor for looking past my disabilities and still allowing me to occasionally/frequently coteach techniques to the young '*Karateka*' (*Martial Arts* students)!

('*Arigato gozaimasu, SENSEI!*'[5])

As I am quite athletic, I kinda need physical activities to balance my extraordinary neurological talents! My wrestling further complemented my already astute understanding of the how's and whys of 'biophysics'. (EVER the optimist, I'm still trying valiantly to move stuff with my mind, for "I AM 'The One'." ('Twas a Neo reference from *The Matrix*.)

Regarding my quasi-telekinesis, I won a "Halloween costume Contest" in 2015 by

---

[5] 'Thank you very much, TEACHER!' in Japanese

dressing as mental Miracle Worker Professor X from *X Men*. (How appropriate! RELAX! I did not shave my head. But, I think my motorized wheelchair won it for me. YEP. I just sensed that.)

As a child, I played community soccer for four seasons, community basketball for another three, youth gymnastics for two years and freshman football at age 14. I was an active member of the Boy Scouts of America for ~four years. But, ultimately, due to a scheduling conflict, I had to choose one or the other: Martial Arts or Scouts? I chose wisely. (Karate won.)

European 'futbol' (soccer) is just in my blood almost literally! It's almost all I did when I visited my father's homeland (Turkey) across the Atlantic as a child "way back in the day".[6] Since I had not yet become comfortable enough with the language, I chose to express my happiness via my feet:

('*Tekme Atma.*'= 'PASS the ball.' '*Topu!*' = 'shoot it!') I have the utmost respect for the stamina/conditioning/and strategy soccer requires! As a former left-middie (midfielder), I speak from experience. (ACTUALLY, I am right-footed. In soccer, coaches generally/usually position their best defenders to guard the left side, 'cuz most players are right-footed. SOOO, our top defenders on our left were ready for opponents' top forwards on their right.) Using the same logic, my brother was a left defenseman, despite his also being right-footed.

ALAS! When I first tried organized folkstyle wrestling my freshman year of high school, it was as if my brain started playing "Beethoven's Ninth". I'd found my calling. In high school, I wrestled at 119 pounds, 125, 125, then I discovered alcohol. (At 17?! Ssshhh!) So, senior year, I wrestled at big, fat 135 pounds! Right about when I became a recognizable wrestler, I welcomed the mutual attraction to and liking of the opposite gender.

I had no/zero complaints!

(Perhaps that was why so few fans attended my matches. HHHMMM. Were y'all scared?!)

"BOOOOO!" screamed my groin.

---

[6] "Back in the day" refers to a MONDAY. In Turkey/Turkish, 'twas a 'Pazartesi' (phonetically > 'Pah ZAR teh SEE')

3.
Finding My Niche

IN HIGH SCHOOL, I stumbled into my cliques of hardcore scholar-athletes and NERDdom to the Nth degree. I was, and still am, a ginormous dweeb! Nonetheless, I was not constantly bullied (and teased and beaten up), mainly 'cuz of three reasons:

1) I was a commendable Wrestler. (High schoolers tend to kinda fear messing with wrestlers. And, there's this false assumption that "Wrestling' is gay", 'cuz "they're rollin' around and grabbin' other guys." THAT's obtuse, homophobic, and ridiculously incorrect! "GRABBING" is forbidden. Believe me, I tried! Not!)

2) I was not the stereotypical nerd – hunched over as he hurried to class with his huge backpack. (However, I do constantly push UP my glasses.) I was/am more a "ladies' man"! (My ex-girlfriend to me: "What's with ALL this 'Pina Colada butt Lotion'?!"[1])

3) I could talk my way out of any altercation.

ODDLY enough, even though I certainly have the strength and Biophysical know-how to win any/all serious confrontation(S), I've never actually been in a physical/legitimate fist fight. My words "won" (past tense) me many a "battle." I've sparred for practice thousands of times in classes and/or tournaments. But, I've never had the intent to harm!

So, I established myself as a prominent leader in the ongoing battle for Geek tolerance and respect. HOWEVER, even then, I guess I was not the every man. (NOW, I'm actually far from it!)

My four full academic years/16 report cards/96 classes in a top Florida high school of

---

[1] From the HILARIOUS movie *Ladies Man* with Tim Meadows.

nothing but 'A's enriched me with a '4.9451' Cumulative Grade Point Average as (arguably) the top student of 508 graduating members of the class of 2003.

(HHHMMM, THAT'd be the TOP 0.17%)

(So, I'm JUST your AVERAGE Joe – NOT!)

"We 'RISE' by 'LIFTING' OTHERS."
– ROBERT INGERSOLL

My ensuing valedictory was top notch (as I'm told). My principal rejected 1, 2, 3, 12 drafts of my speech, actually said to my face:

"Well, you can't be both smart and funny." So, my lucky #13 speech was MY way of saying, "Up yours! EAT it!" Everyone complimented me on my insightful and comical messages!

But, if I were to add anything in hindsight, I'd include my thoughts on honor and legacy:

I'd like to think that many of my peers thought of two main points during our studies here:

1)   We must honor the many noteworthy students before us.
2)   We must seek to establish a commendable legacy in academics and/or athletics for future kids.

To continue my thoughts, I am currently trying to create/leave a memorable legacy of success and triumph against/over my major neural hurdles.

4.
Home Is Where You Make It

AFTER THE NUMEROUS PRECEDENTS I set in high school, I sought to bring my genius wrestler army of one team up to Philadelphia. I applied to only one college, and 'twas out of state, and, it is/was not exactly "run o' the mill". (I'm talkin' Ivy League Penn.)

(My top finishing/'summa cum laude' at a tip-top high school in Florida provided me with such excessive pride that I was that confident in my academic résumé. Am I wrong? AM I wrong?!)

As it turned out, the University of Pennsylvania gave me a resounding "'Wrong'?! Hellz naw! Welcome in!"

(That's the Ivy League Penn Quakers NOT the Big Ten Penn State Nittany Lions! UUUGGGHHH! That's SOOO AGGRAVATING, when people somehow all too often mess that up/confuse the two! Do y'all see a "STATE"?!)

Since my powerful determination just tends to instinctively kick in randomly, I continued my academic excellence as a bioengineer at the Ben Franklin-founded University. I also continued my athletic success as president of the Wrestling club and my social tendencies as new Member Chair/Pledge master for the 'Sigma Alpha Epsilon' fraternity. Since I'm really funny, I was also Eminent Chaplain[1]/Funny Man during my entire stay in

---

[1] Since RELIGION was NOT a MAJOR focus in MY fraternity (To EACH, his OWN), and we needed an *official TITLE* for the HUMOROUS *way of LIFE* I so PROMOTED, the *CHAPLAIN* was REchristened.

the Brotherhood (of the Guzzling Liquor - NOT of the Traveling Pants).

My fantastic ability to converse and entertain combined with my commendable humor made me rather memorable in the greek system of the Northeast. While IN school, my fraternity brothers built AND named a long rectangular table "The A.J. Kaynatma Table for Competitive Drinking" to address a MAIN concern of the ACTIVE college life. AFTER GRADUATING, I learned that an ENTIRE ROOM was REnamed "The A.J. Kaynatma Arena for Alcohol Abuse". As is APPROPRIATELY noted in the film *The Sandlot*: "HEROES come and go. But, LEGENDS live FOREVER." (YES, I AM implying that MY Greek life tenure was LEGENDARY.)

(After REwatching *The Sandlot* recently for the UMPTEENth time, I decided that PERHAPS I would be A.J. 'The BRAIN' Kaynatma. SAID nickname EVEN has the SAME cadence/syllable # as the FAMED Benny 'The JET' Rodriguez.)

Since I love to socialize and make an ass of myself, I participated in the "econ scream" every spring semester during my college tenure (2003-2007).[2] During said "scream", each student enrolled in 'Macro/Micro economics' is INFormally encouraged to blast loud music while streaking' through the (large) Quad. (WINTER would cause SHRINKAGE!) I only took econ once, but I love to push the envelope of decency and appropriateness![3]

Efficient with my time management, I still managed to balance my [movie-esque] 'beautiful mind' with/against my fraternity life and wrestling commitments with a dash of affection for/from the ladies.

---

[2] I NUDE screamed and streaked EVERY Spring semester, because I COULD. (I LIKE ATTENTION.)

[3] I didN'T JUST run NAKED. I LIKE ORGANIZATION and/or a ROUTINE. ONE year my roommate and I made a four-minute [NAKED] DANCE routine. ANOTHER year, I went to Penn's STORIED Nursing school and requested CRUTCHES for a PAINFULLY SORE ankle. (I had DELIBERATELY twisted my LEFT ankle a day earlier, as a SACRIFICE for the GOOD of the TEAM! When I *SET my MIND* to DOING a task, I have the DETERMINATION to ACCOMPLISH it. In THIS case, I really WANTED to *make an ASS of myself*, as a **FLAMBOYANT scene**.) So, I STREAKED while SLOWLY HOBBLING on crutches BUTT-ASS NAKED.

'Twas especially tricky/puzzling to balance my time senior year between my academically excelling in bioengineering, rowdily partying in my fraternity, instilling joy and respect as pledge master, romantically entertaining my girlfriend (at the time) from a nearby school and joyously organizing my post-college occupation. But, I accomplished all, 'cuz that's just what I do (or did)!

Hopeless romantic that I was/am, I established a very serious, but goofy, symbiotically-affectionate, coed relationship with a female from a nearby school (Mary C.). Apparently, smart was (past tense) the new sexy. (AUDIBLE sigh) She provided a welcome intimate distraction from the constant academic rigors of Ivy League life. However, when I moved south for my job, she suddenly/surprisingly changed her mind about following me. : (Apparently, she wasn't as serious about our future together as she led on.

I was devastated by the dumpage! She was gorgeous and appreciated my humor! Heartbroken, I seemingly soullessly sleepwalked through work and school *and Martial Arts*, until I found (who I thought was) my soulmate.

Unfortunately, I do not recall all/many of my glorious Greek tales from my post-high school but pre-paying job days. But, just know that I was almost always joking around and/or playfully causing TROUBLE. (That's just how I orchestrate the symphonic compositions of my life: promoting playful trouble.) Even though I was attending such a commendable and well-respected Institution of higher Learning, I still lived by the motto:

"Work HARD. Play HARDER."

Long story short: I Thoroughly enjoyed my time away from the hustle and bustle of South Florida. And, this time away in the (geographic) distance continued my ongoing passion for the sciences and numbers.

(e.g. My major of Bioengineering and my blood alcohol level from fraternity parties)

5.

MAXIMIZING MY JOYS IN THE IMMEDIATE POST-COLLEGE LIFE

IMMEDIATELY AFTER MY triumphant four-year tenure at Penn, I began my occupational career at a Petroleum Distribution company back home in South Florida where I met my (supposed) soulmate/heartthrob.

I had a great in/connection, 'cuz not only did I intern there two summers, but the company owner (Call him Mr. S.) was/is the father of a high school wrestling teammate of mine. I happily served as official Operations Engineer in the Fort Lauderdale office for ~1.09 years (~13 months), before shit really hit the fan.[1] I was being groomed/training to be a site Manager, which would've been a gargantuan promotion!

Always seeking more learning, I graciously accepted Mr. S.'s offer to fund my Graduate Schooling while simultaneously continuing my JOB at his Fort Lauderdale-based site. So, I had to organize my schedule to maximize my time management amongst day work, night school and a live-in girlfriend[2] and Martial Arts commitments. ('Twas quite the "hand-full" of "activities"!)

Needless to say, I proved to be an exemplary (metaphorical) juggler! I was enjoying my soaring up the Leadership ranks at work. I was happily excelling in grad school (~3.82

---

[1] By FAR, the WORST occurrence of my LIFE was my SUFFERING a Traumatic Brain Injury (MORE later).

[2] Technically, I lived in her apartment at the time.

GPA in an Accelerated MBA program).[3] I was ecstatic that my girlfriend[4] was so enthused about living with me! I was proudly and energetically kickin' ass (pun intended.) as a "Karate and Jujitsu" instructor.

Not to brag (but kinda yeah!), but I relished the fact that all of my coworkers really liked my unique conglomeration of irreplaceable insight, wonderful wisdom, intelligent intuition and Astounding Ability at Allowing Aerosol Activations. Alliteration aside. I was quite the impressive soon to be site manager.

Business School was almost foreign to me a Biomedical engineer. But, I saw the light at the end of the tunnel for what it meant at my job. (Plus, I am/was very culturally fluent: I travelled to family in Turkey often, and I was a member of the 'Sociedad de Honor Nacional Español' in high school. How 'bout that pun of "foreign"?!) So, I pushed through the difficulty. (As bright as I was/am overall, I am not bombastic or stilted enough to think that I know everything! Everyone has his/her area(s) of expertise. Mine are math, Karate, Jujitsu, physics, fitness, film quotes and card counting (SSSHHH!).

I love(d) my now ex-girlfriend! : (

I treated her with many a dance, romantic trip, lovely dinner, comical movie and boisterous laugh! But, she also weathered umpteen *shit storms* with me. Whoever said you can't/shouldn't date a coworker is ridiculous! With our seemingly constant time together, our relationship prospered! Of course, we did not tell Human Resources. (SSSHHH!) At work I was a model/tip-top employee. But, before[5] and/or after work, 'twas as if I were listening to "It's 5 o'clock Somewhere" with champagne and strawberries and chocolate sauce. (I shan't lie. I may or may not have imbibed a bit/tad of alcohol strictly socially during the work week. Was that safe? Was that responsible? Well, I tried to stay sober and clear minded near days I had to scale/climb 200-foot-HIGH tanks. So, yeah. I'd say that my time management regarding my optimum state of mind was rather exemplary!)

I cared for/about her so, so, SOOO MUCH that at some point in late 2012, I proposed marriage to her. She accepted! (YEEESSSSS!)

---

[3] One teacher gave me 'B+', just 'cuz he claimed that I "did not cite [my] sources". after I wrote a nine-page paper for a three-page project describing/defending my thinking, he changed my grade to an 'A'.

[4] We live(d) together.

[5] At that time, we'd only "been together" for only ~7.23 months.

(Tangent, which is a SPEECH/MATH pun!) Shortly after earning my black belts, I began my teaching career in Karate.

My time as 'SENSEI' was very spotty at first, 'cuz I soon had to leave for college ... in Philadelphia. Needless to say, I'd soon locate, establish and settle into my niche as a smartass, but fun and knowledgeable, Martial Arts instructor.

In lieu of my joyful energy in my new attempt at high school wrestling, i soon incorporated ground work into my self-defense teachings. Consequently, I put *two and two together* and began my studies in the world/realm of Jujitsu or ground fighting. My Martial Arts Professor has extremely high ranks in both 'Shuri ryu' Karate and Jujitsu, so I did not hafta travel far[6] for the alternative aspect. My Professor, my fellow Instructors and my students all eagerly gobbled up all of the "Karate + Wrestling + Jujitsu'" techniques I designed. ('Twas quite rewarding psychologically!) Did I mention that during my ~8.5+ years of teaching (since ~March '03, excluding a lengthy hospital/rehab facility stay), I never once accepted any monetary compensation for passing on my Martial Arts knowledge? So, 'tis kind of a volunteer service. I prefer the moral/ethical gratification of knowing I'm better preparing kids for the unpredictability and craziness of the numskulls around us.

The antithesis of a numskull would be my most serious/long-time/recent girlfriend (~5.44 YEAR relationship) Yes, she unfortunately dumped me. SOB story. : (How 'bout that "transition"?!

As testosterone-filled and intimacy-starved and super masculine 'Y' chromosome possessor as I am, I rank impressive INTELLIGENCE just *slightly above* amazing aesthetic appeal for a long-term mate. Said woman is a remarkable combination of both virtues! Once again, smart is the new sexy. (So, why am I – a commendable and helpful/generous genius – still so alone and unloved?! HHHMMM, maybe I'm too smart?! To the point that it's offputting?!)

To tell y'all the truth: I wish I could say something suave and debonaire and inspirational. But, that wouldn't be my style.

My opening line to Ms. *Poundage* my longtime beau was at the water cooler at work.

---

[6] My dojo was an ~eight-minute drive from my house at the time. Then, 'twas ~21 minutes away. Now, 'tis ~28 minutes away by car. (I've moved my "dwelling site" a lot and even less frequently my dojo location changed.)

She didn't recognize this similarly aged new guy (me). Sooo, she walked up to me and pleasantly semi-snapped:

"(AUDIBLE sigh) What do you do here?"

My reply: "Uuummm, I'm important."

Then, I walked away.

That worked!

I learned: 1) Keep your audience guessing. 2) Leave 'em wanting more. 3) Subtly hint at your power.

6.

"A Day That Will Live in Infamy"

(—Former U.S. President Franklin Roosevelt)

SO, ALL THAT was my pre-injuries background.

Interesting?! Now, I'll describe what I can remember of my second life.

As I have no/zero recollection of any of the details of that horrendous, life-threatening travesty, I'm forced to piece together other people's stories and/or (police) reports. So, my tales are inherently not personal and unbiased.

On my way home from a black belt (ONLY) workout, I was driving an S.U.V. (I forgot the exact company) my *Ford Explorer* (?) on a local highway (I-595), when my front left tire exploded and shredded! 'Twas in the early afternoon of July 6th, 2008.[1] It turns out that not only was said tire technically defective, but 'twas expired! (A car tire's expiration date is actually posted on the outer mid-rim of the tire! So, WARNING! Check 'em!)

However, I did not know this at the time. : (

Believe you me! I would've checked.

At that moment, my entire life came to a crashing, violent thud! (pun intended.) People always ask me:

"Why weren't you wearing your seat belt?!"

To which, I reply in my head: "Contrary to popular belief, I was and always do! 'Tis just

---

[1] Numbers guru that I AM, I remember the date, 'cuz it's "7/6/8" OR "July 6, 2008".

that the laws of physics seem to deny your pithy understanding of automechanical science and movement.

(How the combination of the Strapping angle of a subpar safety buckle and the angle of elevation of an extreme impact caused driver flight can provide little to no protection in certain automotive accidents)

Well, begrudgingly, hell froze over, as monkeys flew outta my BUTT!

How's that for crude imagery – primates parading out of a 'gluteus maximus'?! Wrecked him (RECTUM)? Damn near killed him! My 3-wheeled car swerved off the road, as I flew out over my buckled seat belt, out my open window and onto the busy highway. I may have been not entirely focused on my driving, as I pondered how awesome it was that "College Boy"[2] just "took 4 other, older black belts to school"! I'm speaking facetiously of course! I just mean that I *reeked of self-confidence*, as I intently *scouted* the busy traffic.

Regardless! Not even racing great Jeff Gordon could drive/steer his way out of a blown tire! (Maybe Dale Earnhardt could, 'cuz he's hardcore old school. ("Old school" like John Stockton and his short shorts! maybe.)

(Tangent! How unfortunate was the name of NASCAR driver "Dick Trickle"?!)

As good as that terribly eventful day began, it turned frighteningly/poisonously sour pretty damn quick!

Oh, sweet irony!

Alas! I lay dead-esque along the busy highway, hoping that I would not be run over. Needless to say,

HOPE is a GOOD thing maybe the BEST of things.

(Can I get an "AMEN!"?)

(To not confuse any of y'all, I mentioned the theological practice only for emphasis! Ya see, despite my academic domination in a Catholic high school, I'm way too obsessed with science, free will, deduction and proven facts to be any form of a "religious NUT!" I'm a "hope-full"/optimistic, probability oriented realist.)

Now I can semi-jokingly berate myself for not *shoulder-rolling*, when I struck the road.

---

[2] During my away time up at school in Philly, my fellow black belts of various *'dans'*/degrees playfully nicknamed me "College Boy".

(Uuuggghhh! How could I not?! Have I learned nothing during my ~24+ years of studying *Martial Arts*?!)

(I'd bet that I did not even break fall or exhale properly!)

(A.J., I'm not mad, just disappointed.)

In the aftermath of my debilitating accident, I've fallen victim to a unique, hair raising form of PTSD. 'Tis Positively Training after Sidestepping Death. (It's like sero negative Lyme disease or bipolar disorder in that there's not really a way to see it or to diagnose it through tests. You've just gotta take my word for it.)

('Tis a RARE offshoot of Post-Traumatic Stress Disorder.)

7.

GOTTA SOMEHOW TURN
MY FORTUNES AROUND

Someone (far wiser than myself) said: "It takes incredible forces to accomplish incredible things."

On that note, what's the force that drives/pushes you to move forward along your *path of enlightenment*?!

"Cheese n' Rice!" So, I lay on the highway bloodied, comatose with a bones jutting out of my left shoulder. But, thankfully, I was alive on the road. So, the paramedics soon scooped me up and brought me to the hospital. Obviously/rightfully, I traveled to the emergency room, where doctors performed intensive surgery on my nasty left shoulder, severely destructed left hip, horribly injured left knee and exposed brain.

: (

Basically, I was a human pin cushion!

Much of my neural damage was done to various lobes of my cerebral cortex.[1] Overall, my frontal lobe still functions ADMIRABLY, as I still excel in conscious thought, reasoning and decision making. However, my prefrontal cortex was significantly set askew, as my memory retention and processing are very subpar. Only parts of my parietal lobe were unaffected, while others now suck. My hearing (and maybe vision) has actually dramatically improved! (SSSHHH! My sister just flushed the toilet in Turkey. SSSHHH! It

---

[1] This medical info comes completely from my own research. So, don't quote me on it.

sounds busy. Ah, yes, yes. She's in populous Istanbul.) (DAMNIT! I still cannot hear a lady whisper sweet nothings in my ear. Damnit!) Also better is my spacial navigation. I hafta maneuver my motorized wheelchair everywhere in my very spacious, one story (minimal walking > no stairs) 'casa'. On the opposite end of the spectrum, I lost my sense (stop laughing, Mom!) of TASTE.

Again, my temporal lobe was only partially terminated. My hearing has improved. My smell rarely functions. (Strangely, I'll sometimes smell my fecal output, as I rest atop my porcelain throne. This rare but encouraging and disgusting nasal detection is likely due to bad smells' generally/usually being more odious/stronger than their pleasant counter-parts.) : (But, my nasal passages are clearing up/improving! The only instance in which my olfactory detection is not appreciated is when I'm aboard 'mi JUAN' ("my JOHN" = slang for "toilet"). However, I do feel slight ambivalence, when I excrete a particularly putrid fecal frenzy, 'cuz I can actually smell my gagging digestive output. I can actually semi-smell my feces better the more solid my dung is.

My occipital lobe function may have also slightly improved. I seem to require my glasses for distance **less** frequently. I'm focusing better. My astigmatism has marginally decreased. (YAY!)

My hippocampus essential for memory function and sexual urges is one of the few neural areas capable of actually promoting nerve regeneration! Thus, I get really excited (pun intended.), when I become aroused! So, there is hope! (It's SCIENCE!) Although, this replenishing ability is impaired by stress related "glucocorticoids." Ergo, I've gotta just roll with the punches more.

(Don't sweat the small stuff!)

Minute inspection of my neural x rays revealed that my amygdala connections were way more widespread from the right amygdala than from the left. This side preference is indicative of a heterosexual male and/or a homosexual female.

(That would explain my great attraction to the 'XX' chromosome possessors.)

Further analyzing my hippocampus, y'all can deduce that I'm not just seeking a ro-mantic affair, but, I'm also searching for a memory liason to guide me to open new doors to old thoughts.

(Ya see, I cherish ol' stories about my goofier days. I'm hoping that some *verbal recounting* of my past tales might *initiate* sumthin' in my *memory recall!*)

My parietal lobe is relatively (hhhmmm, what's the technical term? ah, yes.) *OUT of WHACK*: My spatial senses are decent. (The minimal damage to my house walls may claim otherwise.) I aptly regulate some sensory info that actually arrives at/comes from my brain. I can get happy or mad or goofy. But, physically/neurologically, I just cannot cry.

: (

No, it's not some misogynistic/overly mannish persona! My T.B.I. just does not allow my eyes to create those fluids. (SSSHHH! I sold my tear ducts to the local medical school to raise enough $ for legal fees. SSSHHH!) Even in my most unfortunate and saddening times (e.g. my longtime beau's surprising, still completely unexplained separation and my father's unexpected passing), as rattled and heartbroken as I was, I could not shed a tear.

(That unintentional nonvisible sadness is in itself a tear-jerker.)

I inadvertently internalize much/all of my emotions.

Overall, my improved senses of hearing, touch, vision, focus and reasoning/processing have over compensated for my diminished senses of smell, taste, speech and solo standing.

NOTES: I did all that Neurological research myself post-accident. So, it holds credence in that I am a biomedical engineer. But, I do have a *Traumatic BRAIN Injury*. So, don't necessarily quote those brain facts.

(Actually, do cite them! I am that confident!)

Speaking of "over compensating," I've noticed that my arms have become very strong. My remarkable leg power used to characterize my Karate, Wrestling and Jujitsu dominance. But, now, with essentially no ability to move my legs, my arms have gotten quite strong!

(FURTHERMORE:
- TASTE = BAD > VISION = BETTER
- SMELL = BAD > HEARING = BETTER
- VOICE = BAD > THINKING = BETTER
- WALKING = BAD > SLEEPING = BETTER)

Sooo, after awakening from my accident caused coma, I fell into a medically induced coma. (Why the medical chiefs needed two separate comas/unconscious states of mind to complete my surgical corrections I know not. Actually, the doctors could justify their inducing a second coma. It would decrease some of the immediate pain in recovery.

But, my anger usurped my reasoning in writing that. A second coma?! More *LOST time*?! Really?! Was that actually necessary?!

I also do not know how long my respective comas were. Lemme check my files/notes/diary (Oh. Wait. I'm a dude! Ergo, I meant journal!) (I'm fingering through my files. Oh, wait. How could I have taken notes, when I was unconscious?! Then, what the hell is this book?! Oh, it's my copy of 'Goodnight, Moon', 'cuz I'm a child.) So, let's just guesstimate that each coma lasted between three days and 50 weeks ($\rightarrow$ 3 DAYS < X ~0.97 YEARS)

(Is it that obvious that my turbulent surgical history has deleted almost all respect I had for the surgical profession?!

MY degree is in Biomedical Engineering. and, since it's from a highly respected Ivy League institution, that makes my medical understanding pretty damn impressive! 'Tis aaalmost doctor-esque.)

(I kid. I kid! I have the utmost respect for the at least 8+ years of biomedical studies that medical doctors hafta do! I only did four.)

By the way, I'm not bitter! (SARCASM) I simply crunched the numbers on necessary versus aesthetic surgical mishaps.[2]

But, nevertheless, I marched onward (metaphorically). One personality trait of mine that may have actually improved since my devastating accident is my indefatigable determination. I face numerous obstacles every time I move! But, I always give my 110%, After I analyze the physics and angles to hypothesize the ideal procedure. (IF you're gonna GO, go ALL OUT.)

'Tis that never say die attitude that fuels the converting process of my thinking from idea to hypothetical to possibility to hope to mental application to imaginary visualization to physical enactment to kick ass success to CELEBRATORY JIG.

---

[2] As a senior in high school, I actually chose to study and ace all year 'Advanced Placement Statistics' as an elective! (NERD!)

(Yes, despite my caucasian ethnicity, i used to cut a little rug on the dance floor!)

(That was the general step by step breakdown of my process for confronting an issue.)

Physically, I've had to overcome non-working legs, a BAD ~11/16ths of my LEFT arm, a BAD ~5/16ths of my LEFT hand, a BAD ~two fifths of my RIGHT hand",[3] surgically LIMITED LEFT shoulder movement, DRASTICALLY severed VOCAL cords, MANY severed NERVES and a Traumatic Brain Injury.

Mentally/neurologically, I've dealt with very inconsistent (if at all) brain to muscle' message/impulse receptions. I've *trudged through* countless *pieces* of a subpar memory. My live-in girlfriend of six years just unexpectedly/inexplicably/unceremoniously *ended us,* leaving me painstakingly helpless. Plus, I have to *weather* the constant frustrational *storm* of depending on others' help for menial tasks. Plus, my T.B.I. has unfortunately minimized my patience thus decreasing my sociability

Socially, 'tis very difficult to not be a social pariah, when I rarely go out of my comfort zone/house ('cuz of the physical awkwardness) and struggle to use a telephone. (I still occasionally use a letter board by pointing to letters on a board to spell out my thoughts in-person.) My semi-active Facebook friends seem to be my only saving grace. I've gotta understand that nobody else has nearly as much *free time* as I do. So, I should not feel so *low,* when others can't join me.

Another example of other's unsuspecting/unknown deceit toward me would be my learning of a former fraternity brother (3 years older), who claimed he started a charity/fund to pay for my recovery costs. 'Twas supposedly going to accept monetary donations from my *brethren* to help fund my recovery process. Upon my intense monetary investigation, my banker[s] knew nothing of said (faux) "fund". So, this former Fraternity brother/*Eminent treasurer* (I'm guessing that's why his lie seemed so believable.) cheated numerous unsuspecting, young gentlemen out of 'X' dollars.

(BOOOO!)

Said *brother* and I never really *got along.* I'm hoping that he did not seek payback on a comatose former *associate.*

---

[3] As a junior in high school (pre-accident), I was goofin' around before a wrestling match, when I fell very awkwardly and broke my right forearm. It required surgery. Consequently/unfortunately, the surgeon nicked my ulnar nerve. Since then, I've been unable to fully open my right hand.

Thus, I've had a lot on my plate![4] The fact that I still have tons of obligations (e.g. *Martial Arts* Teaching (The children are literally our future.), Business organization, big house management, employee satisfaction and (I shrug.) Oh, yeeeaaahhh my rehabbing) illustrates just how strong my back must be to sturdily withstand all that heavy responsibility.

Consequently, I frequently host parties to better communicate with the outside world. I shan't LIE: I do frequently *scout* the female guests for prettiness and personality plusses due to my super hyperactive hippocampus and amygdala.

I've gotta highlight my virtues, in lieu of how obvious some of my vices are. My necessary wheelchair and needed voice generating device ('DynaVox') help a LOT.

If it weren't ridiculously illegal, offensive, chilly, uncouth, socially unacceptable and currently physically impossible, I'd go 'Econ SCREAM'-ing often. (That would highlight either virtue or vice, depending on the victim! Beauty's in the eye(s) of the beholder.)

Above all, I've gotta remember: "Never stop never stoppin'!"

Life doesn't/won't get any easier. I'll just hafta get stronger! With my formally working out/exercising three times/days per week plus two *Martial Arts* classes per week, I'd venture to say that I certainly do my all to keep my body busy!

The legendary artist Michelangelo brilliantly said:

"The greater danger for most of us is not that our 'aim' is too high and we miss it. But that it is too low and we reach it."

---

[4] That's a humorous pun, 'cuz I actually eat all my nutrients and vitamins and medication via a "test tube attached to my stomach" I occasionally eat via mouth (in speech Therapy as Lip, Throat and Tongue practice but nothing is "ABSORBED.")
: (

8.
I Am a "Marked Man"

THERE WERE/ARE NUMEROUS CONSEQUENCES and repercussions physical, emotional and/or psychological of my dreaded/catastrophic "Traumatic Brain Injury."

Physically, I have a large skin toned, ~6-inch scar (ladies, contrary to your thoughts, "~SIX inches" is ginormous!) along my left inner shoulder from my surgery. Internally, there are nine screws embedded in/attached to my left shoulder. I have a much smaller ~1.5-inch surgical slice mark on my left inner hip.

There's an even smaller surgical aftermath on my left inner knee. The less visible the permanent scar, the greater/higher the quality/skill of the surgeon. Nevertheless, scars serve as a reminder that the past however horrific 'twas was real.

Emotionally, I'm deeply saddened that I cannot live up to my own rather lofty but realistic/attainable expectations. Pre-injuries, I thought/hoped I would become a happily married family man/socialite/petroleum Distribution Site Manager who doubles as a genius!

Psychologically, I really struggle at times to remain positive with so many unfortunate travesties happening in my mid to late 20s. My previous plethora of friends has significantly decreased in quantity.

(QUALITY > QUANTITY?)

(My understimulated hippocampus disagrees.) (Cue the "BOW WOW chicka BOW WOW" music.)

My T.B.I. has drastically diminished my memory storage capabilities. My imminent 'Shodan ' ('black belt') test for Jujitsu has been unknowingly delayed. Most of my favorite sports teams have been sucking in the early "2000 teens". By far the worst of all feelings is that my former/ex-fiancée suddenly and inexplicably won't even talk to me!

(Without so much of a reason why – STILL!)

Nonetheless, I've gotta keep trying with anything and everything! The biggest risk is never taking any. In other words, Grow some BALLZ! Y'all too, ladies!

(Relax, estrogen possessors! I just mean, display some testosterone in a slang way.)

However, I am neither hesitant nor ashamed to admit that my psyche was so messed up that I saw a necessary and brilliant NeuroPsychoTherapist for awhile in 2014 through '17.

Virtually the only mental weakness I now have is a very spotty, unreliable memory intake/capacity. Although, since I'm a visual learner, faces rather than just names trigger recognition, but, alas, no tales. (I recognize faces but not why.)

As an optimist, I like to remind myself of the motivating words of quarterback Shane Falco in the movie *The Replacements*:

"Pain heals. Chicks dig scars. Glory lasts forever."

But, since no ladies can see my cranial "scar" on my unshaven head, don't tell me I'd hafta buzz my beauteous locks (of cranial hair) just to get some (female) ass/sympathy!

I do occasionally stand naked in front of my big bathroom mirror, grab my hairy pectoral muscles and ask aloud: "Would you fuck me? I'd fuck me."

(I'm mocking "Buffalo Bill" of 'Silence of the Lambs'.)

I can't stand (pun not intended), when IGNORAMUSES confuse empathy with sympathy! It's infuriating, when some doofus says to me: "I know how you FEEL," 'cuz face it you don't have the SLIGHTEST CLUE!

A coworker of my ex-housemate[1] asked him about his previous living conditions with a Traumatic Brain Injury victim (me). His reply: "About the only thing we know about that guy right now is he's independently wealthy, well-educated, and totally insane."

(—Random Cop in *Se7en* talking about John Doe)

---

[1] I'm considering hosting a "FRIEND-aissance" party with my ex-housemate and I dressed as Teenage Mutant Ninja Turtles to represent the storied artists "Leonardo (da Vinci) and Michelangelo."

Upon hearing of his explanation, I exclaimed: "Way to quote *Se7en*! And, I am 'CRAZY like a FOX'!"

Furthermore, true beauty's in the eye of the beholder.

Besides, you hafta see me in my element of teaching proper form at Martial Arts class. Since I have usually forgotten much of the order of the "prearranged set of fighting movements" or *'KATA'*, I've developed a new appreciation of proper form and efficient movements.

9.
BEGINNING RECOVERY

SOOO, I SPENT MOST OF MY IMMEDIATE time after my terribly catastrophic accident after my two heart breaking, gut wrenching comas after my re-
paratory surgeries (~4.25 years), semi-recovering at some random Neurologic
Rehabilitation Services of Florida (*N.R.S.F.*)

My time there was physically beneficial. I kinda felt (and still feel) like an infant: (RE)
LEARNING how to stand and walk and piss and talk (separately) and laugh and mock
and rhyme, as I check stock. So, even as a severely disabled T.B.I. victim, I'm multitasking
much to the dismay of my mother, who abhors the concept! She believes: "If you're
multi-tasking, then your attention can only focus on one thing at any one time. Sooo,
you'd always be 'half-ass'-ing something."

Aaahhh, yes. 'tis a very TRUE, mathematically sound argument for most people.
However, I'd like to think that my own mother knows that her firstborn progeny is mentally light-years[1] (metaphorically) ahead of most people. As was the case/deal in my 'Calculus' classes, I'd complete a test toward the middle of the pack time wise usually. But I'd
always be among the top scores. (In this case, I rated *quality over quantity*.)

My time at the rehab facility was also tremendously mentally/psychologically helpful.

---

[1] Contrary to the TIME frame the name "light year" implies, the term is actually a unit
of DISTANCE.
(5,850,000,000,000 miles = ~6 trillion miles)

My *Traumatic Brain Injury* as the name suggests was so dramatic, significant and mind boggling that I lost almost all of my already mystifying/dazzling intelligence! (Actually, That's a flat out lie! I'm still MATHEMATICALLY, SCIENTIFICALLY and LOGICALLY well-minded. My main mental discrepancy is a spotty subpar memory.) I've come to accept my (metaphorical) mental drop to being a FAUX-*HEMI-DEMI-SEMI-QUAVER of a* "*normee*"[2] (me). Consequently, I now take three showers a day, to wash off the (imagined) filth of thinking regularly. Ironically, my time at said Neural Rehab facility made me more mentally/psychologically unstable and paranoid!

My words may seem condescending. But, NNNOOOOO! 'Tis just that my T.B.I. has kinda forced me to become very hesitant to accept change. And, after ~23.25 years of (generally/usually) being in the right (Yes, even as an infant, I'd just kinda know who my family was, what prime #s were, where my mouth was while eating, when I have to evacuate my bowels, why Americans don't use the metric system, and how to convert Thanksgiving leftovers into a gourmet omelet.[3]), 'Tis a thorough puncture in my pride to admit that I'm often ignorant/un informed.

(AUDIBLE sigh)

My fears/worries were confirmed, when my mom and I deduced that the rehab facility had created zero/none of the "therapeutic devices" it claimed it would get when asking my mom for money for ~four frickin' YEARS! So, the SUBpar institution repeatedly STOLE my money and continuously lied to my mother.

Upon calculatin' all my lost cash ('Twas A LOT!), I begged my mom to "get me the hell outta there"! After learning of the deceit, dis honesty and (technically) robbery, my mom obliged. So, I VAMOOSED from my living NIGHTMARE.

(WHEW!)

Me to N.R.S.F. "how and why did y'all keep 'faux' rehabbing me for so long?!"

N.R.S.F. Executive to me: "You had certain dis advantages."

ME: "I know my vocal cords are damaged."

N.R.S.F.: "Yes, that and you're insane."

ME: "You're yet again delving into 'the realms of semantics'. Besides, since you're

---

[2] A supposed 1/64th of a normal, *run o' the mill societal DOLT*.

[3] Now post-accident, I thought of a great recipe that I need to try for some *breakfast pizza*.

talkin' semantics. Beauty's in the eyes of the beholder and vice versa."

My settlement from my lawsuit against the tire company funded my purchase of a large, easily accessible house loaded with handicap accommodations! So, I'm not a big fan of leaving my humble abode (Aaah, sarcasm!). (I will! But, I don't like to.) Therefore, I try to host many parties in hopes of showing friends that I am sociable via my letter board: fun, witty, entertaining, and generous!

Also, 'tis essential/paramount especially for me to always remain "BALLZY".[4] I will never get better, unless/until I'm willing to take some chances. Set high standards and goals for yourself. With the right preparation and focused determination, you will reach them. My preparation involves alotta mental calculations. The fact that my hypotheses are usually correct further proves that I am quite the neurological anomaly with extreme *mental strength*!

(Sarcastic chuckle) Immediately after my accident's [necessary and impending] surgical repairs, my doctors proclaimed that "what saved [me] from being a nonfunctioning 'VEGETABLE' or even death is [my] incredible mental strength"! For example, while I was supposedly comatose in the hospital post-surgeries, the *Murses* (= MALE nurses) were arguing over who threw the "pick six" to Larry Brown in Super Bowl XXX. I murmured "NEE O'ahhl". My first semi-words post-accident were the correct naming of the GOAT of Super Bowl XXX: Neil O'Donnell. (Tis not like I could just look up the answer! Some things you just KNOW.)

I believe it was the ever so wise Tigger of 'Winnie the Pooh' who deduced: "Life is not about how fast you run or how high you climb but how well you BOUNCE BACK."

---

[4] RELAX! 'Tis slang for "BRAVE."

10.
SOME HOBBIES JUST STICK

SADLY, MY **T.B.I.** has both drastically diminished my plethora of past memories and dramatically limited my neural capacity for future thoughts. 'Tis this neural detriment that kinda forces me to live in the NOW!

I've gotta make NEW, REFRESHING memories! Sadly, I LACK NEARBY peers with da *BALLZ* to HANG out.

: (

Strangely, four of the first things to return to my mental "lockbox" (*Saturday Night Live*) post-accident, injuries and surgeries were my humor, my movie quotes, my "knowledge of sports stats" and ('Tuh BEE!' > Phonetic Turkish for 'of course!') my mathematical comprehension. (Actually, 'tis scientifically accurate, 'cuz past "T.B.I." victims have shown that they usually maintain their strengths and interests.)

Now, I still teach *Martial Arts* to kids. Thankfully, they usually do not try my *patience*. Occasionally, I'll get down on the mat to demonstrate the 'Jujitsu' techniques that I designed. But, I don't need to show 'em myself, 'cuz my assistants are fully competent and capable. (Whew!) I had a really sore left hip, and it kinda hurt, when I'd lie down in the supine position for 'Jujitsu' practice. But, since I've been better "weight shifting" and compensating when I "walk",[1] it's been feeling much better! As a biomedical engineer, I correctly predicted that I just needed some "R and R" ("Rest and Relaxation.").

---

[1] Always when I put walk in quotation marks, I mean "slowly shuffle stepping while leaning on and pushing a "walker" like I'm 76 years old.

Semi-layman (BioEngineering me): 1 – Medical doctors: 0

I meet with my two "'Martial Arts' underlings" (HahaHA!) on occasion to practice said "techniques" to make sure they "get the (respective) premise." I still watch many movies preferably "comedies." Supposedly, "laughter" is the best medicine unless the person suffers from severe asthma attacks or cardiac issues. I still watch almost any sport even 'swimming', 'rifle shooting' and poker. As is my reflex, I always "crunch numbers" of the odds of winning hands. I still host parties from time to time. 'Tis a comfortable, relaxed, familiar atmosphere that's really close by!

I'm not gonna brag here about "kickin' ass" in *Martial Arts* class. So, let's just say I kicked every ass I faced. (Not literally!)

Unfortunately, I'm just not biophysically able to actually wrestle or even swim in my own pool! So, I use these "cant's as motivation for/in my ongoing "fights."

'Por Ejemplo',[2] I thought I couldn't swim, (pause for effect) just 'cuz of worry about my "G tube." 'Au contraire!' My main nurse said that the central issue is that there are many animals like frogs, iguanas, lizards, and small snakes getting into/onto my pool/patio area. They poop and pee a lot. If any animal's bodily waste got near my G tube, it'd be catastrophic like I was eating their feces and/or drinking their urine.

EEEWWW!

So, I am more than willing to pay an exorbitant amount for a patio screen from the surrounding trees, bushes and water.

"I've gotta think about the good of the team!"
– ANY DECENT ATHLETE.

The probability of the potential benefits of any aquatic therapy far outweigh the possible drawbacks of "water exercise."

(Again, my storied academic history with 'probability and statistics' is rather extensive

---

[2] SPANISH for 'For example' I TEND to speak in FOREIGN languages (e.g. Turkish,/Spanish/Japanese), when I REALLY get UNcomfortable.

and commendable.)

I still amaze/astound my mom and friends, when I just randomly "rattle off" cinematic quotes that are somehow pertinent to the discussion *at hand*. Pre-accident, I could recite the quote, by which character, from what movie and the plot circumstances from many a film. Now, I at best can recite most of the quote, give two possible Speaker options, guess the film title but know the plot. ('Cuz I thoroughly understand film plot)

"Swimming" is a fantastic form of exercise! 'Tis an excellent (biophysics related) type of kinesthesia. The water provides a small amount of resistance against my moving limbs. 'EH-VEH-RE-TIYM!' "Swimming" is the best type of exercise in that it works all ~620 muscles.[3] It used to be my favorite form of (one person) calisthenics. As a 13-year-old "Boy Scout of America", I earned the "mile swim" merit badge at summer camp in North Carolina by swimming ~76 consecutive, non-stop laps in an Olympic sized pool. Plus! I live in Florida!

As yet another form of "over compensation," the "amygdala" of my brain has been overly stimulated. The "AMYGDALA" is the area of the brain that controls all emotional and sexual behavior. So, despite my inability to publically express my extreme feelings of HAPPINESS or SADNESS, I still POSSESS JOY and SORROW "on the INSIDE."

'Por Ejemplo' the two most (emotionally) "painful" moments of my entire 31+ year life were the sudden death of my father and the sudden, still unexplained breakup by my former fiancée. I don't care who teases me: I would've cried! I *permanently lost* my long-time *best pal,* and I somehow *screwed the pooch* with my potential *life partner.*

:(

In a romantic relationship, I like to establish *jobs*. From time to time, my EX would *overstep her boundaries.*

:(

(I.e. she was an "acute angle," while I am "obtuse". But, together, we are "supplementary.")

(Damn, I'm witty with the math puns!)[4]

---

[3] This EXACT # is DEBATABLE. I'm just goin' with the number the "HEAD" of my "Martial Arts" system, 'cuz he IS a doctor.

[4] Evidently, I have few *limitations* or embarrassments.

11.
BANKRUPTCY

JUST KIDDING!

(Although, if I were not so diligent and skilled at Quantitative Analysis, *N.R.S.F.* (just a pseudonym) would've made me BEEEEEroke!)

With my stellar, responsible, and obedient, "Banking team of 'Economic Handlers'", I do alright.

(Aaahhh, gotta love that "reverse hyperbole" or sarcastic exaggeration"[1]) Actually, I do contribute "a lil' sumthin'" to my economic success.

Ya see, as of July 31st, 2016 ~8.07 years since my accident, I've profited ~15.27% of my initial investment via the stock market on/about my 30th birthday (April 8th, 2015). So, technically, that'd be ~$24.51 profit per day, if I worked 365 days a year. I'd be "gettin' hosed"! 'Cuz that's only be ~$3.06 per hour!

(Ya see, I really get "numbers"! Legitimately, I could've been a successful statistician. But, how little intimacy do math geeks actually get?!)

(Well, before my last breakup, I'da proudly disagreed!

But, now, I've gotta side with the numeric assumptions and statistical tendencies.

: (

Ya see, my 'Macroeconomics A.P.' class senior year of high school was very helpful! However, I guess my familiarity with the "financial material" wasn't as strong as I would've

---

[1] I'da thunk that "over exaggerate" would be a word, 'cuz I'da associated that with hyperbole. But, That'd be a bit redundant.

hoped, as I "only got" a 'C+' in my 'Finance and Accounting' class for my accelerated M.B.A. program, but I (technically) needed a 'B ' for MY degree. (Oh, well. I'll figure out how to "count" the credits toward my electives, so I don't "lose the credit time".)

In hindsight, my pursuit of a business degree was a huge waste of time and effort! Further "pulling my weight", I'll occasionally assist my mom by (all mentally) "balancing her checkbook" She'll just give me the "list of Transactions" (money in versus money out), I'll compute each's respective sum and equate them.

That's my way of (silently) showing my appreciation for her "breaking me out" of that "'N.R.S.F.' prison"!

This chapter title is a big joke, as my catastrophic accident did the exact opposite monetarily. Now, in my spare free time, I just research potentially successful (usually Biotech) companies, invest $X, monitor 'em and lick my lips as my money soooars!

I think I might now have enough $ to "pay [my] ATTENTION". (barely).

12.

"IF AT FIRST YOU DON'T SUCCEED,' DUST YOURSELF OFF AND TRY AGAIN"

– AALIYAH, "TRY AGAIN"

AS "SHITTY" AS MY LIFE may (often) seem, 'tis paramount to always "keep my head up"! Miracles happen every day. I've just gotta keep looking and trying! As a "science freak", I've long been a staunch proponent of the "'Trial and Error' then Learn and Apply" experimenting technique. Now, I just utilize it more.

> *"No amount of security is worth the suffering of a medio-cre life 'chained to' a routine that has 'killed your dreams'."*
> **(—MAYA MENDOZA)**

Despite my court ordered exorbitant material wealth, there is no frickin' 'way that I'd ever give up/trade my amazing legs for $$!

("HIND sight's 20/20", right? Shut up, Conscience!)

I'm considering gettin' in my bathtub, fillin' it with cash then having the discipline to not use my legs, as i bathe in DOLLA, DOLLA bills, YO! (what a strip show!)

Carpe Diem! ("Seize the day!" in Latin)

I tried reenrolling in graduate school. Pre-accident, I had a ~3.82 GPA in my business studies. Post-injuries, I just felt way, way too frustrated, confused, and helpless at my having to depend on other students to take notes for me and ask questions for me. So, I took turns angrily pulling out my hair and correcting the teacher's math. (Jeez, he was terrible at basic, non-accounting mental math! But, I shan't judge! To each his own.) Ultimately, I decided to value my happiness and pleasantry over/higher than an unnecessary degree.

So, I again (temporarily?!) withdrew from grad school after completing my half assed 'C+'. The teacher's calculations were so pitiful that my grade could've been anywhere from a 'B ' to a 'C+' to a 'C' to a 'C '. Regardless, I passed a 'Finance and Accounting' class as a management major in an "accelerated degree program" at a respected Business School (Huizenga School for Business) with a Traumatic Brain Injury and without the ability to take notes! Soooo, I tried the academic realm as a possible social outlet. But, as I should know (beforehand), not everything in 'academia' comes easily for most students. So, (unfortunately) they'd hardly have time to "shoot the shit" with me.

Eh, bummer! It turns out that I passed with only a 'C+'! That shit's way below my (lofty) standards! *"C'est la vie."* I have to accept that my ways of testing are way different from what they used to be. And, besides, actually choosing to "take an 'accelerated program'" and passing it are commendable enough!

Hhhmmm. Perhaps my constant goofiness and shenanigans while still acing every class upset some of my peers. "Eh, fuck it, *Dude*. Let's go bowling."

– Walter Sobchak, *The Big Lebowski*

> *"And I've dropped out, I've burned up, I've fought my way back from the dead.*
> *I've tuned in, turned on, remembered the things that you said!"*
> **– EDWIN McCAIN, "I'LL BE"**

Why is it that we can remember the past but not the future?
(Whoooa! I think I just "blew my mind!)
That's so *deep*!

(And, *that's what SHE said!* The assist goes to KAYNATMA!)

> *"I went to 'the woods' because I wanted to live deliberately.*
> *I wanted to live deep and suck out all the marrow of life."*
> **–HENRY DAVID THOREAU**

In my case/example:

"The woods" are the questionable realms of grad school. But, Beware! "Sucking out marrow" does not necessarily require choking on the bone! Life has times that call for caution and times that call for daring. It takes insight, intuition and sagacity to know the difference.

Ergo, all my doings take me a lil' longer, partially 'cuz I always calculate odds beforehand.

"Living deliberately" > "Behaving socially."

"Live deep" > "Be friendly."

"Suck out marrow" > "Befriend classmates."

Overall, 'twas a well-intentioned attempt. But, ultimately, this T.B.I. has unfortunately torn down countless dreams of love, *Martial Arts*, Science, Socializing, Traveling, Friends and Family.

Nevertheless, I must slightly alter my goals, all the while hoping for the best!

I.e. Instead of leaving business school at the time, I weighed my happiness priorities and decided to stick with the grad classes only to simultaneously write for the school paper. My blogging has lit a fire of desire in me for writing/telling my amazing and inspirational tales.

For the longest time (~26.08 years), I've only possessed an academic yearning for quantification.[1] But, my blogging inspired me to develop a new mental passion. It certainly helps that I'm somewhat familiar with the protagonist in this here autobiography.

(Cough cough! I'm choking on the sarcasm!)

("He's a good man and thorough!" – *The Big Lebowski*)

('Tis I!)

---

[1] I'm fluent in numerology.

I guess I'm kinda like a 'lifelock' employee. Only instead of "protecting against 'Identity Theft'", I focus on self-development. The company/product name just seems kinda like my constant, permanent quest for self-betterment.

13.
EVERY DAY'S A NEW DAY

'DA CONTINUED TO DRIVE around with one expired tire. 'Twas just aesthetically unappealing, not mechanically unsound.

Don't judge! "To each his own." Actually, hhhmmm, I will "judge", 'cuz I'm directly
affected by the Mechanic's Numeric genocide. This is HORSESHIT! I'd feel like a
soggy, shit sandwich, if (and when) I mess up a lesson. I feel I have a responsibility to give
my kids ("students") the best I can. (But, I hopefully will teach my genealogical/actual
kids the proper info to keep them well-informed!) Even though it's not usually my fault,
I know 'tis of the utmost importance to accept responsibility. I'm kinda built like a brick
shit house in that I shoulder alotta blame.

(Ha ha ha! There's a double entendre or pun on "shit house", 'cuz I have broad shoulders on a slim waist and a propensity for semi-frequent bowel bonanzas.)

(TENTATIVE) Day-by-Day Schedule	
MONDAY:	Payroll (for seven employees) (Every other week) Speech Therapy (hour long) Workout (hour long)
TUESDAY:	*Upper body* Workout (hour long) NeuroPsychoTherapist's Meeting (hour long) (Every third week)
WEDNESDAY:	Rest Speech Therapy (hour long)
THURSDAY:	"Martial Arts" class (~1.75 hours)
FRIDAY:	Speech Therapy (hour long) Workout (hour long)
SATURDAY:	"Martial Arts" Class (~1.75 hours)
SUNDAY:	Rest Plan weekly schedule/activities (I constantly think of new techniques for Karate class.)

14.
SOME OF MY FREQUENT TASKS

"All in all, the goal of my planning and doing is to find the true meaning of life 'PEACE of MIND'."
– BRUCE LEE

AS A FELLOW **"MARTIAL ARTS" EXPERT** to a much lesser degree, I hold everything Mr. Lee said in very high regard!

Not only do I mentally plan/visualize and act out all my sparring/self defense techniques in Karate/Jujitsu class, but I hafta prep for all my movements. I hafta ensure my safety and comfort using physics and probability, before I "tackle" a new task. E.g. before every walk, I hafta enact a plan, visualize it and follow through. I see my "Weight SHIFTING". I "see" my "straight-backed" posture. I "SEE" my non-"pigeon toed" gait. I used to only look down at the ground. Now, thanks to repeated practice walks, strong mental power and requested ankle stretches, I almost never hafta glance down at my feet for "psychological stability."('Tis my "telekinesis.")

Those were all examples of "mind over matter": I'd see a "physical drawback (of mine)" and kinda will it away. In lieu of my continuous quasi "telekinesis," my ex-housemate/current buddy quotes *Star Wars* about Me: "'The force' is strong with this one."

"Whatever the mind can CONCEIVE and BELIEVE, the

MIND can ACHIEVE."
– NAPOLEON HILL

Of my numerous self-goals, I always make sure to at least start 'em! I'm big on the *trial and error* tactic for *procedural analysis* with a steadfast emphasis on *trials*. I could kinda "rest on my laurels", and just be content with my being alive after that life-changing (almost life-ending) debacle of a car crash.

But, my perilous psyche does not let me take the easy way out! I "trudge onward" regardless of the numerous/countless "setbacks"! You improve not by always winning but by insightfully adapting after losing. My car accident would be a catastrophic loss of my legs. So, I'll just continue to adapt to my lower observation angle in my wheelchair.

(In other words, I'll continue to hope and work for my independence.[1])

Actually, I kinda prefer to be busy to avoid random thoughts about the numerous negative turns my life has taken! I long to hang out with friends! I need to distract myself from my incidental concentration on the many recent negative aspects of my life by somehow focusing on my supportive friends! I like to live vicariously through them. I refer to my closest friends as "MY 'Insane Clown Posse.'"

Since I cannot yet taste, I like to constantly "eye" what my peers dine on at restaurants. Then, I "rate" the nutritional versus desirable "value" of the "food input" to determine if I'd order said cuisine.

So, seeing and feeling my physical changes/success gives me great feelings of motivation and accomplishment. Despite my (temporary) inability to (independently) walk and (cogently) talk, I feel grand and proud of the notable progress I've made in the last (as of September '16) ~8.21 years.

My feats are particularly astounding, when one considers that rarely does a "T.B.I." victim show any significant improvement after two years. As further evidence of my

---

[1] For a number of years after my accident and comas, the ignorant government rescinded all of my [supposedly] Constitutionally protected "rights" (e.g. "marry", "vote", "own housing", manage my own finances, etc.)

"anomaly ness", most of my dramatic, visible improvements have occurred, after I "grad-
uated" from "Therapeutic school"[2] to "independent recuperation."

(e.g. eating via mouth, semi-smelling, semi-tasting, "walking" with minimal assistance,
three different, intense, hour-long workouTS per week, *Martial Arts* teaching)

Time-wise, that'd be all after ~4.3 years of uneventful, (faux) guided therapy.[3]

I especially enjoy walking with just a cane and a trainer's holding/stabilizing my left
arm/elbow!

I frustratingly show y'all this timely Self-Therapy.

Speaking of potential suffering, I could have "turned the table" of certain harm, on
March 15, 2003, I earned a Martial Arts black belt (actually, Surprise surprise! 'Twas
two!). As a direct result, I had to "register my hands as 'lethal weapons'". Since I used to
(pre-injuries) always prefer my herculean leg power to my more believable arm strength,
now I kinda hafta compensate. 'Tis all about "making the best out of what you have."

Ergo, have I become even more "fatal"?!

---

[2] *N.R.S.F.* actually told my mom about me: "He's so advanced mentally that we don't
know what to do with him anymore." (AUDIBLE sigh)

[3] Did I mention that the stupid American government took over four frickin' years to
realize I am in fact "not dead!"? During that time, the American government had
stripped me of all of my (supposedly) Constitutionally protected "in alienable rights"!

15
LONG TERM GOALS

I wanna swim and WALK,
laugh and TALK,
tease and MOCK
and find the "KEY" to my "leg LOCK."
My determination will cause friends to GAWK.
My gait will NOT warrant a MOCK.
I just successfully put on my SOCK.

GOOFY RHYMING ASIDE. I really wanna redevelop all o' my senses including walking. Despite the fact that the numbers/stats are against me, I've kinda developed a habit of rising up over (metaphoric) "hurdles". (I've never run track. I was never notably fast.) Even in Martial Arts, my teachers would compliment me on my "unique blending of speed and power." Legitimately, however, I'd tip the scale slightly more to favor power and intensity over speed and fluidity. My Martial Arts Professor even asked me in early 2016 to write and present a speech to the kids about "remaining headstrong and overcoming adversity." So, I did. Professor liked it so much, that he subsequently asked me to present it to the adults' class. So, I did. I guess I'm sorta/kinda an informal motivational speaker. (Legitimately, that positive reception of my relentless "triumphing" over distress provided further motivation to share my tales on a larger scale.)

Sooo, I started writing.

Ultimately, I really wanna find a (female) *life partner*. Mother of my "offspring" and "JOKE partner". Ideally, these three characteristics would be "all rolled up" into one

"Wonder Woman"!

To those who devote all of their hope and faith to an "outside being": you have been assigned this "mountain" to show others it can be moved. (That's just what I do!)

I guess I'm "agnostic" like my father was. "Religion" was just never really emphasized or even mentioned in my childhood home. 'Tis not that I have any less respect for theologians. 'Tis just that "I don't swing that way." I feel that I am more "in control" of my own life. But, to each, his own. (My "independent thinking" is further evidence of the "nurture" theory in child-raising.)

I have alotta material wealth that I want to share with a family I co-start! I'm very interested in establishing a legacy.

In the meantime, I'm enjoying *writing*. So, I'll continue that.

(I hope that's good!?!)

16.
SHORT TERM ACTS NEEDED FOR LONG-TERM SUCCESS

I am determined to kinda "rub the 'nose' (of the organization that "gave up" on me) in my [metaphoric] 'shit'! As sophomoric as that plan may be,

"The best 'revenge' is 'living well'."
– JERRY, *SEINFELD*

Ergo, I'll just continue to enjoy my success in biophysics learning, healthy eating via mouth, constant speaking, tiring yet awesome "walking" and successful "lavatory venturing."

Between ~April 8, 2015 (my 30th birthday) and August 31, 2016, I'd made ~14.51% of my initial investment as profit from the 11 stocks that I selected! 'Twas a rather large investment, 'cuz I know I'm still really frickin' smart (I did my financial homework. T.B.I. be damned!). It's my money (So, I'd have no one to thank or blame but myself.) and I needed a "project" to monitor!

Ya see, I was able to determine certain economic trends and business patterns using algorithms that I learned in 12th grade "Advanced Placement' Macroeconomics."

The major issue I learned from my (AUDIBLE sigh) barely passing that business class is 'finance' regards trend analysis for future transactions, while 'accounting' involves more recording of past transactions."

(There was way too much finance jargon for a T.B.I. victim to dominate as he usually does. Alas, I shan't make excuses! Gotta just play like a champion!)

I don't have delusions of grandeur. I have an actual recipe for "awesomeness."

'Tis as follows:

1) Provide constant effort.
2) Add 2 Handfuls of pizazz. (Not "pizza")
3) Scoop a spoonful of sugar (to help that medicine go DOOOWWWN)
4) Produce wise decisions.
5) Watch the clock for opportunistic timing.
6) Mix all together.
7) 'Voila!' This should yield eventual happiness and (objective?) awesomeness.

(Repeat over and over again)

'Tis not that I took my legs for granted preaccident. But, since then I have certainly gained a greater appreciation of all they do.

> *"Sometimes you hafta experience what you don't want in life to come to an understanding of what you do."*
> **– MANDY HALE**

It's all about showing, displaying and expressing gratification and appreciation! I.e. I am extremely thankful, when my employees do the little things to ensure my satisfaction. Ergo, I am quick with my verbal and monetary *thanks*.

Since I do not (yet!) drink, every time a group of my friends sit around and imbibe beverages, I offer a toast: "To knowledge and legs!"

Since the *'Karateka'* ('*Martial Art* Students') are usually already standing, I give 'em the option of addressing me as "Oh, Captain, my Captain", If they wanna be fancy and formal and "stroke my inflating ego" and impress me with the Walt Whitman quote. Or, they may simply call me by my Japanese title of *'Sensei'*.

17.

'TIS FAR BETTER TO TRY AND FAIL THAN TO FAIL TO TRY

"Don't worry about 'failures'. Worry about the chances you miss, if you don't even try."
– JACK CANFIELD

I am rather disappointed in myself, having earned just a 'C+' in my post-injuries academic career.

(However, 'twas an "accelerated program" for a business degree (an area in which I am barely familiar) for fun. So, it did produce a few new social connections.)

You've gotta be optimistic! Focus on the good aspects of any ordeal!

(Would it not be prudent to make a humorous reference to perhaps my going to a secluded area to "teach" folks to better "concentrate"? Too soon?!)

"You miss 100% of the shots you don't take."
– HOCKEY LEGEND, 'THE GREAT ONE', WAYNE GRETZKY

We tend to regret the things we didn't do more than the things we did do.

After a meeting with my two advisors at business school, I had to reconsider my future there. I stayed as a "student" temporarily, so I could continue to write for the school newsletter. Shockingly, the writers' "advisor" "dismissed me", 'cuz she's a close minded, tyrannical *beeyotch* who sucks at life! So, I wrote a separate article explaining said wrong-doing. But that psycho *witch* has apparently not heard of the First Amendment of the United States Constitution, which grants and supports American citizens' (my) right to "freedom of SPEECH" and "freedom to VOTE" AND "freedom of PRESS", 'cuz not only did she fire me from the school newsletter and the writers' (not her!) meeting, but, she called the police on me and threatened to "kick me outta school"! Little does she know (about anything) that I just joked with the Po Po at her expense!

(Me to the cops: "I'm terribly sorry you guys had to come down here, just 'cuz a wuss couldn't handle her 'Premenstrual Syndrome'." They just laughed heartily and wanted to make sure I was okay. Ha ha HA!)

Sooo, what were the only two things I learned from the aforementioned debacle?

Always ease the mood with humor.

Thankfully, there are still people who don't abuse their power, do respect the handi-capped, and do possess a sense of humor!

There's a gargantuan difference between "giving up" and "knowing when you've had enough! Thus, I chose to disassociate with that school!

I was researching math stuff late one night. I was getting very sleepy.[1] So, I wrote myself a note, before I "hit the hay". When I awoke the next morning, I looked down at my left forearm, I saw

"$6.02214085 \times 10^{23}$" on my left forearm. I debated whether I should contact my der-matologist to examine my new *mole*.

I am unlike anyone else in that I am willing to laugh at myself. (Sometimes, I've gotta laugh at my own jokes, 'cuz they're funny!)

---

[1] There's a distinct, almost obvious difference between being "sleepy" and just being "tired":

Being "tired" indicates muscle fatigue and a lack of enough oxygen in/to said "muscles"

Being "sleepy" mainly indicates "extraocular muscle" fatigue and a desire for "sheep counting".

18.
TEAM WORK > SOLO ACTS

AT THE HEART OF MY "BATTLE" against my Traumatic Brain Injury, it's my solo fight. But, there's no way I could've made such phenomenal progress[1] on my own! (I know I'm good, but not that good.) Thus, I made sure to hire a top notch group of high caliber helpers around me. highly successful Facebook creator Mark Zuckerberg said, "[the best entrepreneurs] surround themselves with other highly successful and motivated people."

I cannot anymore (post-injuries) teach a "Martial Arts" class by myself. I need my "voice" and "legs" (in other words, "sempais" or 'assistants") to explain and show the concepts/techniques.

Yes, I devise/design/orchestrate all 52+ self-defense techniques myself using only my mental imagery of Attackers and Defenders and their respective reactions to biophysical stimuli. (Hhhmmm, should I turn that into another book? Hhhmmm, I'd rather not.)

Instead, I'm gonna make a DVD of the how to for ~26 of my "Karate + Wrestling + Jujitsu" techniques, 'cuz my "Martial Arts" professor asked me to organize one. ("Score!")

I'm always working. But, technically, I am jobless. The name/term "job" just implies

---

[1] Break down the word:
'PRO ' > 'POSITIVE'
' GRESS' > 'MOVE'
(How DELIGHTFULLY ironic! I interpret "MOVING" as "WALKING".)

negative feelings toward the activity, like one has to accomplish a specified task for acceptance, approval, and money. Personally, I prefer "occupation", 'cuz it just seems more optional.

E.g. pre-accident, my job that I made FUN was as an "Operations Manager" for a Petroleum Distribution company. Additionally, my occupation was as an unpaid "Martial Arts" Instructor.

Post-accident, my job in which I pay employees biweekly and get paid monthly is to operate a self-"Health Care" entrepreneurship. Additionally, I still maintain my occupation as a 'Sensei' for KIDS' *Martial Arts* classes. My main occupation that occupies 100% of my awake hours (~75% of the day) is rehabilitation.

I've observed and concluded that I don't need more than the approximately six hours of sleep I get per night. (~Midnight to ~6:00 am) I never feel sleepy! Granted, my muscles tend to get tired. But, 'tis never an issue for my eyelid muscles.

Yes, I am "an Army of One" in my ongoing battle against this T.B.I. But, as smart as I was, I cannot will not "win", if I try "by myself"! I need to bombard myself with wisdom, intelligence and logic. I've always emphatically impressed that correctly operating an insightful strategy will trump "out muscling one's strength" any/every day that ends in 'Y'. Very few successful plans can be applied using just one person.

19.
AM I 'THE MAN WITH TWO BRAINS'?

THE COMBINATION OF MY INJURED AMYGDALA and my inability to cogently speak makes my random actions seem to be semi-*nonsensical*, 'cuz said "actions" rarely match my words. I don't like to blame my sporadic *numskull ness* and constant forgetfulness on my "T.B.I." But, occasionally, logic and medicine leave me no choice. I shan't lie: pre-injuries, I was rather genius-esque. Post-injuries, my overall intelligence has notably decreased, but my hindsight vision has drastically improved. However, better hindsight causes increased regret.

Pre-injuries, if I made a bad decision, I'd feel sorrow, analyze what I could've done differently, "walk it off" and prepare for next time. Post-injuries, when (not "if") my judgments are shitty, I "drown myself in sorrow" (Well, technically, I'm not drowning in sorrow, 'cuz I neural psychologically cannot cry.), Soothe my nerves with sports stats, analyze what I could've done differently and prepare for next time. Nowadays, I'm incorrect entirely too frequently for my liking. (But, who actually enjoys being "DEAD WRONG"?![1]) Coming from such a WELL-documented history of a surplus/excess/overabundance of trivial and useful knowledge, I encourage others to seek to inspire others, as I hope to do:

Your words are more important than your thoughts, so start inspiring people.

Post-accident, my inability to consistently write legibly really "adds fuel to the fire"

---

[1] Isn't that term "dead wrong" a double negative?! Sooo, does it actually mean "Correct"?! How 'bout "alive right"?!

of my supposed *extreme randomness* 'cuz I can't "jot down" notes, as they come to me. That's why my blog and this book have been so instrumental in my psychologic rehabilitation. They serve as an outlet for me to vent on my thoughts and feelings. So, thank you, "Mr. G.", for creating my blog! Everything, including this writing is very much a stream of consciousness.

The path of the hero is a lonely one.

Does that mean that once I find my "significant other", I will cease to inspire?!

That shan't be my case/deal! My somewhat recent romantic life has been extremely "UP and DOWN." Yet, I've continued to express my inner-self with others via "Martial Arts" teaching, math tutoring, blogging and book writing.

20.
OR, AM I EERILY LIKE "RAIN MAN"?

'll get the obvious similarities between "Raymond Babbitt" (of the brilliant film *Rain Man*) out of the way right off the bat:

We both have (different) brain issues that make us socially awkward.

We're both the firstborn of a successful family.

We both know entirely too much about math and sports.

I, like "Rain Man," am absolutely stunning with numbers!

E.g. If you add the numerical value of all seven Roman numerals, what is the sum? 1666.

(> MDCLXVI, in which "M = 1000" + "D = 500" + "C = 100" + "L = 50" + "X = 10" + "V = 5" + "I = 1".)

I noticed a couple TRIVIAL patterns:

111111111 x 111111111 = 12,345,678,987,654,321

12 + 3 - 4 + 5 + 67 + 8 + 9 = 100)

E.g.

QUESTION: If I had continued my organized football playing in college, for what award would I have aimed?

ANSWER: I played quarterback. So, I'd be "aiming for" the "Davey O'Brien Award."

QUESTION: The late Muhammad Ali developed what neurological disorder after years of taking head strikes?

...

ANSWER: Parkinson's syndrome

(I would consider that a *"Traumatic Brain Injury."*)

QUESTION: What are the only five European nations to have ever won soccer's "World Cup"?

...

ANSWER: Italy, Germany, England, France and Spain

(Unfortunately, Not 'Turkiye')

QUESTION: What is the common term for the sports related ailment 'lateral humeral epicondylitis'?

...

ANSWER: "Tennis Elbow"[1]

QUESTION: What is the only city in the world recognized to be in two continents?

...

ANSWER: Istanbul, Turkey

(GEOGRAPHICALLY, ~HALF the city's in EUROPE. While ~10% of the POPULA-TION is "European." 'Tis the fifth most POPULOUS city on the PLANET.)

'Rain Man' and I both have successful younger brothers.

we're both socially awkward with the opposite gender.

I have actually successfully used the pick up line: "Are you on any PRESCRIPTION medication?"

And, it WORKED! 'Cuz I made SURE to include HUMOR and MY SEXY face in the INQUIRY.

(Thank YOU, "Ms. L."!)

---

[1] Is there any common sports related shoulder injury I could use as an excuse for my *"heterotopic ossification"*?

"H.O." is the process by which additional/extra bone forms outside of the skeleton. I have the extra calcification in my left shoulder. According to my detailed research, *"H.O."* can be caused by a *"Traumatic Brain Injury."* However, since my brain is not in my shoulder I think, I sarcastically chuckle.

21.
Or, Am I a Some Sort of Unique "being"?!

'LL ADMIT: YEAH, I AM VERY ODD, strange and just weird. However, those have more of a negative connotation, while I see them more as blessed virtues, of which I must be proud! We've gotta embrace, cultivate and promote each of our respective uniqueness!

I quantify everything! Well, I always have. 'Tis just that now I always search for patterns to try to increase efficiency and decrease required trip time for future tests.

I'm very (too?) sports oriented. Rather than following political *mumbo jumbo*, I prefer to focus my attention on trivia filled atmosphere of athletics! I'll watch baseball, basketball (NBA and NCAA), football (NFL and NCAA), wrestling (NCAA not that *horseshit*/fake WWE crap), soccer, mixed Martial Arts ("MMA"; 'UFC'), poker and/or anything that's on the "boob tube". (When desperate, I've even watched swimming/diving, equestrian and golf. But, I draw the line at *cricket*. Some sports are just too foreign and too stupid even for me.

I have quite the grab bag assortment of tendencies that all based from/began with mathematical or biophysical roots.

I tend to almost always begin my "walks" with a right footed step. Pre-accident, I'd usually lead with my right side, 'cuz it's my better half, and I'd like to start strong. Now, I understand that I've gotta constantly test my left leg's strength and stability. So, I still step first with my right foot. Now, I just have a different reasoning to explain my bio-physics.

... All in All, there's a method to my madness. I'm very numerically inclined. I link almost everything with numbers. It used to help my memory. Now, I use my quantifying as a type of "image association."

22.
COMMUNICATION IS KEY

Since post-accident I still cannot speak consistently and cogently, I developed some hand gestures. Plus, my buddy created a keyboard-esque "letter board" to better "communicate" my thoughts. Rather than learning "sign language" with only ~65% of my two hands working, I kinda hafta have a way of "making my feelings known." Otherwise, I'm like "Helen Keller 2.0" only smarter and masculine and, my hearing is "supersonic" according to my mom and my vision is usable. If I ask for something to be repeated, it's almost always because I am so taken aback by the request that I'm hoping that when repeating the ridiculousness of the request becomes apparent to the speaker. (So, my request is more for you.)

I actually have/own a shirt that says/reads:

"Oh, I'm sorry if I looked interested. I was just thinking about 'drinking beer." (Can I get an "AMEN!"?)

I miss not the actual alcohol imbibing or the drunken stupor that eventually inevitably accompanies it. But, I treasured the social gatherings and care free atmosphere that alcohol kinda promotes.

Since I originally did not have a *letter board*, upon my *waking from* my second coma, my buddy of "~9 tenths of my life" (since age 3) Grant Engel designed (from a computer keyboard) and constructed a *communication board* for my usage. 'Ya see, had he not done his *homework*, then I'd likely not be able to talk for awhile if at all.

With this voice disability, I've developed multiple *gestures* to speed up my "communications": eye-rolling; audible sighing; right thumb up; EMPHATICALLY smiling; yawning; resting my right temple next to my closed right fist; with my eyes shut; pointing to my left leg with a disgruntled look on my face; holding up my right index finger horizontally; then swirling it/rotating it clockwise.

So, even though I do not always speak my mind, I can almost guarantee that I'm processing how to remain 1, 2, seven steps ahead of y'all. Then, the most difficult part is trying to explain the intricate logic of my reasoning. But, I'm sorry to admit that I've kinda had a long history of *dumbin' it down*. 'Tis not that I'm condescending or egotistical in any way! 'Tis simply that it can be *'muy dificil'* for a "T.B.I." victim such as myself to explain his assumptions and conclusions.

Unfortunately, none of y'all can truly understand (thankfully?) how frustrating it is to have many great ideas but to not be able to say 'em! Sometimes, it's like a flashback to my *high school* days, when I'd try to explain my quantitative analyses to the cute girls in my 'Calculus' and 'Statistics' classes at my private religious school.

Minus the aesthetic appeal! Sad to say, most of y'all lack the forbidden beauty of a *Catholic schoolgirl* fantasy.

: (

You are your own best teacher, 'cuz you know all your preferred methods of learning, your questions, your tendencies and studious nuances.

According to physics, the shortest distance between any two points is a straight line. But, according to sociability, the shortest "emotional distance" between two people is a smile.

I've gotten relatively good at thinking *ahead* according to my schedule, as I am not a fan of surprises. I've gotta plan stuff and *look ahead*, 'cuz the alternative would be to "look back", and that's just remembering. Unfortunately, my "T.B.I." has made that (remembering) undeniably difficult and unreliable. I try valiantly/earnestly to explain my reasoning and processing.

Some of my peers (e.g. my mom, my ex-housemate, my speech Therapist, my *Martial Arts* Professor, my NeuroPsychoTherapist) actually prefer me to either try to speak or use my 'DynaVox' mechanical speaking device. The only down side of my (English only) 'DynaVox' is when my thoughts are in Turkish or Spanish or Japanese. So, it does not compute/translate the correct message.

23

USE THE NEGATIVES AS FUEL TO FIRE UP SOME POSITIVES

THE MOST OBVIOUS EXAMPLE would be my cataclysmic car accident. duh! That tragic catastrophe traumatically shoved my weakened mind and body through a physical, mental, psychological and romantic upheaval.

Physically, I lost possibly forever my once impressively powerful leg strength. I used to be known for and complimented on my strong kicks and pillar like stances in Karate class. Now, I try to regain at least a portion of what I once had – by frequently enduring deep squats as home work along the wall bar in my shower. With my incessant work, I'm slowly regaining some of my leg strength. With my obvious progress, I repeatedly remind all my trainers: "F.Y.I. I appreciate what you're doing. But, I'm more concerned with my lack of flexibility than I am with my muscle development. I know I am strong. I just have a very limited range of motion."

Mentally, what with my T.B.I.-caused diminished memory capacity and decreased handwriting legibility, I realized just how much I relied on my own not those of an unknowing other student's spectacular notes. Yes, pre-accident, I was ridiculously smart. But, more and more, I've come to realize that I might've had a bit of a selective photographic memory. Now, I'm very dependent on my making drafts drafts of my projects.

Psychologically, I began to really question my karma. Hhhmmm. I think that I'm a good person overall. But, I may be a tad bit biased.

I mean, the most serious "offense" for which I was actually caught (HahaHA! I kid! I joke about my surreptitiousness!) was rear ending a station wagon on my way home from high school my senior year. Thinking quickly, I chose to translate for the cop. Ya see, the other driver/victim was Hispanic and spoke zero English. The policeman spoke zero Spanish. As an active member of 'La Sociedad de Honor Español', "entendí ambos" (> 'I understood both'), I acted as translator/interpreter between the two parties. As my eventual reward for serving as "International Liaison," the cop graciously thanked me and just gave me a warning. So, I used 'mi comprensión del inglés Y español' ('my understanding of both English and Spanish') to alleviate the awkwardness of the terrible situation that was obviously my fault.

Anyway, with such a deluge of *shit storms* seemingly following me between 2008 and 2013, I was desperate to *right my wrongs*. I'd really begun to doubt the (supposed) good aura surrounding me.

One time, I got seriously frustrated with my night caregiver, 'cuz after ~15 minutes, seven unanswered bell rings and four of my yells he still did not even reply, so I bent forward and reached down to successfully put on my socks! (YEEESSSSSSS!) I use my unfortunate conditions as motivation for future improvements. (I've gotta!)

Romantically, my best, most intense, longest lasting "intimate relationship" (~5.44 years) inexplicably ended "because" of my injuries! She won't admit it. But, unless I'm some obtuse, apathetic dip shit, (I hope I am!) I cannot "read between the lines" as to why all of a sudden, she was so bewildered that she ended *us* and refused to discuss my ignorance (not knowing)! She's a good spirited, moral person. So, I'm hoping that she's just uber busy with her job.

With my terrible luck, (No, I shan't use that word, 'cuz I'm too, too, toooo numerically and probability oriented to believe in "coincidences." Everything has a reason or explanation.) Now, I am not condescending or stilted enough to claim that I know all, 'cuz I don't. But, I've experienced alotta good things and far too many bad feelings not to express my views.

24.
MIND OVER MATTER

A **S SEMI-PROOF OF MY "DILIGENCE",** for ~a month in mid 2016, I "worked" my left ankle by constantly stretching it and rotating the foot outwardly, as I lied in bed at night every night for ~4 months (~120 times). Using, a 90-degree straightened foot as my "0 angle", the range of motion for my left footed/ankle increased from ~30 degrees (I was kinda *pigeon toed* as a direct result of knee surgery and ~7.84 years of compensatory walking.) to ~45 degrees. Granted, I dare not take all the credit. Various ankle stretching by trainers at my gym certainly aided my increased foot and ankle mobility. Sooo, 'KUDOS' to them!

I kinda hafta be creative nowadays. pre-accident, I'd practice Karate or swim in my pool or practice wrestling or shoot hoops anything kinetic to amuse myself. Now, with my physical limitations, I hafta constantly mentally exercise! Rather than watching alotta television, I prefer to plan stuff like my daily schedule, "Martial Arts" techniques, employee transportation, blog writing, etc. There was a time, post-accident, during my tutoring service's existence, in which I'd design assorted math problems. Now, I prefer to write non-math. (Whoa, whoa, whoa! Am I sick?!)

Relax! I still quantify everything, when I'm tryin' to relax and sleep. But, during the day, I focus more on my writing.

(I've started my book. Therefore, I am committed to finishing it.)

(AUDIBLE sigh) I'm like the sun.

(I point to my noggin.)

I can't turn this off.

I hafta apply my biophysics knowledge to every one of my daily activities. One of the numerous negative consequences of my "T.B.I" is a very faulty and randomly haywire digestive system. As a direct result of my "eating" via "G tube" and my stomach's not *processing* food from my mouth, I hafta" take in" and "absorb" my bodily nutrients via a gastro tube attached to the inside of my stomach, but jutting out of my lower abdomen. Due to my now faulty digestive "process," I take a small dose of a minor laxative usually everyday. This stimulant intake varies according to my daily schedule.

('Tis accident prevention.)

Whenever I prepare to stand up or sit down, I hafta instantly guesstimate my angle of elevation or depression using leverage, momentum, acceleration and trigonometry. Still possessing both my algebraic and biophysical expertise, I tend to always use the same concepts and formulas. Using this repeated setup, I feel that I'll eventually gain enough "muscle memory" to overcome my weakened leg nerves and walk sans assistance.

I revised/edited a popular Kenny Chesney song 'When I Close My Eyes', in lieu of numerous onlookers complaining of my mistakenly assumed "sleeping" while repeatedly doing a 'pull, stand and sit' exercise:

'Eyes CLOSED, Brain's still OPEN'
"There are MANY THINGS
That I MUST DO
TRY as I MAY,
I caN'T MAKE nerves GROW.
But, y'all MUST watch OUT.
If you doN'T, you might SHOUT:
"Every stride I SEE
Looks quite 'STAY BUHL.'
Every stumble I HEAR,
It caN'T come from YOUR GAIT.
I've GOTTA be SMART!
For ALL goals, YOU 'play' PART!"
(A.J.:) When I close my eyes,
I 'SEE' my 'WALKS'
THROUGHOUT my BIG GYM.
'Painting my THOUGHTS'
THROUGHOUT the DAY

KEEPS mind CLEAR and WELL.
ALWAYS good TRIES
Come, when I close my EYES.
My INNER-self KNOWS
I can ONLY WAIT.
But, DEEP in my HEART,
I want MUCH MORE!
I'm NOT givin' UP!
I NEVER HAVE!
DESPITE NON-TALKING,
And/or NON-WALKING.
Wherever I BE,
It's TOUGH to NOT SEE.
When I close MY EYES,
I 'SEE' my 'WALKS'
THROUGHOUT my BIG GYM.
'Painting my THOUGHTS'
THROUGHOUT the DAY
KEEPS mind CLEAR and WELL.
ALWAYS good TRIES
Come, when I close my EYES."

Albert Einstein defined "insanity" as "doing the same thing repeatedly while expecting different results." Well, I'm comfortable with my routine of steps for all I do, 'cuz I've found what comfortably works for now.

I am under the impression that eventually my leg nerves will regrow and rebuild themselves with time, effort and persistence. Sssooooo, I believe that time will eventually reward me for my patience and determination.

Does that make me insane?!

...

ME: "Be quiet, A.J.! What do you know?!"

25.
SCIENCE > COMFORT

OFTEN, WE/I NEED TO ACCEPT the inevitability that *Science > Comfort*.
Frequently, I'll accidentally place my legs/feet in an awkward position as I prepare for my *walks*. I'll want to step first onto my left foot, b/c my right foot is stronger and more stable as an *anchor leg*. But, I've gotta *test* my injured left leg's strength and stability. I'll constantly, subconsciously put my left leg in an uncomfortable position. (AUDIBLE sigh) Nevertheless/ultimately/"in the long run", I need my left leg to show its power and endurance[1] and to "stand the test of time" (Pun intended!).

It's beyond irritating, troublesome, and potentially dangerous"[2] to have a plastic tube surgically attached to my inner stomach, "jutting out" of a hole in my lower abdomen by which I ingest all of my liquefied nutrients.

But, wait! There's more!

My Main nurse did inform me that it is possible to have one's G tube removed! Granted, the tube is mainly taken out in less severe cases. But, just the fact that the procedure has been done successfully is encouraging!

(My back's gettin' tired of breakin' new ground and settin' precedents.)

(Ya know what's not tired?! My sarcasm switch!)

(I've always "had a thing" for 'mujeres hispanas'.)

The power of my discipline/restraint, and scientific/nutritional wisdom dwarfed that

---

[1] You won't/don't learn, until you try.

[2] "Potentially dangerous" is the general term for any illegal move in folk style wrestling.

of my curiosity, as through over ~8.52 years I have not pulled said tube out of my stomach.

(GREAT self-control!)

Don't say that I couldn't! I simply choose not to destroy my only current form of nutrition intake.

(My scientific wisdom outweighs my "desire to appear badass." Whew!)

My pain tolerance is through the roof! Pre-accident, I successfully completed the last ~third of my 'shogun' ('black belt') test with a separated shoulder of my better (right) arm! Post-accident, I have numerous deadened nerves throughout my body that prevent me from feeling or outwardly expressing some things, i.e. extreme sadness, empathy, slight pain.[3]

Every time that "nature calls" "#1", and I "walk" to my bathroom, I spit my excess saliva into the toilet. But, I don't "hock a loogie" *like a testosterone infused MAN.* : (

Instead, I stand leaning on the hand rails in front of my "porcelain throne" and try to let saliva drip from my partially open mouth. I usually get out three spit bombs. But, that spit dropping usually takes between ~two and ~seven minutes to overcome the adhesion between the saliva and my lips. Thus, my "lavatory trips" are especially gratifying.

So, that's at least ~four to ~nine minutes of supported "standing" plus the ~40 steps of "walking" from my bed or ~60 steps from my entertainment room, all multiplied by at least four different treks per day. (Hhhmmm, so that'd be (~6.5 (average of ~4 and ~9) minutes + ~2 minutes (pre and post-urine walk), ALL multiplied by six, because I do, on average, 4 to 8 lavatory treks per day, that'd be ~51 minutes of urination induced standing per day.)

We've all heard wrestling horror stories of "cuttin' weight": not eating and constant running and all too frequent spittin'. But, luckily, I sweat a lot! So, back when I actually cared about my body's gravitational push against Earth ("weight"), I was always motivated to exercise more.

---

[3] With my weirdo body, it's all or nothin'.

26.
STILL LEARNING AND APPLYING

EXISTENTIALISTS SAY, "Nothing happens, 'til you've hit rock bottom." Well, I couldn't be much "lower" physically, emotionally, psychologically, and metaphorically sooo, I'm always open to new things. I wanna "begin anew."

Only, I need a "muse"!

Bein' the hardcore nerd that I am, I'm forever learning! Seeing as I don't have or want a Biophysicist livin' with me, I hafta teach myself. As I've completed my academic studies, (I highly doubt I'll ever return to optional grad school.) I train myself in life applicable sciences. that'll definitely do!

"The biggest enemy to 'greatness' is 'good enough'."(*My Martial Arts* Professor) Never "settle." Along those lines, my trainers openly consider me a bit of a perfectionist. I disagree. I'm just so used to (my) maximum efforts and positive results that I've just grown *accustomed to* earning that "'A' for effort".

(Perhaps, that explains my all/96 'A's in a top high school: I TRY.)

I'm not gonna LIE: I kinda need inspirations for my (optional) studying. I was so obsessed with the smart guy show 'The Big Bang Theory' that I began to question everything and determine myself why it is what it is.

Seeing as the average "human attention span" is ~eight minutes (8.16), I calculated: THAT'd be

489 and 3/5ths seconds OR

~2/15 hours OR

~1/180 days OR

~1/65,700 years

(PLUS I'd hafta factor in the eight Leap Years of my life!)

HHHMMM, so, I really followed that show for ~1.2684 x 10^ 7 years times my ~31.52 years of age, which is about right.

Now, I've transferred my attentive dedication to the genius show 'Scorpion.' In addition to the plethora of wise deductions, there are 'dos mujeres calientes' on the team! So, they make the "dweeb talk" tolerable. (Ssshhh! I actually enjoy the nerdy repartee. The aesthetically appealing double 'X' chromosome possessors are merely a delightful bonus!)

I've even suckered my new housemate as of ~September of '16 into thoroughly enjoying the brilliant writing, tremendous "character development" and beautiful ladies! (Speaking of my new housemate, within his first week in my abode, he nicely, genuinely asked me how to present his project findings for his new i.t./computer job.)

My brother to me:

"With your bad memory and subjective views, where do you get your writing points?"

My reply:

"A voice in my head talks to me. Of course, 'tis in Portuguese, so I need a translator. Then, when I ask "the voice" (in my head) her relationship with 'España', (knowing my fascination with latinas, my amygdala ensured that my constant inner voice is female), she replies with

"Eh, así así."

So, I quantify practically everything to determine general patterns for future applications. I counted the average # of steps/strides I take every morning, when I walk to my bathroom to brush my teeth in my manual wheelchair, then I walk to my motorized chair.

(~45.67 and ~51.25 steps)

I count how long my "urinal stream" is when I stand to urinate into 'mi Juan', and I monitor the color of my secretion. (It's always between 11 "mississippi"s and 17 with an average of 13.3644 seconds with outliers at 6, 8 and 22 seconds. Plus, the light yellowish hue indicates that I don't "hold it in.") I don't "hold it in", 'cuz 1) I know that's BAD for the urinary system and 2) it's a possible prelude to a "U.T.I." ("Urinary Tract Infection.") Also, multiple "treks" if there is a "false alarm" mean more practice "walking." And, what's the saying?

"'Practice' makes (close to) perfect."

I always count the # of brush strokes when I brush my teeth twice a day. (20 RIGHT LOWER BACK, 20 RIGHT LOWER SIDE, 20 LEFT LOWER BACK, 20 LEFT LOWER SIDE, 20 LOWER MIDDLE, 20 RIGHT UPPER BACK, 20 RIGHT UPPER SIDE, 20 LEFT UPPER BACK, 20 LEFT UPPER SIDE, 20 UPPER MIDDLE, 20 TONGUE)

I always brush *with the grain*, 'cuz I know that's what dentists PREFER.

Through my ~31.62 years "aboard Earth," I've never had a cavity orally. (Knock on wood.)

I always count my number of deodorant swipes two different times a day (pre-daily activities and post-shower). Since I cannot yet smell, I just guesstimate my needed amount 10 swipes "in the morning" and 8 swipes "after my shower." Besides, my long-time beau said that I "don't smell." I'm just always wet from perspiration.

(Reminder: I am a male. So, there's no sexual pun with that "wet"ness comment. 'Tis merely an example of my heightened/stimulated amygdala operating always finding an intimate alternative.)

I find my attention to detail regarding quantifying anything scientific" both entertaining and noteworthy. Some people think I'm too intellectual, and that bothers them. But, I think it's a fabulous way to occupy my time!

('Tis a helluva lot better than lying in bed and letting my nonstop mind dwell on missed opportunities!)

The great Sir Isaac Newton spent more time writing biblical interpretations than he did analyzing physics principles. How's that for questionable Time Management?! (Newton was an Englishman in the 17th century with an atrocious wig. That probably forced him to DRINK! I think it's a fair assumption that he enjoyed the BRANDY.)

I was a Fantasy Football virgin before the 2016 NFL season. Now, I have two teams in two different leagues, thanks to a buddy's connections!

I used to tend to walk/step "on the balls of my feet", 'cuz I was always taught that that tactic allows for quieter movement. Well, I used to pride myself on being very "serpentine ninja"-esque. But, (sniffle SNIFFLE) No more! I guess I'd just now step rather heavy footed. So, I *went back to the ol' drawing board.* Per the advice of my gym owner, I tried the "heel to toe" approach. Sure enough, it is quieter to an extent.

Self-Analysis:

I think I was a bit too relaxed. I'd stride first on my heel. Then, I'd slam my heel against the ground to establish a strong right anchor for my next left footed/legged stride. With my supersonic hearing, 'twas a cacophonous echoing throughout my gym facility!

So, after months of self-stepping trials, I decided to try the heel first approach. Sure enough, 'tis an improvement!

Granted, 'tis not silent. But, at this point in my life, I'm just searching for progress not perfection.

Then again, my *Martial Arts* Professor says: "If you aim for 'perfection', you can't be disappointed with greatness."

After 24+ years and a *Traumatic Brain Injury*, apparently, I still know my self-defense. My *Martial Arts* Professor recommended that I make a DVD showing my assortment of (~51) "Karate/Wrestling/Jujitsu" techniques, 'cuz they're so "Unique and Helpful!" (His words! It's not that I need recognition! But, it sure as hell feels good!)

27.
I'VE STILL GOT MANY QUIRKS AND MORE

DESPITE MY **TRAUMATIC BRAIN INJURY,** I've still got many nuances that highlight or emphasize my mental oddities and strengths.

"C'est la vie." Actually, 'such is not life", 'cuz despite the name of my brain injury my injuries are mainly physical, while I remain mentally commendable.

(I am a proud puzzle encapsulated in an entertaining enigma joking around as if I were a jocund jester!)

'*Por Ejemplo*', I'm still obsessed with monitoring my health: I organize my daily schedule around my five weekday feedings and four weekend meals.

(In spite of my having less "free time" on weekdays, I need more meals/nutrition/energy supplements on those five days to help me *push through* my additional activities.)

('Tis a real smorgasbord of assorted minerals, vitamins and enrgy boosters. My "caloric intake" is actually greater/higher/healthier than yours. So, who's laughing now?!)

(Ha ha HA!)

(I AM.)

On my workout days (Monday, Tuesday, Friday), my caloric intake is ~3,000 calories medicinally/"via G tube." On the other four days, my calories are limited to 2,500. This numeric organization is necessary to provide me with more calories and thus more energy. The caloric number is strategically below 3,500 to maintain my steady weight of

~142 (+ or 2) pounds.

I always watch wide-eyed, as the nurse *takes my blood* via syringe and checks my blood pressure via sphygmomanometer.

(Then, I create random patterns with the digits > 120/80 > 3/2 > ("TEN x # of MONTHS per YEAR"/"SQUARE of 'my mom's # of siblings' x 'my maternal grand-mother's # of offspring'"))

(> "10 x 12"/"4^2 x 5")

Like an *old fogie*, I've arranged an early dinner (~3:00 pm) everyday to avoid drastically slowing my metabolism by eating right before sleeping. And, it allows me more time to host some fecal festivities before I retreat to bed.

(It helps indirectly my gastrointestinal system that I'm a bit of a "night owl", as I usually fall asleep between midnight and 1:00 am.)

I'm a big fan of television shows about smart people, e.g. 'Scorpion' and 'The Big Bang Theory.' I find scenes especially humorous/entertaining, when I A.J. Kaynatma can directly relate to a scene. (That happens more often than I care to admit.)

Besides my constant counting, I'm very interested in any and all sports, but particularly those which I have actually played: wrestling, football, basketball, Martial Arts (Yes, it is a "sport", in which I took third in point sparring as a 13-year-old!), and soccer.

Even though I temporarily cannot yet taste, I still "look down on" disapprovingly at anyone who likes anything with mayonnaise.

I am an avid sports fan. One might characterize me as a "fanatic" or a "sports nut." I meticulously, ardently follow the varying levels of success of my favorite teams. This dependent happiness can be good. But, correlating/connecting my level of life contentment to the production of a sports team over which I have zero influence or control is not healthy.

Since I'm still very obsessed with statistics it boggles my mind how so many people could still be convinced of the existence of coincidences! Said ignoramuses are obviously unfamiliar with the "Law of Large Numbers", which explains that the average of the results obtained from a large number of trials should be close to the expected value, and will tend to become closer to the expected value as more trials are performed.

I definitely/indubitably prefer my " ool" to the ocean.

28.
SIZE DOESN'T MATTER

LADIES, PLEASE FILE the chapter title in your 'Life lessons' folder.

It's how you use what you have.

Even especially the little things can "pack a big punch"! I've never been one of large stature. As of now, I stand ~5' 7.25" and ~141.1 pounds (~64.09 kilograms). When I actually trained in *Martial Arts*, I'd almost always hafta spar against a larger dude. Ergo, I'd seek to prove that "strategy" beats "power." However, pre-accident, I was a unique, enviable combination of both! Ya see, I was and am neither lightning quick nor musclebound strong. I pick the appropriate instances of when to use either.

Now, I'd warm up to a song:

(To the tune of Muhammad Ali's taunts:)

"Fly like a HELICOPTER. Mar like an ankle SPRAIN. Y'all caN'T UNDER estimate my greatly[1] *injured BRAIN."[2]

Personally, I've encountered countless doubters. More than any physical pain in my

---

[1] Clever pun on the meaning of "great": both "vast/all encompassing" and "awe inspiring"!

[2] More so now post-injuries, I tend to spend alotta time mentally prepping, before I follow through with a sparring attack.

legs or shoulder or skull, you know what hurts the most?! The lack of RESPECT!

When sparring in Karate class and when grappling in wrestling practice, my peers and I discovered that I had a commendable combination of speed and strength. Since I understand both ends of the spectrum," my designed techniques incorporate "all angles of self-defense."

(I'm sorry, kids. But, there's "no half-assing!" You've gotta know all aspects for my teachings!)

An ongoing theme with all my lesson is

"'Tis better to know too much than not enough."

So, I'd rather OVER prepare 'em, than UNDER "set 'em up."

Commendable speed breeds/causes/leads to stellar strength. Transforming one's quickness into muscle is certainly noteworthy!

The surgical scar on my left shoulder is only ~3.46 inches long. But, you ladies might say that that would hardly leave a lasting impression. But, as any "real estate" agent would tell you:

"It's all about location, location, location." Ya see, that "surgical aftermath" is located on my left glenoid and left acromioclavicular joint. But, it affects so much more! My shoulder and arm rotation has been significantly and sorely reduced. Additionally, its angle of elevation has largely decreased.

So, as the "penile challenged" buddy would plead:

"It's not the size that counts, but how you use it." I've never really thought about that.

I jokingly teased my "upper body" trainer recently, 'cuz he kept watching me raise and rotate my left arm and saying, "wow! I'm impressed!" My response:

"So, you underestimated me. Maybe next time, you'll estimate me."

There is a popular widespread misinterpretation that a bigger brain contains more intelligence. Although the extra "neural real estate" certainly has the potential for "above average wisdom", intelligence depends much more on how efficiently different parts of your brain communicate with each other.

Pre-accident, my peers used to tease me about having a big head. My brain and cranium are not that large, just I used to sport a buzz cut So, compared to the rest of my rather barren head, I'm sure I looked "HHHYYYUUUUUUUJJJJJE!"

29.
TEAM WORK

YES, MY REHABILITATION ultimately depends on my (concentrated) effort and my (focused) strength individually. But, some guidance and assistance now and then certainly makes me grateful!

What's the saying? "two minds are better than one." well, 'tis especially true, when one of said brains is "traumatically injured." even though I am still very smart, it's always helpful to hear an outsider's opinion to get that third person's perspective.

My main nurse helps me biweekly organize my employee work hours for my/the payroll. seven employees > four caregivers for 168[1] weekly hours, two nurses for 33 weekly "meals", one speech therapist for three weekly sessions.

Additionally, said nurse helps me organize and set up my weekly schedule.

(JEEZ! With so MANY meals and NOT walking, HOW am I NOT hideously obese?!

Fine! I'll tell ya: my main nurse calculated my medicinal caloric intake according to my necessary caloric output. It's very scientific and over my head.)

(Not!)

My *Martial Arts* professor not only psychologically supports me, constantly compliments me and asks me for help in front of the young 'Karateka' in class, but he's helping me act out and produce a technique DVD!

Yes, I always do the majority of the work for any task. But, I almost require minor

---

[1] While typing up my biweekly payroll, I always check my numbers > 7 x 24 = 168 hours/week, 4 + 5 + 5 + 5 + 5 + 5 + 4 = 33 "meals"/week.

assistance to satisfactorily complete a feat. (.I am not a perfectionist. I'm just used to having and reaching high standards.)

E.g., my 'Sempai' speaks during my co-teaching *Martial Arts* classes. My caregiver wipes my butt after a "fecal frenzy." Nurses "feed me" via *gastric tube* 4-5 times a day.

My trainers assist me in my upper and lower body workouts by directing me on how to perform various exercises. With their guidance and supervision, I then perform said leg and arm mobility techniques accordingly.

I've repeatedly told my trainers: "No offense to what you're doing which is great, but I know that I'm already strong. I'd like to be more flexible." so, they in turn stretch me.

(ASK, and you SHALL receive.)

But, I know a good workout is a combination test of both one's muscle strength and limb flexibility. Plus, I like to also include work on my endurance and conditioning.

My ex-housemate used to (help) organize my social activities. We'd host parties, attend basketball games, attend baseball games and attend mutual friends' parties.

My new housemate informally kinda should help initiate some social interactions. He's off to a good start, as within his first month, we'd attended one of my high school's football games for "alumni night."

My caregiver(s) assist me with my everyday ordeals: getting "out of"/into bed, rinsing out my mouth after my teeth brush, changing my clothes (my left side is still embarrassingly weak.), putting on/taking off my shoes and socks, supplying me with two distinct "folds"/"sets" of toilet paper to wipe the left over spit from my mouth and left over urine from my penis, wiping my ass after a timely turd (unfortunately, my "toilet chair"[2] was not constructed trigonometrically for "self-wipeage".), rinsing those impossible to reach body parts when I shower.[3]

Therefore, it takes alotta work to somehow make this (I point to my face then circle around my whole body.) presentable? Hhhmmm.

4 Caregivers + 2 Nurses + 2 PHYSICAL Trainers + *1 Martial Arts* PROFESSOR + 1 NeuralPsychoTherapist + me (player/coach) =

'Determined Dreadnoughts of Destiny'

---

[2] My surgically repaired left hip and nonfunctioning legs do not allow me to stably and comfortably sit flesh to porcelain atop my "Dung Depository".

[3] Again, I sit in/on a "shower chair", when I'm taking my daily ~20-minute shower.

So, with 11 players, we'd be quite the formidable football team. I'd be the quarterback and middle linebacker, 'Cuz I am a/thee constant "team leader". Yes, I get all the recognition and accolades and respect appropriately. But, I make sure to always "thank" my "teammates" whether verbally or monetarily.

Truly great leaders make those around them better. I THINK about THAT before EVERY "Martial Arts" class I TEACH. I LIKE to think that my still teaching Jujitsu inspires observers to "tackle any foe" no matter how daunting the task may seem!

30.
A GOOD WORKMAN DOESN'T BLAME HIS TOOLS

I **CERTAINLY DO NOT ALWAYS SUCCEED**. At first, I admit I would get very frustrated with my unsuccessful attempts. Like a spoiled, ornery child, I would blame my caregiver(s) for not "helping me" enough. But finally, I've settled into/with a splendid group of understanding folks! Yes, I've surrounded myself with a responsible, dependable, trustworthy group of "tools."

I've had to fire a few employees, mainly 'cuz you've gotta "gel with" your coworkers and your boss.

(Yes, I am technically "THE BOSS". But, sometimes I consider us mainly coworkers, 'cuz we're aiming for the same goal > the common good. Afterward, I make it more apparent that I "run the show.")

In the midst of the procedure, I am merely an accomplice. 'Tis a bit of "utilitarianism", 'cuz essentially it's "the greatest good for the greatest number." If the boss (me) is happy, the contentment will just "trickle down" the "Occupational Leadership hierarchy.

I abhor using my T.B.I as an excuse, when any trial is unsuccessful. On the other hand, when the outcome is favorable, I do like to point out that, in overcoming this obstacle, I additionally had to fight off my own "neurologic discrepancies". Thus, even though "[the T.B.I.] cuts both ways", I like to admit only one.

I could just give up after any one of my many unsuccessful attempts at anything. But, to use the suburban slang of 'da (I push up my glasses.) Well-maintained communities: "that just ain't – Excuuuse me – is not quite how I roll (literally in my wheelchair.)" I'm much more comfortable finishing a task as a closer than I am beginning one as a starter.

My personality was definitely not always like that. Pre-injuries, I liked to start solutions, 'cuz I was so creative and resourceful that I'd easily devise an ingenious solving procedure. Now post-injuries, I'm just far more dependent on others' guidance and instructions. After using the initial instructions, I create my own procedure using logic, biophysics and reasoning for future tasks.

As time passes and my nerves improve, I try to limit my dependence on others to accomplish any task. I used to steer clear of pain. But, now, in lieu of all my deadened nerves, I actually welcome discomfort and maybe minor pain.

(Ya see, pain is just weakness's leaving my body. Thus, I will tolerate a scant amount of muscle ache, 'cuz I view it as merely a reminder that I'm still alive!)

31.
BEING THE NERD I AM, I ALWAYS DO HOMEWORK

I ALWAYS LEARN NEW STUFF at 'NeuroFit 360', at my dojo, at social gatherings. I then file the lessons in my memory folder for future applications.

E.g. subconsciously, I (always) wanna start my gait with my left legged stride. But, through my numerous treks at home, I've downgraded that "vice" from a tendency to merely an inkling. I repeatedly try to speed up my walking pace, so I'm not sooo painstakingly slooooowww. While walking, I try to maintain a straight forward gaze without staring at my feet. Since I've ashamedly forgotten many Karate 'katas' (= 'KAH tahs' = 'prearranged fighting moments'), just watching the kids "perform" said 'katas' motivated me to create/design/write my own (as yet unfinished) Jujitsu 'kata' plus my DVD.

Reviewing some of my conversations with friends, I'd say that I do tend to *monopolize the talk to just be about me.* (It ain't cute, A.J. How ya gonna attract a female?!) It's not bragging! It's just my own way of expressing my feelings of pride and accomplishment, kinda/exactly like my blogging.

I researched some *engineering terms*, and I devised a joke. 'Cuz I NEEDED one:

"A *Möbius stripper* takes OFF her clothes.
They then get right back ON."

I thoroughly enjoy mind stimulating/thought provoking movies (*The Usual Suspects, Multiplicity, The Life of Pi*) and television[1] shows (*The Big Bang Theory, Scorpion, Saturday Night Live*)!

I plan my weekly schedule, record my biweekly payroll and plan my daily forecast from in bed. I work better, when/where I'm most comfortable. Contrary to what many observers think, sitting in an uncomfortable wheelchair is tiring![2] No, 'tis not sleep inducing! 'Tis merely constant poor muscle positioning.

Yet again, I sought to revise another popular song, Sandra Dee from a cinematic favorite of mine, *Grease*:

'Wow. A.J.!'

"Scoff with dismay, I'm just A.J.

I tend to provoke a 'yay!'

I'd bet that I talk slightly before I can walk.

'Tis nerves of me, A.J.

Watch me 'beat' my 'T.B.I.'

When speaking, I try to stay eye to eye.

Won't ever quit.

So, doubters just sit!

I just won't be denied!

I don't slack. (No!)

Or, quit. (No!)

I abide by 'phy ziks'. (Noice!)

I strive on despite many misfires.

(Stand and bow)

Swallow your damning doubt,

Or, I'll make ya pout.

Would y'all 'talk shit', if I could argue?

Mocking his legs, A.J. constantly begs

---

[1] I could just say "TV." But, I wanna make things tough for my speaking, so I try to say, "TEH LEH VIJ IHN" during every speech therapy session.

[2] "Tired" simply refers to muscle fatigue. "Sleepy" refers to a desire to "count sheep" and eyelid fatigue.

To not buy new thighs on 'list of craigs'!

Legs, show a sign

To keep 'faith in line'.

'Tis wow ing A.J.!

Legs, please, legs! Get me up!

Soon, I'll drink from a cup!

Keep being a clown,

Even when I feel down.

Hey, doubters. I'll beat this 'T.B.I.'!"

32.
ALL WORK AND NO PLAY
MAKE A.J. A DULL MAN

THAT CHAPTER TITLE is purely/only hypothetical. To combat my constant theorizing, I've gotta keep and stay busy! Ergo, I try to schedule many parties and outings. 'Tis a bit tougher lately, 'cuz my current housemate is kinda antisocial. But, I (AUDIBLE sigh) accept that, 'cuz he's nice and responsible. Sooo, I'll just hafta take it upon myself.

This added "social burden" (naw, "burden" has a negative connotation. How 'bout "duty"?!) will be a major difficulty that'll likely be frustrating, 'cuz no one has the free time that I have. Nevertheless, I'll do it, 'cuz i must.

I consider "Martial Arts" activity (technique creating, video planning, coteaching) as "play". So, I am very glad I got reacquainted with my "Martial Arts" crew, 'cuz my dojo really is my "second home". Plus, all the kids 'calm' me, 'cuz I may not be the most sophomoric/immature person there. I still create techniques, as I always did, I just can no longer explain and perform my reasoning.

(My assistants do that!)

Technically, I don't have a "job". But, I'm always working on my legs and nerves. As I actually enjoy the slooow but steady progress I'm makin', I'd consider my "occupation" in name only "Leg Nerve redeveloper". Said "regeneration" occupies ~18 hours/day, 7 days/week, ~52.14 weeks/year.

Despite my being "job" less, I still pull in a rather sizable salary.

(Thank you, law team and judicial system for supplying me with the monetary kindling to fuel my inner fire for Neurological rehab!)

So, I like to find different ways to "give back" to the community: Give a painting to 'Salvation Army', teach free "Martial Arts" and math tutor for free.

I love to play! But, it is considerably different and difficult to play with out legitimate leg strength and a coherent voice box. All my social activities are awkward, if and when I hafta use either my 'DynaVox' or my letter board. Typing just takes longer than trying to speak. (Sometimes, my voice can lack coherence or cognizance). 'Tis especially uncool, if said playing is *in bed*. Knowing how important *bedroom games* are to my hippocampus, i really/tirelessly try to express my concerns verbally!

33.
WAY TOO COMMON MISCONCEPTIONS

NEARLY EVERYONE IMMEDIATELY "dismisses me" as "mentally weak", when he/she hears "Traumatic BRAIN Injury". I'm sorry, I'm not sorry for my "cognitive dominance" that "probably saved [my] life" according to my supervising medical doctors. This T.B.I. has been a painfully humbling experience! I was never very humble pre-accident. (I mean, I was certainly/definitely not pron e to bragging and boasting. I was/am just usually right with my analyses.)

If I had a nickel, for every time some ignoramus called me a "retard", I'd have "a butt load" of money!

My brother: "A 'butt load'?! How much is 'a butt load'?!"

Me without hesitating: "About a thousand dollars. Sooo, that'd be about 20,000 'retard's."

Post-comas, I was *under the impression* that "rebuttal" was some *yoga pose*, and pronounced, "Re-BUTT-ALL". Ergo, my hyperactive *amygdala* constantly wanted arguments, so I could witness some good *counters*.

Many people falsely assume that "all wealthy people are cheap." well, I am most certainly not![1] I am definitely "frugal" in that I am wise of/privy to the final destination of my investments and why. I've become sooo desperate that I even desperately/ashamedly

---

[1] Between housemates, I found a large painting of a bunch of horses. Said painting was not mine nor my ex-housemate's. So, I'm givin' it to goodwill.

temporarily joined an online dating site. However, when it became apparent that the ladies were only after my money, I quickly "put the kybosh" on that experiment. The ladies misinterpreted my semi-boasting of "I'm 'very wealthy' in my pants!"

(Isn't it obvious that I'm "rich" anatomically and not necessarily monetarily?)

(I don't even carry a wallet anymore!)

Even though 'tis more difficult for me to express myself face to face and tougher for y'all to interpret my lack of tone variation, I undoubtedly prefer communicating in-person over online. The likelihood of an unspecified misunderstanding are inordinately higher for/with nonverbal back 'n forth than it is for face to face talking.

I use my manual wheelchair, when I'm out of my house. This decision is not because I am lazy at all, but because I have hand injuries that prevent my fully opening my "upper appendages".

('Tis also why I don't[2] learn SIGN language.)

Plus, 'tis embarrassingly inconsiderate, inefficient and illegal how many public locations do not have "Handicap Access"! Just the thought of this all too common ignorance is boiling my blood!

(I'm quickly inhaling and slowly exhaling. They wouldn't like me, when I'm angry. "[Turk] smash!")

To all the *Star Wars* fans out there (me included), I pose this query to you:

Since "only siths talk in absolutes" (Obi Wan), what does that make Yoda, who said, "do or do not. There is no 'try'"?!

I'm torn. On one hand, there are definitely various in between levels of effort. On the other, I continue my trials, until I am successful.

(Also, I think/feel/know that I am far too morally sound to be considered an evil "Sith"!)

To combat the all too common misunderstanding that I'm not "all there" (I point to my head.), I like to frequently "cast light upon" my pre-accident various successes. I tend to so often say, "'member when", that it seems like I am "livin' in the past". But, I am merely "pointing out" that my once mighty mental magnificence "got me to where I am today" as in "not dead"!

When an employee or relative or friend or just peer does not listen to my instructions,

---

[2] My mom teases me, 'cuz I still use the word "SHAN'T" (= "SHALL NOT").

I sigh loudly, roll my eyes, repeat myself one, two, four more times, then I try to explain my thoughts verbally. It may look like I'm very angry and spazzin' out. But, I'm just ridiculously frustrated!

Some rude dolt of an observing parent stupidly yelled that I was sleeping at my gym. Me to observing stooge:

"Here's a 'Jeopardy' answer for you, dumbass:

'He wasn't sleeping.'"

...

(AWKWARD SILENCE)

...

ME: "First, your response must be in the form of a question. Secondly, 'how did the most active patient at 'NeuroFit 360' perform 12 'Sit to stand's while asleep?'"

As my speech therapist keenly noted, while I was eating:

"[I] close [my] eyes, because [I'm] really focusing on chewing and swallowing."

So, I revised a song:

(To the tune of Kenny Chesney's 'When I Close my Eyes':)

     'Eyes CLOSED, Brain's still OPEN'
     "There are MEH nee STEPS
     I didN'T TAKE.
     But, THAT's just 'CUZ
     I know we'll MAKE
     It THROUGH this TOUGH ORDEAL!
     SHOW me that IRON WILL!
     Every time I WALK,
     I kinda FILL with GLEE!
     Every time I TALK,
     I test my intelligibili-TEE.
     As time SLOWLY ROLLS,
     I shaN'T drift FROM my GOALS.
     My eyes MAY be CLOSED,
     But, my BRAIN's OPEN.
     With BETTER FOCUS,
     WALKING's what I SEE.
     Even AT the GYM,
     While I WORK my ARMS,

My mind'll WANDER,
When I CLOSE my EYES.
(AUDIBLE sigh)
Yes, I WILL ADMIT:
Progress IS 'SLOOOH'.
Optimism STAYS HIGH!
Nothing has CHANGED.
I'm STILL thinkin' 'I WILL',
Like I ALWAYS HAVE
BACK in the DAY,
In my mental PRIME.
Whatever I DO,
It takes me LONGER
To 'VIH-JHUH-liyz' IT,
'Cuz I CLOSE my EYES.
LEGS, with my eyes BOTH CLOSED,
Your STEPS I SEE.
So, there ARE 'misFIRES'
and 'DEAD' MUSCLES.
Nonetheless, KEEP TRYIN'!
I KNOW you're STILL THERE!
My brain's STILL OPEN
Even WITH eyes CLOSED."

34.
NEW MENTAL TRIALS

PRE-ACCIDENT, I'd never really gave much of shit about music. Some people claim that it's fun and relaxing. After starting to rewrite well-established songs only post-accident, I'll agree with the first part. I wouldn't be a legitimate judge of "relaxing", 'cuz weirdo that I am, I find mathematics calming/soothing. During the creation process, it's not relaxing, 'cuz I'll struggle to find a rhyming word and/or a sentence with the correct syllable #. But, after the conclusion, that feeling of accomplishment is relaxing.

With my oft extolled academic years behind me, I must seek new forms of neural entertainment.

(The television is great! But, anti I started with Martial Arts technique design.

(I've started with help making an informative technique DVD.)

Next, I (with help) began my blog.

(www.ajkturk.blogspot.com)

"The dude Abides."

From A.J. to you. The blog posts are arranged from newest on top to oldest.

Soon, I ventured into song parodies. (.A book of new parodies different from those here will be created.)

Then, there's been my all encompassing autobiography.

Finally, there was my Editor's recommendation of splitting my tales into sections.

What have I learned?!

There is a method to my madness!
(Cue the dark and sinister laugh,)

35.
THERE ARE GOOD DAYS, AND THERE ARE BAD

JUST TRY TO LIMIT/MINIMIZE the "not so great" days. Probability and statistics undeniably imply that not all instances may/can be ideal. Hence, the phrase "'shit' happens" became popular. Accepting the fact that sometimes stuff just doesn't work out according to plan, please always maximize your effort.

An optimist aims for and hopes for converting the "maybe success" into certainty. A pessimist only sees the potential/possible "negativity" as inevitable.

I like to start and end each day with/on a POSITIVE note. (E.g. Emails, athletic stats, *NUMB3RS* show, *The Tonight Show with Jimmy Fallon*, crunches) I've certainly had my share of terrible days. But, I just focus more on my better days! I concentrate on my 'Shodan' promotion, my valedictory, my accepted proposal. To a much lesser extent, I like to recall my completion of the "50-mile bike ride" and "mile swim" at Boy Scout camp (in North Carolina), my qualifying for the 2003 Florida State 2A wrestling tournament, my romantic dates.

People say that "you learn more from your failures than from your successes". I disagree. When somethin' goes right, I file the procedure in my "how to" memory files[1] for

---

[1] Even THOUGH my ACTUAL memory is SHIT/UN reliable, my MUSCLE Memory is AMAZING!

future applications. I mean, why else would there be terms, "consistency", "repeated success" and "favorite"/"underdog"?!

When you do not give up, you cannot fail. Hence, the common "self teaching" concept of "live, err, learn and reapply" was born.

Keep your mind occupied!

(I.e. When I was ~seven years old, my mom gave me a 'Slinky'. I applied kinetic physics and concentrated pressure to straighten it, which brought my first "grounding" punishment.)

Personally, my favorite days for relaxing/"shootin' the (proverbial) 'shit'" are Monday and Saturday. On Mondays I get to watch my favorite show about (Boston accent) 'SOOPUH SMAHTEEZ' 'Scorpion'. On Saturdays there's hilarious 'Saturday Night Live'.

36.
BEWARE OF THE MANY MEDICAL FACADES

TOO MANY "DOCTORS" MOSTLY "medical" ones falsely/ridiculously present themselves as "infallible gods".

(SKOFF! HAAARUMPF! Ha ha HA!)

Nothing could be further[1] from the truth!

Numerous "medical head honchos" are so teeming with egotism and stubborn ignorance that they fail to "listen to"[2] the actual symptoms.

They create their usually erroneous diagnoses without taking in and processing all the medical facts.

(AUDIBLE sigh)

First off, there was the horrendously botched surgery on my right forearm. The surgeon unknowingly/mistakenly (I wanna say "carelessly" or "haphazardly" but, those feelings are more outta spite and discontent.) Sliced my right ulnar nerve.[3]

Ya see, I've been unable to fully open all of my right fingers with out assistance from

---

[1] "FUrther" denotes "degree of intensity". While "fArther" denotes "distance".

[2] There's a distinct difference between actually "listening to" and processing details and just "hearing" something.

[3] The ulnar nerve in the forearm controls opening the hand and fingers. While the radial nerve controls closing it.

my left hand. But, I've coped with and adjusted to my limited hand movement. The very next year, I had my best wrestling season ever despite my having at that time only ~7.68 good fingers.

Next, there's my complicated digestive system. Bravo to my G.I. doctor for successfully "connecting" my stomach to a "G tube"! But, he's gotta "make up his mind" about what's healthy for me!

He said that I "should have solid bowel movements at least every other day".

Jeez! I know many of the statements I make seem like "poppycock". But, I cannot be that "full o' shit"!

What's worse is that my subpar doctor assigned me to "imbibe" via my G tube liquid "bowel stimulant"! My main nurse defended the doc by explaining to me that "the body can convert liquids into solids".

'Tis just one of the miracles of science!

(Need I remind her how odd/weird/un characteristic/wei rd my body is?!)

So, I tend to feel rather hesitant about asking for a Bowel Stimulant after 3 to 4 days of excretory inactivity.

On the other hand, said "G.I. doctor" messed up big time, when he approved of my swimming. My "gastro opening" got infected from my pool water.

(Notice the 'P'/PEE/URINE from the animals.)

I suffer from a major "Traumatic Brain Injury". Yet, I'm still smarter than approximately 78.7% of the people I've encountered.

(So, y'all can/should "hang your head in shame".)

One of my doctors audibly laughed to/in my face. He questioned why I did what I did (squats) in lieu of my bad hip.

Sooo, I spelled out:

"As a Biomedical Engineer, I might know a little sumthin' about Biophysics."

Then, he snickered and stammered under his breath: "Yeah, RIGHT!"

(I will not return to his office.)

I emphatically apologize for seeming to be a jerk! I'm just constantly "on the defensive", 'cuz nearly everyone thinks less of me, when they hear "T.B.I."

I'm just so used to bein' thee "TOP DAWG"! I can't say that I like or am used to being "looked down upon".)

37.
My Joyous Past Prepared Me for an Eventful Future

THE FIRST **~23.33 YEARS** of my "event full" and mentally/academically spectacular life provided a legitimate foundation for my severe neurogenic injury and the ensuing ~8.34 years (thus far) of determined responsibility.

My numerous and well-documented success stories prepped me well for the ensuing catastrophic drops. Despite my personifying the epitome of optimism, I'm also a realist in that I recognize that not "all things can/may/will be good or bad". Hence, I believe in karma and/or balance.

Since I was ~7.42 years young, I've been excelling in Karate. My ~24.08 years (and counting) of studies have taught me the importance of discipline, respect, determination, will power, practice, balance, repetition and studying.

After tons of mental highs, I'm wise enough finally to know that I couldn't possibly always be correct! After many athletic "wins", I've accepted that I have "lost" a big one physically my set of legs! psychologically, I was so emotionally stable and on a "feelings peak", that I "semi-saw" the inevitable "psyche 'drop'".

My valedictory status showed and proved to 507 other students, their parents, an exemplary educational staff and me that I'm kinda/sorta/"eld-a-bit" smart! Boy, have I appreciated my having such impressive instincts, insightful judgment, keen applications and clever teaching.

When it's raining and overcast, I gauge whether my manual wheelchair and me can "weather the storm". It depends upon the amount of time I'll be outside and uncovered.

(So, I always bring my big umbrella.)

I daily gauge when I should get up and out of bed to begin my morning. I hafta "do alotta crunches", recheck my daily schedule, check my email and start my daily blog. Then, by ~11 am every morning, I'll walk ~34 steps into my bathroom to either stand and urinate into 'mi Juan' or sit in my manual wheelchair to brush my teeth, change my clothes, shave my face, trim my goatee and begin my day.

I've gotta respect my time management skills!

(I.e. I just tried to visualize a calculator's showing of "how I've always been aesthetically appealing" to hetero sexual women by story:

"There once was a girl with 69 boobs. (Type '69' into the calculator.)

She had too, too, too many. (Type '2' three times.)

She went to 51 St. to see Dr. X. (Type '51' and a 'MULTIPLICATION' sign.)

He gave her 8 operations. (Type '8' and the '=' sign.)

(Turn calculator upside down.)

I achieved a "lack of 'man boobs'" mainly from "almost two and a half decades of 'Martial Arts' training". This physical studying consisted of at least 1.5 hours/class, at least 3 days/week, at least 40 weeks/year, 24 years > at least 4,320 hours of formal class to learn not teach.

Along the STME lines, I greatly desire a female's doubling the odds against "my overcoming my T.B.I.":

They're ~2,659,004 to 1.

Sooo, if I were to double '2,659,004', that'd be 5,318,008 upside down, which is "BOOBIES".

(I♥ my 11,513 days "aboard Earth".)

Despite my greatly disliking the teacher's (my "high school" principal's) hatred of me, her teachings in 'macroeconomics' combined with my own morally straight conscience set me up as an efficient and understanding entrepreneur.

38.
'TIS A LIGHT
AT THE END OF THE TUNNEL

EVENTUALLY, MY DISABILITIES SHALL PASS. My paralysis has already been like an 8.33+ year "kidney stone"! But, it will pass. I've just gotta continue my neurologic therapy and physical workouts.

On that note, originally, I went to my leg gym three different days per week each for an hour and a half. However, after ~0.33 years (> ~4 months) of that, I recognized my limits. I switched/decreased my exercise time from ~4.5 hours per week to 2 hours per week. (Only Mondays and Fridays, each from 3:00 to 4:00) then, in late 2016, the owner of said "leg gym" asked me to switch back to three days per week. I however knew/know the limits of my body's strength and endurance. Sooo, I graciously declined. Most importantly, though, he asked me, 'cuz he liked my energy, power and enthusiasm, and he hoped my zest for exercise would "rub off" on other patients/customers/"clie nts".[1] My philosophy on life:

"If you're gonna go, go all out."

I would say "'Tis all or nothing". But, that seems very/too circumstantial to be applied

---

[1] Yet another thing that irked/bothered me about my initial rehabilitative facility was that workers there would always refer to me and other patients as "clients" or "customers." As if we brain damaged, medical help seekers are/were nothing more than "paychecks with eyes."

to my recovery process or rehabilitation in general. That's why there are fractions and percentages.

Since I am a mathematical nut, one of the few joys I get nowadays, as I monitor my slooow but legitimate nerve rebuilding progress is to note/mark the trigonometric maxima and minima of my various limbs.

The most appropriate "Fortune cookie" I've ever received read:

"Think with your head. But, follow your heart."

Now, if only I could find a lady who shares my passion for "practice 'multiplication'".

Since I like to describe my bedroom as

"This is where the 'magic' happens", I've practicing my prestidigitation to make my words more literal. But, then, I begrudgingly realize that I can't do much "sleight of hand" with my surgically botched and nerves severed hands.

(Aaawww, SHUCKS!) I'll just continue to marvel mademoiselles with my math magic! Alliteration aside, I think that (my) mysteriously magnificent "sleight of mind" is weirder.

Ya know, I "rued the day" once. I didn't get much else done.

"C'est la vie."

(Of course, the day in question was July 6th, 2008. So, my time was unfortunately cut short by my "falling into a coma." Sooo, is that really fair?!)

One day, I'm gonna look back at my "insanely difficult times", and be glad I did not give up! The (metaphorical) "juice" will be well worth the (neurological and muscular) "squeeze"!

"Don't confuse the ability to 'PREDICT' with the ability to 'CONTROL'."

('NUMB3RS')

I.e. I predict that my leg nerves will regenerate strong. But, unfortunately, I cannot control that. Although with enough willpower and effort, I can and will eventually triumphantly jig around my big house in celebration of my "defeat of" my "neural hurdles."

If I had learned one thing in my studies of 'Non Linear Algebra in Multi Variable Calculus', it'd be to always account for variable change.

Upon "deep"/intense reflection, I'd hafta agree with the thoughts of Jeanette Winterson:

"To be ill adjusted to a deranged world is not a breakdown."

I have the courage, determination and willpower to confidently declare:

"I'm hurt. I ain't dead!"

39.
FURTHER STREAM OF CONSCIOUSNESS

AS I DON'T REALLY FEEL LIKE FINDING if and where I mentioned these points, I'll detail said issues now. (That's why there's an "Editor", right?)

So, my main nurse and I were discussing how my appointment with my physiologist went. I stated that he mainly just confirmed what she's been saying about wound care and eating. The main/only point that I gathered from my meeting was that it is definitely possible to medically/surgically remove [my] G/peg tube.[1]

My mom claims "[I] hear only what [I] wanna hear..."

With my "supersonic hearing," I can only wish it were more selective. I hear all. I just tend to dwell/focus on[2] the more positive points/aspects.

---

[1] After my appointment, my main nurse corrected my interpretation of her analysis by stating:

"[MY] feeding tube is kind of a 'peg tube', because there was minor 'surgery' done to attach the tube to [my] stomach with a balloon. But, it's kind of a G tube, in that constant 24/7 feeding is not necessary. So, it's a very unique blend."

[2] I researched the phrase. According to its definition, the phrase dwell on doesn't carry a negative connotation, as I thought.

40.
MY HINDSIGHT >> MY FORESIGHT

FOR ALL THOSE not *fluent in mathematical jargon*, ">>" translates to "much, much greater than."

Since my judgment is still very, very questionable, I unfortunately tend to misjudge situations and behaviors, when I'm in certain scenarios. I'll mistake *kindness* for *romance, sadness* for *humor invitation* and/or *uneasiness* for *fear*.

Then, it's not until afterwards when it's way too late, that I realize my stupidity! I'll be teeming with regret!

: (

(MORE in *Volume III*)

AFTERTHOUGHTS

In hind sight of all I've been through,

I ask myself:

"Who's crazier me or everybody else?!"

I know I'm ridiculously smart. It's just psychologically very frustrating that all too many common folks lack the understanding to grasp the concept of a "semi-mute genius."

Tough times never last long periods of time. But, tough people do!

As an indirect result of my accident, I've lost much/most of my leg power, all of my romantic/symbiotic love, ~33.37% of my astonishing intelligence (That fraction is correct. I did the math.) And almost all of others' respect.

Thus, I must "begin my 'second life' anew"!

> "Once your point of view is changed, the very thing which was so frustrating, becomes a clue to the truth."
> – **ARTHUR CONAN DOYLE**

Embrace/treasure your unique ness. Never fear highlighting it! We all have problems with varying levels of difficulty. 'Tis the ways we "attack"/encounter and eventually solve 'em that makes us different.

Personally, I confronted/attacked my T.B.I. "HEAD ON." (Pardon the pun.) But, that's just how I "fight": all systems go!)

Don't trust everything you see.

Even salt looks like sugar.

Ergo, I strut as the "salt", and a "retard" as I have so ignorantly, mistakenly and stupidly been called is the "sugar."

"Don't 'judge' a 'book' by its 'cover'."

Wise "John Bridger" of the fantastic movie *The Italian Job* mentioned some memorable/priceless advice that's my next "project" for the "big picture":

"Find someone you want to spend the rest of your life with, and 'hold onto her' forever."

I believe it was the ever so wiiise "Tigger" of *Winnie the Pooh* who deduced: "'life' is not about how fast you run or how high you climb not how well you 'bounce' back."

As a semi/quasi-mathematician, I always search for the "elegant" answer. I've gotta realize that human behavior is rarely if ever "elegant."

> *"Life isn't about finding yourself. It's about creating your-self."*
> **– UNKNOWN**

(As an example of my "recreating myself," I keep a daily/nightly blog: http://ajkturk.blogspot.com.)

> *"You can't 'heal', what you don't acknowledge."*
> **– JACK CANFIELD**

My body is one of the few cases in which
"the parts are greater than the whole."
(In other words, I am an "A-hole.")
Don't wait for the perfect moment.
Take any/every moment, and make it perfect.
You have three choices in life: You can watch things happen, make things happen OR

wonder what the hell happened.

"'Health' is like 'money'. We never have a true idea of its value, until we lose it."
– JOSH BILLINGS

Hindsight's 20 20: I'm sure there were some tasks that I could've done with my legs, but I chose to use my hands, 'cuz I felt more coordinated with the latter. Now, I hafta continue semi-ignoring my legs. I loved my ex-lady. But, I must've done something wrong to/for her. (I know not what or how!)

You'll never find anyone remotely close to

"Altan Javit Kaynatma."

The jury's still out on whether that's good or bad.

But, it's the truth.

"I want people to realize I'm just human. And, I make mistakes. And, I want people to be able to forgive me if they're willing to do so."
(USWNT GOALIE HOPE SOLO)

To encourage further work, I say:

"Your words are more important than your thoughts, so start inspiring people."

Thus, I'm making a DVD showing of my Jujitsu techniques, in hopes of inspiring others to "hold nothing back in defense of [your] life, [your] family and [your] country" (MY dojo's School Creed).

Dear KARMA,
I begrudgingly accept the fact that I had to sacrifice a sizable fraction of my brilliance, a quizzically high degree of my memory storage capability and nearly all of my leg strength and

flexibility in both my lower appendages to spare my life.

But, I think you're a crazy/doubting pessimist, if you think I'm gonna let these injuries be permanent! Through my rehab, I'll admit that I've struggled. But, I've become more well-rounded in accepting my faults, highlighting my virtues and strengthening my weaknesses.

I'm still a remarkable brain, a commendable athlete (to a much lesser degree), a sociable party animal and an affectionate lover. Also, I'm now a respectful entrepreneur, an empathetic teacher, a reluctant semi-"hermit" and a generous giver.

Sincerely yours,

A.J. Kaynatma

A Note From the Author

THIS DAMN *T.B.I.* has brought me (almost) nothing but mental frustration, physical anguish and psychological (almost psychotic) dismay!

But! I've *made the best* of the *cruddy* physical state I'm *in* to tolerate and even prosper in my disabled *state*.

I'd hope that you, the reader, already read *Volume I* — The MENTAL CRESTS and TROUGHS of a 'Turkish Knight' with a *Traumatic Brain Injury*: Life's chock-full of **extrema**. That way, I can skip my extensive history.

Nevertheless, I'll detail the physical aspects of my **pre**-injury life and how/why I'm **trying** to recover a portion of my once enviable athletic prowess.

Currently, I am *under construction*. Ultimately, it's a full-body *Project*. But my *physical progress* is way more obvious than my *mental* improvements, because **it**'s external and therefore visible.

Y'all can't see my mental and psychological *advancements*. So, they require more explanation. Since I always want and appreciate guests, I recommend visiting me to witness just how I function throughout the day.

Just to warn y'all, I may shift tenses from time-to-time and/or points-of-view. But, these incidents are inadvertently done merely as attempts to remain objective. Ya see, I **know** just how amazing I was and am.

I desire to make my excellence rather clear to y'all without seeming egotistical or bombastic. (Of course, my *stilted* language doesn't help my cause. But, 'tis merely my seeking of synonyms to clarify my thoughts for you, the reader.)

(The key word here is *"SEEEEMING."*)

Alas! Dag-nabbit! After I'd written ~nine chapters of this second **Volume**, I accidentally deleted my draft of this **Volume**. So, hopefully, history does **not** REPEAT itself. (Said time-singularity would also apply to my catastrophic accident.)

Please *drift into* a sophomoric attitude as I have, when reading of genitalia and *intimacy*. Though I am currently *quantitatively* ~**31.66** years old, maturity-wise I'm still a rather sophomoric pre-adolescent. So, I find *genital*-based puns rather humorous.

(i.e. *ballzy* = brave) Please do not be offended!

I've felt a bit censored lately. It's almost as if my severely damaged oral nerves were trying to silence me. Strangely and enigmatically, my logical comprehension, cognitive understanding and mathematical applications are now my **virtues**. While physical prowess is now a weakness.

(AUDIBLE sigh)

On a lighter note, just know that I **was** a commendable *MATHLETE*. (*Perfect* Math S.A.T. and S.A.T. 2 scores, 8 years of competitive wrestling, ~24.32+ years of *Martial Arts* training). Since my high school's construction in 1936, I am still the only valedictorian to also be a four-year wrestler. Textbook *scholar-athlete*.

Now, I'm vigorously—yet healthily—trying to regain a fraction of the physical and intimidating strength I once **had**. 'Twill be tough, 'cuz so much of my strong action was derived from my hip movement. However, my tumultuous accident directly caused my need for extensive surgery on my left hip.

Metal pin(s) were surgically installed and later surgically removed. So, my reduced/limited hip movement is partially medically caused. Plus, constantly sitting in my wheelchair kinda prevents my generating much/any force from rotation.

My physical accomplishments have been numerous and laudable, if I do say so myself. (I'm gonna blame the fact that I can't get this damn *dirt off my left shoulder* on my botched right forearm surgery, clipped right ulnar nerve and resulting always loosely clenched right hand. 'Tis *slang* for *no sweat*.)

Thus, as I tend to favor my right hand for anything and everything, I hafta compensate (constantly) by varying my finger placement. And, when *shaking hands* upon first meeting someone new, I'll extend my right hand out past my colleague's hand, then *drag* it back, extending MY fingers through *push-pull* principle of biokinetics. As a result, my right arm has grown quite strong. My left arm has become annoyingly weak.)

Sadly, as I've **semi-sat** for all these years, a few of my muscles have semi-atrophied from nonuse. But, I've compensated admirably.

I've tried to date my accomplishments as often as I could, 'cuz my long-term memory's so bad that I'm selfishly using my book as my life's bookmark.

The calendrical-*dating* also shows just how long this *book-writing* process can be. I, the author, have tried to stay diligent and committed to this *project*. But, I, too, have a host of other obligations—mainly, my physical rehabilitation. This natural tendency to *date* my accomplishments kinda cuts **both** *ways*, because it's made me painfully aware how often I bother my *helpers* (Editor, Illustrator). I feel incorrectly that I'm *pressed for time*. That's ridiculous, A.J.!

As with my entire *rehabilitation process:*

It's about the end *result*, not the *process*.

Ergo, I've written more stories and exercised more (crunches, *neck-ups*, finger stretches) to better occupy *my time*.

Alas! Frequently, it's less about the *timing* of some of my accomplishments and more about the *fact that* I actually did 'em. 'Cuz technically, according to popular medicine, I should be dead.

If I were a religious man, I could *thank God and all that is holy for keeping a* kind and watchful *eye on me*. It's not that I'm completely Atheistic. I just think that if there's an *evangelical other-being, he's* got sumthin' against me.

But, I'm *far too scientific* to support that theological *mumbo jumbo*. No disrespect to any and all *believers (making the sign of the cross: "In the name of the Father, and of the Son, and of the Holy Spirit)*, I'm just, personally, not a religious man.

Holy water? It's just not my *cup o' tea*. I prefer a large glass of grapefruit juice! Or, I did when I wrestled.

(AUDIBLE sigh) Times change. Regardless, I've gotta continue to *give life my all*.

1.
DOMINANT BACKGROUND

SINCE I AM A MATH NERD/AFICIONADO/CONNOISSEUR, I've long sought a kinetic **balance** for my commendable mental brilliance.

(I pause to push up my glasses.)

Sooo, ~24.34 YEARS ago, at the tender age of ~7.44 years, in September of 1992, I decided to join a Karate class at the local YMCA. It turns out that 'twas an instrumentally genius choice!

(If I do say so myself)

As it turned out, at ~17.07[1] years young, *Martial Arts* would become my main kinetic distraction from the rigors of my mental skirmishes. I enjoyed wrestling too. Since I'm done with *school*, I need to seek other distractions.

Practice makes *close to* perfect. With over 24 years of *training* and *muscle memory*, skill becomes *reflex*. Aaahhh, *muscle memory*!

Over the next ~seven years, after my septenary-birthday (ages 7 to ~14), I *juggled* a few different sports, while simultaneously *kickin' alotta ass* in Karate class. (Pun intended.) I played community soccer for two or three seasons as a pre-adolescent. I always positioned myself as the left-*middie*. But, I am right footed.

Why is a right footed soccer player positioned on the left side of the field?! Perhaps he's just that *damn good*. Actually, my coaches told me that it's 'cuz I'd never **stop** running. I was everywhere.

---

[1] I earned my first two black belt(s) and thus, became an instructor.

Most *'futbol'* teams have their better strikers on the right, 'cuz most players are right footed. Ergo, the better strikers are positioned on the right. To combat this tendency, teams will position their better defenders on the left. Like my Karate-sparring, I've always been better at defending than attacking. I'll go on the offensive if and when I hafta. But, for the most part, I prefer to wait for you to attack.

So, I can *block and counter*. Rarely, did I devote my time and energy into attacking something. I'd merely ignore it. I'd respond in the **same** manner in my Jujitsu defense. OR, on the soccer field, look for others to assist.

This *callisthenic work* of constant running on the soccer field instilled and developed my terrific endurance early on.

I also tried youth basketball for ~two seasons. I was too young to incorporate much strategy. But, the feelings of extreme competition were ever present. Again, I was more into the assists than my baskets.

'Twas not that I lacked the skill or creativity to *get open*. I just preferred the over-whelming feelings of pride I'd get from setting up teammates. I sought to position myself better for teammates to score. Both soccer and basketball triggered my *internal fire* for rivalry and trigonometry.[2] Those early wants of competitive clashes and angle manipula-tion have hung with me and *stood the test of time*.

High school began. I got right to work. Freshman year I tried (American) football, 'cuz I'm obsessed with the game. Goof off that I am, I busted my left big toe while foolin' around barefoot up in my high school wrestling *room*.

(Or, was that later? Constant prankster that I am, my *laundry-list* of hospital visits all get *jumbled into* one *painful* stay.)

Sooo, I decided to shift gears to a different full contact sport with no *protection*/zero *padding*.

Said *padding-less* venture was folk-style wrestling. During my very first *practice* with my school team, my coach asked us all if anyone had wrestled previously. I gulped hard and mumbled my response: "Yeah, with my emotions!" As time passed, all eight years of high school and college were partially dedicated to wrestling.

(I devoted some of my college life to my obsessive hobby, 'cuz I knew of the necessity of dedicating *much* of my brilliance to my 'Bioengineering' studies in the oft-commended

---

[2] The study of angles.

Ivy League institution.)

In addition to my being President of the Wrestling *Club*, I also commandeered the (fraternity) Intramural *Beer pong*[3] and Soccer teams.

My *folk-style* wrestling further *matured* my stamina, which has been a critical part of my present-day *rehabilitation*. (MY) muscles may (temporarily) *forget*. But, repeated trials will hopefully jog *the memory*.

(WOWZA! Has it ever?!)

Well, well, well. I'm glad you asked. One thing that has become *crystal clear* to me since my accident is that there *is a* gargantuan difference between mental memory and muscle memory. Meaning, I can mimic the moves of a Karate-*kata* as I watch students present the forms.

But, I can't teach the kinetic moves of the *kata* in a write up, 'cuz I'm notable to visualize it. I'm just not remembering the move at all. Someone could tell me the next move. But, unfortunately, I now lack the cognitive comprehension to apply it to future knowhow. I now focus more on the "why" for a move. I think about the hypotheticals of "what if."

One aspect of my rehab that's been especially frustrating has been how surprising and unnerving it is to not have the stellar stamina I once had. *BOOOOOO!*

I'll re-emphasize: anomaly that I am, most of my injuries are more physical than mental. (That's excluding my severe psychological *uneasiness*, which renders my judgment highly questionable, I'm sorry to say.) : (

Pre-accident, I was very much a protector in my relationships. Post-accident, I'm much more of a *provider*. 'Tis not just a matter of material possessions. 'Tis just my way of thinking. I still provide *protection*. It's just more along the concept of *avoidance* of than actual *physical confrontation*.

Thankfully, my extremely active and athletic *background* provided me with an overabundance of metabolism. Currently, my lifestyle is rather sedentary.

: (

Even with my current, less frenetic lifestyle, I still maintain a stable bodyweight in the LOW 140s with an **"estimated** *Body Mass Index* of ~14%"(my *UPPER body* Trainer). But,

---

[3] Collegiate/*frat-tastic* name for beer pong is *"beirut"*, as *"beer PONG"* is played with paddles

it's safer. Sooo, it's *for the greater good*. As I am still within two weight *classes* (ten pounds) of my senior year of high school wrestling weight class (135 pounds), I'd say I'm surprisingly healthy!

To be more specific, I weigh ~141.25 pounds. Since muscular tissue weighs ~1.16 more than fat, and it's ~2.2 times denser than fatty tissue is, I'm thinkin' I've gotta gain weight!

2.
MY SECOND *HOME*

BACK TO HOW RELAXED, COMFORTABLE and knowledgeable I feel at "America's Home DOJO"[1] in Hollywood, Florida.

Little did I know as a seven-year-old whippersnapper that I'd go on to earn officially two (informally three) '*Shodan*'[2] ranks. Not only did I learn countless blocks, strikes, and kicks, but I grasped the concepts of '*KATAs*"[3] and self-defense. But, I treasured the ongoing class theme:

The most serious enemy of *greatness* is *good enough*.

'Tis even an excerpt from the "School Creed" at my dojo:

"I will exercise restraint in the use of my Karate knowledge, employing it only in fair competition or in defense of my life, my family and my country."

Hey, way to go, A.J.! I probably haven't heard or seen those words since I was a student in the kids' class! Sooo, I was just an unsuspecting 12 year old, some ~19.34 years ago (The adults don't need a reminder to focus.)

Since I was so skilled at a young age, my *Professor* actually asked me to join the adults' class, when I was just a 12 year old '*midori obi*.[4] ('*Karateka*' are typically **not** permitted to

---

[1] I just overheard someone state that. Sadly, I did not research that. So, don't quote me on that distinction.

[2] 'Black belt' in Japanese

[3] 'Pre-arranged fighting movements' in Karate

[4] Japanese for 'Green belt'

participate in the adults' class 'til age 16. But, I was and still am just that good.)

'Tis extremely odd, that I was very mature as a pre-teen child. But, *now*, as an *early 30s* man, my maturity seems to have *backtracked into sophomoric-City*. 'Tis as If my maturity level (qualitative) is indirectly proportional to my age (quantitative).

In other less mathematical words:

As I grow **older**, I tend to act like a *wordy* **child**.

I am by no means a perfectionist. I just have lofty, but attainable, goals coupled with indefatigable determination. With these *raised* objectives, I, in turn, have developed *inspiring* expectations, 'cuz I'm a confident optimist.

It kinda helps that my catastrophic car accident deadened many of my nerves. Sooo, if I feel pain, there's no beginning levels. It's pretty much

ALL or **NOTHIN'**.

There ain't much in between. My lack of nerve impulses to indicate pain to my brain can be good or bad. Sure, I get uncomfortable constantly. But, my extensive history in the sports *world* taught me long ago the significant difference between actual pain and mere discomfort. So, I know when to stop versus when to just *suck it up*.

For instance, if an unknowing friend bets me that I can't withstand certain pain or tolerate nasty taste, then he'd be *in for a rude awakening*. 'Tis great, if I cared about winning bets. But, that's *below me*. Plus, I have no-one with whom to bet.

Plus, it's **not** *gambling*, when I **know** I'm gonna *win*.

(How do I **still** possess such confidence in spite of such repeated injuries?!)

I like to joke with my mom that I almost always *beat her* in the card game *cribbage*, 'cuz I cheat. But, it's really that I just utilize my rapid *mental math*, astute probability analysis and keen Knowledge of Psychological tendencies.

(EVIL laugh)

(Aaannnd, CHEATING!)

(I can kinda *count cards*. Ssshhh! Just, my memory's *nowhere near as good as it once*

Calamities?! I now have more time to better crunch *the* biokinetics-numbers. So, I can be safer and better prepared with alternative schemes. I aim for precision as opposed to accuracy, because statistically *precision* implies a repeated procedure. While *accuracy* refers to how close the results are to the actual value.

(In layman's terms, I am more concerned with the means than I am with the end.)

was.)

Ya know, I **could** easily "cheat" in any game that involves ongoing and changing score-keeping, 'cuz **my** mental math is always so *dead-on* and trusted. But, thankfully my moral dignity is of a higher degree than that. Then, my skills take over.

'Tis terrible that I don't really acknowledge pain, 'til it's almost too late to do anything about it. On a numeric-scale of pain intensity, I do not really recognize the *discomfort*, 'til it's at least an 8 out of *10*.

: (

I've gotta thank my *Martial Arts* Professor for looking past my disabilities! He entrusts me with co-teaching (with a *'Sempai'*[5]) a kids' class every few weeks. I'm even producing a how-to DVD of **my** assorted "Karate and Wrestling and Jujitsu" techniques! Unfortunately, I'm not performing the ~20 techniques (out of ~54 techniques I have designed. on paper).

My *'Sempais'* do a spectacular job of demonstrating and explaining the *ins and outs* of all the moves. I have a dangerously fickle left hip. So, my main Nurse advised me to not test it.

: (

The hip used to be *metallically supported with surgically-implanted titanium*! But, a lot of self-prescribed *R and R* (Rest and Relaxation) has really helped!

Alas! To be safer, I'm just the critic **behind the scenes**.

But, my *'Sempais'*/Assistants (I have two) play an instrumental role in my teachings. Not only do they act as my voice. But, they physically show when to switch from defense to offense, where to strike and how the body will react.

Further 'kudos' to my *Professor* for his non-technical recognition of my knowledge and understanding. He treats me just as I am – a knowledgeable teacher and skilled *'Shodan.'*

Bummer! I almost forgot how nice and respectful my *Professor* IS. Since my terrible car accident just as I was prepping for my *'Shodan'* test in Jujitsu, he openly tells people about me:

"Oh, he's practically a BLACK belt. He was this close to testing for it. You should see some of his techniques!"

---

[5] 'Assistant Karate Instructor'

(And, with the DVD, they will!)

Said 'shodan'-ranking would be my third black belt. I only know of one other person with that amazing distinction – MY *Martial Arts* Professor.

Post injuries, I still attend *Martial Arts* class either twice or thrice per week—either to teach or to view and assist. Above all my *Professor* stresses that he does not *advance* students on physical prowess **alone**.

(I've only recently decided that this third day shall be allotted to my attending the adult's class. *NO harm, NO foul.*)

My *ground defense* is so **SICK**,[6] that I'd venture to (PLAYFULLY) SELF-criticize as "A.J. puts the **EEEWWW** in *jUUUjitsu.*"

(When I design techniques, I always include alotta devastating *Karate and Wrestling* combos.)

Finally, I'll emphasize that my weakest areas are my legs (obviously) and my psyche.

---

[6] "SICK" is slang for "very good".

3.
WHAT I COULD'VE BEEN

JUST PRIOR TO my devastating car accident on July 7, 2008, I was training in *Mixed Martial Arts* (MMA) to hopefully join the UFC (Ultimate Fighting Championship).[1] I was actually driving home from a *black belt* workout that Sunday, when *the SH*T hitteth the fan.*

I was a rare mix of bone-crushing brawn (I know how to break any/ALL of the 206 bones in the human body.), jaw-scratching brains and knee-weakening charm. Now, I mostly utilize my incredible intellect and benign banter via my Splendidly Special Speech-generating device. Alliteration aside. (AUDIBLE sigh) Currently without a *significant other* to impress,

: (

I hafta settle for trying to surprise myself.

(SCOFF! Good luck!)

(Hey! It happens! Especially post-accident)

Many of my nerves—**not** muscles—are supposedly dead. But, I am such an *oddity*, that sometimes my neural-muscular connections will just *click*. Like most of my *Martial Arts* opponents, I wasn't dead. But, I could definitely deduce I'd been in a *fight*. Little did I know how *intense* my impending *crusade* would be.

One recent evening while I was in bed, my left ankle started itching. 'Twas my bad/left

---

[1] Additionally, I was training/practicing for my *black belt* test in *Jujitsu* for my THIRD *'Shodan'* rank.

leg. So, rather than calling over my Caregiver/employee for reaching/scratching help, I stretched down far to my left calf with my right hand to slowly reach my itchy left ankle!

My eventual ankle-scratching is a symbolic representation of my ongoing mental battle against my T.B.I.: *Good-things* come to those who *wait*. *Good work* takes *time*. (Unfortunately, patience is a *virtue* I currently lack.)

I was further surprised that I had forgotten just how much I'd advanced in *Martial Arts*. Apparently, I've earned a 1st-degree black belt in *'Shorei ryu Karate'* (I remembered THAT), a **2nd**-degree black belt in *'Sh**URI** ryu Karate'* (That was **news** to me!) and a high-ranking brown belt in Jujitsu (that was also news). My teacher reminded me of these impressive achievements after my accident.

Possibly the **only** good physical thing to result from my life-destroying accident was/is my new dependence on my arms. **Pre**-injuries, I'd distinguished myself in the *Martial Arts* world by my exceptional leg power, speed and fluidity.

Now, I've had to use my arms more. My upper *body* trainer has instructed me to increase my *Range of Motion*, to tone my growing biceps and to develop left finger movement.

Back in my *wrestling and **Martial Arts** prime* (Sooo, in ~early 2003), a schoolmate complimented my physique:

"How do you maintain such a statuesque body while constantly cooking such *scrumptious delectables*?!"

(He was a fellow *sophomoric Dude*, a saxophone player in the school band. He lacked **any** form of *athletic tendency*.)

At my job as *Chief Operations Analyst* for a major *Petroleum Distributor*, I had to remain ever-ready to climb an oil tank 200 feet to adjust a (sometimes) faulty *Tank Monitor*. My near-flawless job proved one of the few cases in which *a good workman* **can** *blame his tools*.

Though I may be a tad (VERY) biased, y'all hafta account for changing weather conditions (extreme rain and wind) and/or neglectful product drivers.

I always made sure to check everything during my *monitor inspections*, 'cuz it was such a (metaphorical) *pain in the ass* to drive ~90 minutes to a disorganized oil site, to scale a ladder to some 150+ feet up, to examine the electronics/mechanics of a *Tank Monitor* then to descend said ladder.

Apparently, I did some exemplary work with said *Tank Monitors*, as **I was** in *training* to be a Site Manager.

(MORAL: Engineers **can** do more than just *crunch numbers*. Some have Social and Managerial skills.)

Ssshhh! During my sophomore year of college in Philly, I was *thrown out* of a members-only sauna for *not being naked* **enough.**

(AUDIBLE sigh) I **had** a smart, funny, generous, gorgeous longtime girlfriend before my traumatic accident and ensuing injuries. She stayed with me even after my cataclysmic accident and resulting injuries for awhile.

I love(d) her, so much so that I proposed marriage to her.

She accepted!

(YYYEEESSSSSSSS!)

I still don't understand why!

(I cannot even remember this (tragic) event happening.)

But, she **dumped** me just two days prior to my 27th birthday in 2012.

We'd lived together again for only ~six months (October to April) post-accident. We'd celebrated zero birthdays together since my 23rd in April of 2008. So, I was **due** for some *hootin' and/or hollerin'.*

Such *heartbreak* from her **inexplicably** ending *us* has **negatively** affected all I did and DO. Thus, mathematically speaking, of the 11,590 days of *my existence* as of December 31, 2016, April 6th, 2012 was unquestionably the *minimum* or lowpoint.

now (AUDIBLE sigh), I still feel terrible, like she killed my *spirit! And she* refuses to even email me!

Jeez! I haven't been this uncomfortable since I was a *Chippendales* "dancer".

Oh, yeah! I meant, *since I stole chips and danced naked in a bloomingdales.)*

FYI: I use *humor* as a **coping** mechanism, 'cuz my physical disability frequently creates social awkwardness.

My public nudity was **never** without grace.

Sooo, I now have extensive *free time.* Thus, I exercise and *workout* frequently (5 days a week → 3 workouts + 2 *Martial Arts* classes). Plus, I'm kind of a genius. Sooo, is *strong* the new *sexy,* or is it *smart?!*

Either way, "I'm *dead sexy!*"(—Fat Bastard, *'Austin Powers')*

Back when I **could** run and jump and kick, I felt confident in my relationships.

I'd boast with pride, "I protect that which matters most."

(—'The Matrix Reloaded')

Currently, I am **not** *suffering from* any major memory loss, mis-interpretation or coma-caused ignorance. I am merely stating an irrefutable **fact:**

I **will** *walk* smoothly again and *talk* cogently and kiss *passionately*.

4.
MAKE THE BEST OF A BAD SITUATION

EVERYTHING IN MY LIFE since the dreaded accident has forced me to make and try **alternative** plans.

Of course, first I'll try Plan **A**. Then, I improve to a Plan **B**. Over time, my body further progresses to allow for a Plan **C**.

As my improvement continues, I devise more elaborate kinetic schemes: Plan **D**, **E**, **F**, **G**[1] I'd like to think that I will not require **27** different plans.

But, who knows Altan Kaynatma's *Neural Kinetic Rate of Regrowth* in his legs better than I?! I pose this question to y'all! I'm *all ears.*

(Eerie silence)

Thanks to my long and detailed education in *trigonometry* and *Martial Arts*, I can and do apply my knowledge of *angles* to all of my non-wheelchair movements. I recognize *reflexive properties, inverse functions, adjacent angles and tangents.*

The proper "angle of elevation" of my hamstrings' tightening, every time I stand to urinate. The "angle of depression" when I sit after finishing. The best "leverage angle" when I'm lifting at the gym.

Said *angular rules* are essential to maximize my *energy output* and to optimize my

---

[1] Then, I'd hafta go with *Preparation H* for the awkward.

breathing efficiency. I didn't realize how essential proper and frequent *trigonometric inter-pretation* is to efficient *energy production*, until I **now** hafta conserve my *kinetic output*. Thank goodness for my *biophysics* background!

It sucks *to the Nth power* when my brain knows to do one thing but my muscles won't *process* the *neural messages* in time—or at all.

As a direct result of my dreaded car accident, and ~23.24 years of *practice*, my *think-ing-etiquette* altered. According to a very informal *thinking* test I took in late 2016, I'm still very *left brain*-oriented. *How?!* I'm glad you asked. Ya see, in my accident, I suffered numerous *gruesome injuries* **all** along the left side of my body. (e.g. left shoulder surgery with nine screws *installed*, left knee surgery with a *plate installed*, left hip surgery with a *plate installed* but, later surgically removed—'cuz I unexpectedly **improved** so quickly!)

But, alas! Said atrocities were/are **just** physical! I may not be **pretty**.

(PAUSE. I've gotta *hike up my skirt*.)

(LADIES? Judges?)

Most of my *damage* was/is external and *neural*. Since the brain's left hemisphere con-trols the body's right side, and I'm sooo *thick-headed* (SHUT UP!), my right-sided pref-erence remained! Also, as the left neural hemisphere *controls* science, **math**, logic, rea-soning, numerical thought and reasoning, **my** distinctive *virtues* remained.

When I accomplish a *manual* task, it's almost always done with my right hand. When there's no time constraint, and I'm trying to redevelop my hand-eye coordination, I'll first try the activity with my left hand.

Unless otherwise noted, any and all *upper body* are (successfully) completed with my (way better) right arm.

I've always **had to** *work* to maintain my *social popularity*. I'm only now getting the recognition of my *obstacles*. (O' course, said *hurdles* **were** more psychological and inter-nal and thus, *hidden* pre-accident. Now, my *deadened-legs* and *muted voice* are more phys-ical and **external** and thus, obvious.)

There's a *gargantuan difference* between **commanding** respect and **demanding** it. I've always been a staunch advocate of *gaining support via* **action** *as opposed to* **words**. So, as much as I may *talk* in this book, 'tis quite the *inspiration* for y'all to see me *move* at the gym.

I can't understandably speak yet. Sooo, I constantly practice. As I've physically progressed/improved, I've had to make a few concessions to better adjust to my body's timely *progress*:

I deeply inhale before each time I speak. This tactic increases my intelligibility, 'cuz I tend to rush.

I hafta swallow my saliva frequently, so I don't drown! This tactic increases my intelligibility. But, it slows down my message.

Thankfully, I take some *antihistamine* to minimize my excess saliva. As I've never had any allergies, the medicine instead reduces the effects of histamines in my uber-sensitive nasal and laryngeal passages.

This *medicine* doubles by helping my *standing/leg* **Endurance** by further minimizing my saliva. Ya see, every time I'd stand to urinate into my toilet, I'll *spit at least 3 times.*

Sooo, less saliva = longer and more standing.

I think of synonyms, 'cuz I struggle to verbalize words that start with the 'Kuh' sound and/or 'Guh' sound.

This tactic increases my intelligibility, but I'm only avoiding/dodging the problem (of my lack of intelligibility) that eventually I'll hafta overcome.[2]

I've developed a number of physical *mannerisms* to make my speech easier for me and more cogent for others. I'll push down on the right armrest of my motorized wheelchair with my right hand to straighten my back posture and better enunciate. I'll sssllloooooooowww down my *word output*, as my brain *computes clearly* way fast**er** than my mouth can *verbalize understandably.*

When reading aloud, I'll read the entire sentence in my head, to know where to pause beforehand.

Ya see, I **need** a 24/7 editor — someone to clarify **my** actions for the *outside world.* I— as of now, in my *T.B.I.* recovery—lack the patience.

I used to **pride** myself on my phenomenal kicks, stances and leg-power. now, I just hafta depend on my arms so much more. I always knew, but now I experience, what a **necessity** *hip-stability* is to create legitimate power. I can't run or jog or even walk briskly. Sooo, I perform several different exercises often to calm my great desire for fitness.

(E.g. Sit-ups, crunches, reverse sit-ups, squats, bike rides)

---

[2] My next (separate) book includes some helpful *speech techniques* I devised.

Seemingly, I can *control* my own *metabolism*. Despite my aging ~13.5+ years **and** my *berserk* digestive system, I'm still within two weight classes of my senior year high school wrestling days at 135 pounds.

While admiring my *gunz*, I've noticed some great *tone* in my *biceps* and *triceps*. So, I'm still producing **some** muscle and not **just** fat. 'Tis encouraging and supports the medical diagnosis of my *condition* as totally *neural* and *psycho*-related and **not** *muscular*.

Apparently, my nightly *AB crunches* in bed, thrice-a-week bike rides and thrice-a-week formal workouts are *payin' off*. Since I joined my gym, my wrist size has slimmed three watch sizes. Not that I was anything close to *portly* pre-accident, it's just comforting to see *bodily transformations*.

Additionally, my *Speech Therapist* gave me a series of *neck crunching* exercises to practice in bed to better *clear* my larynx and to increase my intelligibility. I try to practice these every other night.

During my editing process, for my 32nd birthday on April 8th, I sought to demonstrate my **33 pushups** at my dojo to further inspire the kids.

Sooo, I had to *practice*:

Every Tuesday, starting March 28, under the *surveillance* of my *upper body* trainer, I did at least **40 pushups** with an increase of **5 pushups** every fourth week. (40, 40, 40, 45, 45, 45, 50, 50, 50, 55)

Then, on June 6th, I successfully *ripped out* **55 pushups!**

Sooo, I used my right hand to *brush the dirt* **off** *my left shoulder*, as if to say, "Ain't no thang."

I'm not nearly as active as I once was. Sooo, I watch all kinds of sports to live vicariously through the televised players.

I was talking with my *upper body* trainer about how welcome and appreciated my **positive** and **optimistic** outlook is. Regarding my (DIFFICULT) *journey*, I said,

"Hey, if it were easy, then everyone would do it."

When he responded by laughing and saying, "I've heard that," I proudly declared,

"I take the road **LESS** *traveled*."

Since I'm now single, I frequently host *PAH-teez*, and display my many dance moves on my '"FESTIVUS' pole"(Seinfeld).

My left hand and arm and leg are often not coordinated enough or strong enough to complete a specific task. (Nevertheless, I always TRY.) Sooo, I compensate by doing al-most everything with my right side.

(I'm considering **changing** the side names just for me: instead of *right* and *left*, now they're *right* and **wrong**.)

I've kinda gotta *live in the **past*** to an extent, 'cuz i had so many fabulous moments. If only I could remember 'em! Above all, I've gotta **accept** the fact that this wheelchair-bound, semi-mute, RIGHT-favoring *SMAHTY pants* is the **new** *A.J.*

On October 31, 2016, I received a very **un**pleasant *Trick and **not** Treat*! While walking a lot with almost just my walking cane at my gym, my trainer stepped aside/away to speak with the owner, unbeknownst to me.

I guess I'm not as well-off as I thought, 'cuz I fell.

: (

Thankfully, I had the presence of mind and *muscle memory* to rotate my trunk clock-wise—AS I FELL—and *break fall* with my right arm/side upon hitting the ground. : (

(Yay for remembering how to fall safely and applying it!)

I like a woman who can *hold her own* in a fight. I love *jujiitsu* and practicing it! Since that's my only doable-form of self-defense NOW, 'tis a nice feeling when someone else can *hang with me* in *my element*.

The combination of my slooooowly **re**developing nerve tissues and my *T.B.I.*-caused *lack of* patience makes my physical status incredibly frustrating and seemingly repetitive to *monitor*.

But, it's the *little changes*, the *minute differences*, *the slight alterations* that make all the difference to an everyday observer such as myself. For instance, I can feel more stability when I *walk*. I can feel the waistband on my shorts growing looser. My left foot is stepping slightly LESS *pigeon-toed*.

5
EVERY DAY MORE *WORK*

AS OF **DECEMBER 31, 2016**, I've had 3,100 consecutive 18+ hour days of intense **work** with zero breaks! Where's the *Labor Union* for THAT?!
(Yes, I'm counting my comatose days as "work", 'cuz I had to fight to stay **alive**!)
An ongoing misunderstanding that countless ignoramuses continue to have is:
"If I don't see it, it's not there."

> *The best and most beautiful things in the world cannot be seen or even touched. They must be felt with the heart."*
> — **HELEN KELLER**

Nowadays, from ages 28 to 31, I liked to kid that I could control my blood pressure and body temperature by just relaxing and staring at the *sphygmomanometer* or thermometer. It's really humorous, 'cuz my numeric estimates are usually about right!
I haven't been sick since... (I shrug my shoulders) I don't know.
(I hope I did not just jinx myself!)
I mean, my legs are semi-"sick."
(No, they're not! There's a gargantuan difference between *illness* and **chosen** *apathy*.)
Currently, my nerves and, therefore muscles, simply choose to not work.
To quote the 'Paranoia' song by *Green Day*:
"I'm not sick, but I'm not welll!"

Granted, there are certain days that I like more than others.

(Thursdays and Saturdays are **GRRRRRREAT**, 'cuz of MARTIAL ARTS class! Also, if and when I host a party, it's more than likely gonna be on a Saturday.) Believe me, my activities are so different, and vary so much that one day does not *bleed into* the next!

Every day's a new day!

Maybe I'll detail my daily schedule.

Or, maybe I won't.

Although I can't literally **taste**, I can metaphorically *taste* my thoughts.

(Such is just one of the infinite enigmatic qualities of **my** *Traumatic Brain Injury*.)

Gonna hafta read more to determine if my rehab is rather/semi/quasi-*eventfull*

OR

If I'm just full o' *shit*.

(A little o' Column **A** and a little o' Column **B**?!)

'Tis a spectacular **start** to my day, when, before my first *meal*, I *walk* ~28 steps to my manual wheelchair. I'll *eat* in my wheelchair, so I'm already squatting in the *pooping position*. Within ~an hour, I'll usually *expel* my *bodily waste*.

6.

BACK TO THE OL' DAILY GRIND

WAIT. **WAIT. WAIT!**

I've already calculated how long it's been since my last day off.

(RIDICULOUS!)

Nonetheless, I'll broadly/generally describe my physical commitments each day, 'cuz I'm nice.

MONDAY

— GYM (primarily LEGS workout[1]) (~1 hour[2])

— SPEECH Therapy (1 hour)

TUESDAY

— UPPER body workout (~1 hour)

— BIKE ride around m' HOOD (~0.5 hours)

— HOME workout of sit-ups, REVERSE crunches and squats (~1 hour)

WEDNESDAY

— HOME workout of sit-ups, REVERSE crunches and squats (~1 hour)

---

[1] My workouts began as primarily **legs**. But, as I improved over time, the training staff continued to *challenge* my entire body.

[2] Originally, my leg workouts were 1.5 hours **each three** days a week (Monday, Wednesday, Friday). But, that plus two other days of *Martial Arts* forced me to recognize and accept my limits.

(Mathematically, I was trying to *maximize* both my *energy output* and *strength display*.)

— BIKE ride around *m' HOOD* (~0.5 hours)

— *SPEECH Therapy* (1 hour)

THURSDAY

— *Martial Arts* class (~2 hours)

— HOME workout of sit-ups, REVERSE crunches and squats (~1 hour)

FRIDAY

— GYM (primarily LEGS workout) (~1 hour)

— HOME workout of sit-ups, REVERSE crunches and squats (~1 hour)

— *SPEECH Therapy* (1 hour)

SATURDAY

— *Martial Arts* class (~2 hours)

— BIKE ride (~$\frac{2}{5}$ of an hour = ~24 minutes)

— HOME workout of sit-ups, REVERSE crunches and squats (~1 hour)

SUNDAY

— HOME workout of sit-ups, REVERSE crunches and squats (~1 hour)

— BIKE ride around *m' HOOD* (~0.5 hours)

Mixed in on assorted, but frequent, nights, I *write* and edit my books.

(HHHMMM, THAT's ~17.9 hours/week.)

(My Tuesday bike ride is a BIT longer, 'cuz I ride WITH my trainer and my mom. She tends to be very sssslooooow. So, I independently take longer routes.)

(17.9 weekly exercise hours/168 total weekly hours = ~10.65% of my week is *workin' out*.)

(~6 sleeping hours/night → ~42 sleeping hours/week)

(17.9 weekly exercise hours/~126 total weekly awake hours = ~14.21% of my awake week is *workin' out*.)

There's a gargantuan difference between *bein' sleepy* and just *feelin' tired*: One is *slumber-desiring*, and the other is just *muscle-fatigue*. My muscles tire nearly every day. But, I can't recall the last time I was sleepy. As powerful as *fatigue* **can** be, my mind is just that **strong**.

(Yes, I **could** reason that my *Speech Therapy* is a *workout* specifically for my lips, tongue and larynx. It's a frequently quoted statistic that "7% of any message is conveyed through words, 38% through certain vocal elements and 55% through nonverbal elements (facial expressions, gestures, posture, etc.)."

—Dr. Albert Mehrabian, 'Silent Messages'

I also incorporate many, various *gestures* to potentially increase my intelligibility: straight back posture, saliva swallowing, facial sight/recognition, *big breath* control.)

Plus, I purchased a *disability-altered, handicap-accessible* bike/*tricycle* that I try to ride around my neighborhood three days/week. However, lately, I've been so busy with my own *speech* and breathing exercises that my *legs should be thankful* if I get out once.

In addition to my physical work, I also have frequent *speech Therapy* sessions (3x/week) and scheduled *NeuroPsychoTherapy* meetings (every third Tuesday). Ya see, now everything has become more physical: More body language, more smile/frown indicators, more head nods, more *eye reading,* more *tone deducing.*

I try to end my week days of *social frolicking* rather early (I'm almost always in bed post-shower by 5:00 pm), just 'cuz sitting in a squatting stance in a not always comfortable wheelchair can be exhausting!

('Tis not sleep-inducing by any means! 'Tis merely muscle-fatiguing.)

Thus, I'm **not** sleeping early. I'm just resting my muscles, as I do almost all of my writing sitting up in bed (~92.74%).

I'm both a *night owl* **and** an *early riser.* I've found that, as I continue to age, I'm becoming less and less sleep-dependent. I mean, I still very much get fatigued! 'Tis just my sore muscles *pleading* for a break.

7.
MISSED OPPORTUNITIES

I DON'T REGARD SITUATIONS as *pass/fail* anymore. I've learned:

*Even in **defeat**, there's always a **lesson to be learned** and **applied** for **future** trials.*

Sooo, a *win*'s a *win*. But, a *loss* **can** be interpreted as a *win*. Just LIKE how a *tie* can be *seen* to an optimist like me as a minor victory, 'cuz Hey! It's **not** a *loss*!

(Hence the phrase: *"I earned an **A** for effort."*)

Actually, even BEFORE my accident, I kinda had this mentality of "struggle or dominate." If I *tried* any task, I'd *learn to master it*. There was no middle ground. Only **expert** or *novice*.

Perhaps/most definitely, I think like this, because of my being so used to finishing *picture perfect/top notch* on all **96 graded evaluations** in high school. (4 report cards per year times 4 years of high school times 6 subjects = 96 grades)

(St Thomas Aquinas % '03 — Valedictorian, 4.9451 cumulative GPA)

Prior to *my accident* and my wrestling career (So, from 1995 to 1999 → just ONE term), I **was** the Prime Minister of (the fictional nation of) *Eatallyakan*.

So, I could've/would've (officially) earned my *'Shodan'* ranking in Jujitsu, probably higher degrees in my Karate rankings and a higher degree of respect as a teacher. Word on the street is I was only *let go* from my *Petroleum Distribution* company, 'cuz I was comatose. (AUDIBLE sigh)

My last girlfriend/EX-'fiancée' confused me, when she said that she did not *end us*, 'cuz of my physical limitations. But, I'm **not** an idiot! I can *read between the lines*: ~4.75

years of occasional physical inadequacy/disability is **not** *worthy of cancelling out* (OFFI-CIALLY) ~5.46 years of amorous bliss neither *romantically* nor quantitatively.

Now, I am not claiming to be smar**t**er than said *meanie*, who's ~2.73 years my elder, 'cuz *to each his own*. I'm merely implying that my math is way **better** than her erroneous *reasoning*.

(It DEFINITELY is!)

(AUDIBLE sigh) Our *ending* may **not** have completely been the fault of **her** stupidity and **her** stubbornness. I recognize that my *psychology* has altered. Thus, my literal perspective has changed, in that my *focal point* is now *lower to the ground*. However, my *amygdala* and *hippocampus* have oddly been **stimulated**. Thus, I've sought **more** *intimacy*, which I'd think would *excite* her!

(AUDIBLE sigh) But, sadly, I thought wrong!

Actually, since she has refused to clarify **any** of her *dumbfounded* (**lack** of) *reasoning* for over ~4.75 years (THANKFULLY, I've been writing the book. So, I've been pleasantly distracted.), so I'm *putting all onus on her*! Despite her stubbornness and my *broken heart*, I **try,** with mixed results, to not let my *forcing back tears* hamper my *rehab* in my gym.

But, I **am** a human! I think. ?!

After my accident, I tried reentering graduate school ~six years after first enrolling there. I signed up for 'Finance and Accounting' in an **accelerated** Degree for my *'Masters of Business Administration'*. Now, I won't name the HIGHLY reputable business school, because just one Administrative *advisor*—**not** a *teacher* nor anyone of authority—threatened me and fired me from the 'Newsletter Writing Team'. Said *female* actually tried to push **my** motorized wheelchair.

Oh, well. Despite my not *being able to write* **my own** *notes*, I understood **all** that the class reviewed. But, with no notes and my *shitty* memory, I *recorded*—NOT *earned*—a 'C+'. Very unhappy and disappointed, I decided to stop class for my completely *optional* degree rather than to continue with a bad temper.

I recognized my unhappiness, my irresponsibility and my potential danger to her! And, I decided 'twould be unwise to continue my studies there.

My deplorable temper aside, I decided that it'd be a better use of my free time to write for fun, than to enroll in some unneeded class for an unneeded degree. (You're welcome!)

As upset, confused and desperate as I now am, I **did** love *Ms. L.* If only she'd visit to witness my **amazing progress** in the last few **years.** I'm struggling to grasp just **how** I can still love her, after she's *hurt me* so bad.

(AUDIBLE sigh) I want to. But, I can't.

(Not to brag, but my improvements—despite my countless obstacles—are really rather inspiring!)

(But, that's more a psychological issue. So, read *Volume III*.)

Alas! (AUDIBLE sigh) Sometimes the *easiest way* to **lose** *something* is to *love it too* **much.**

8.

NEW OBJECTIVES

MY INJURIES HAVE FORCED ME to reevaluate and create new *life goals*. I *think* I need a job. *Not* for monetary purposes. 'Tis more to keep my own body busy. It's not (HahaHA! I said, *"SNOT".*) that I seek a boss. I **am** a *BOSS*! .... I just need **order**. Most importantly, I've gotta move more!

Nooo, I am not some kind of spaz! 'Tis just that I have such an extensive frenetic background, and I still need that kinetic atmosphere! I surprise myself with how outstanding my *Muscle Memory* is! At *Martial Arts* class, I evaluate the *'Karateka'* based on proper form and style, 'cuz I've (AUDIBLE sigh) forgotten most/all of the *'katas.'*

So, long story short, I'd like to earn a third black belt. (This one would be in *Jujitsu*.) But, I dare not **ask** for advancement, 'cuz *Professor* taught me long ago, that that is just *not* done! It's rude and assumptive and just frowned upon.

But, I'll REMAIN **READY**!

PLUS, I'm very CURIOUS as to HOW I might *TEST for* ADVANCEMENT:

— I struggle to speak[1] cogently.

— I can't walk on my own.

— I don't recall what I need to show, or how far I've gone.

Previously,[2] I had a very **physical** and **energetic** lifestyle in every aspect! job wise, I

---

[1] Ironically, I now verbalize foreign words (Turkish, Spanish, Japanese) more understandably than English words.

[2] Whenever I refer to "used to" (the distinctive point in time), I'll be citing before my

routinely climbed tall oil tanks to *play with* the physics, trigonometry and fluid dynamics of *tank monitors* to gauge the amount of product.

Occupation wise, I taught and demonstrated *Martial Arts* to kids' classes. Romantically, I liked to go out for meals. Hobby wise, I'd constantly seek activity like friendly basketball, movies and/or *drunken baseball.*

Now, job wise, I schedule my various activities (*Speech Therapy*, gym, Karate, Neuro-PsychoTherapy) to improve upon my *T.B.I.*-existence. I shan't lie: My main Nurse helps with my scheduling and payroll hours. Occupationally, I still love **teaching** *Martial Arts,* possibly more than I used to!

Now, it provides a fantastic outlet for me to go somewhere where I'm respected and marveled at and even envied. The '*BUSHIDO*'[3] is just so ingrained in my subconscious.

Romantically, I need a female with whom to share my joys! I had a *female friend*—who doubled as my *best friend*—for ~five years. That's about ⅙ of my life (as of then)! I wouldn't say I was *spoiled.*

But, spending so much time with her caused us to develop a *rapport*—an unspoken understanding for how the other feels.

My hobbies have changed. Sadly, I now hafta develop more stationary fun activities, like online correspondence, sports watching and comedic television.

I really want to *test* my ability to move on my left knee. Plus, I try to do sit-ups often.

With the recent acquisition (LATE 2016), I Do very much enjoy *feelin' the burn* in my quadriceps muscles after a bike ride. I've always liked exercising. I suppose ~24.32+ years of *Martial Arts* training **might** do that. I like to *strengthen* myself. Plus, it serves as a great reminder that my legs **still** *work* from time-to-time inconsistently.

Romantically, I need a female with whom to share my joys! I **had** a very *close* girlfriend for ~five years. We shared everything. It really helped that she is/was a medical nurse. So, she could substitute-IN for my *g-tube feedings* if need-be. She semi-understood my biokinetic-explanations about my movements.

(Let's be serious. She was probably just *smiling and nodding* as my *tales* of Newton and leverage and gravity went *flying over her head.*)

Intimately, I cannot move much at all, 'cuz of my *G-/peg-tube*, surgically-repaired left

---

accident—July 6, 2008.

[3] '*The Way Of The Warrior*' in Japanese

knee **and** surgically-reset left shoulder.

In the MUSICAL words of Celine Dion:

"Near, far, wherever you are

I BELIEVE that the heart does go OOOOON!"

9.
RE-ESTABLISHING MY *VERBIAGE*

PRE-ACCIDENT, I WAS NEVER HESITANT to *VOICE* MY opinion. I could apologize for being so boisterous. But, I'm NOT gonna be sorry for WHO I AM! Should I apologize for *lacking shame*?! Um, no.

Whether I was a student in school or a teacher in *Martial Arts* class or a wrestler in a practice, I **never** held back my thoughts. I couldn't *help it* that many of my observations were insightful and poignant.

Now, I'm slightly hesitant to **speak** my *inner-A.J.*, only 'cuz it's actually really tiring to try to make my speech intelligible. Since I've long *held myself to* **high** *standards* (and I've kinda got *Speech Pathology* **in my BLOOD**[1]), I usually ONLY speak—EXTENSIVELY— to MYSELF, my mom and to my *Speech Therapist*.

I've gotta *get* **over** *that*! (But, that's more a psychological issue, to be addressed in *Volume III*.)

I *communicate* with my employees via letterboard, 'cuz *my messages* usually involve my health and well-being. Thus, I **need** there to be **no** misunderstandings.

Finally, actual *talking* requires many seldom-used muscles. So, 'tis tiring. My letterboard looks like a keyboard, which has been printed and mounted on cardboard. In the margins there are a few commonly used words which save me time.

When I actually do audibly speak now, I make sure to apply some ingenious *techniques* learned in my *speech therapy*. Sooo, I try to speak sssllloooooowwwly, take big breaths,

---

[1] Literally, 'cuz my mom's a retired *SPEECH and LANGUAGE Pathologist*

enunciate and use quality posture.

Plus, ~every other night, I do three sets of 15 *neck crunches* in bed to clear my larynx and to increase my intelligibility. (It works!)

Linguistics **+** Kinetics **=** IMPROVED Semantics

(I understand better through mathematical equations, 'cuz that's just how I *SEEEE EVERYTHING.*)

10.
WHY NOT *WATER?!*

I OWN A BIG -OOL AS PART of my house. (There's no *P*/pee/urine.) I chose to have it salt water, 'cuz I understood that the additional *NaCl* would make me more buoyant.

Yet, I checked with my Gastrointestinal Doctor, before I participated in any aquatic adventures. Said medical expert "gave me the go" on the pool parties.

NOICE!

However, it turns out that either the Doc *guessed* incorrectly, or my body is just **that** odd. Lo and behold, after I ventured into *'mi piscina'*, I developed a gastric-infection near the opening for my 'G/peg-tube'.

: (

Sooo, apparently, I can**not** go in any water above (my) navel level (~3.67 feet). I can no longer get into my bathtub.

(SHUCKS!)

I've long been an avid, joyful swimmer. Plus, I actually **own** a pool. So, **not** "being allowed to swim" is particularly *painful*!

Years ago, when I was ~12, I completed the *'Mile Swim'* merit badge for Boy Scouts in summer camp outdoors in North Carolina.

('Twas only ~78 laps of an olympic-sized pool.)

How fantastic *was* aquatic therapy though?! 'Tis just one of the promises that that *good for* **nothing** rehab institute promised to my mom and me and yet never manifested.

(AUDIBLE sigh)

Ya see, the water provides moderate **resistance** to/for any and all movement. Sooo, it'll require extra effort to **overcome** the added *force*. (I understand *fluid mechanics*.) But, NNNOOOOO! I get even less help in my *rehab*! I mean that I get **zero** *physical help*, when I'm *walking*. My trainers just stand behind me, and give *verbal cues*, which my *psyche* kinda needs.

I can't even drink liquids by mouth. Ironically, **all** of my vitamin and nutrient fueled diet are liquids ingested via *G/peg-tube*. I can't drink water. Sooo, how do I **not** get dehydrated?!

Hhhmmm, that's an interesting question. Ya see, my body stays hydrated from the water in my formulated *food*. 'Tis just that I constantly have that *dry-mouth* feeling. My only semi-consolation is that I've always had alotta **saliva**.

That's one way I managed/cut my weight so well during my wrestling-days (1999 - 2007).

Now, I'm just sssllloooooowww to swallow my spit. Sooo, my mouth's more hydrated than it thinks. I cannot imbibe beer or any alcohol, 'cuz my brain and immune system have already been weakened.

(SHUCKS!)

I most certainly was **not** an *alcoholic*. I just like the very relaxed and social atmosphere that *a cold one* inevitably promotes.

11.
WALKING ANALYSIS

THIS ONE'S HUUUUUUUGE!

THAT's what SHE said.

Calm DOWN, amygdala!

(*Walking* sans assistance is a major goal for/of my rehab. So, this chapter will be seemingly *interminable*.)

First off, I make sure my walker is directly in front of me, well within grabbing distance. Next, I place my feet below me, ~shoulder-width apart. (It's physics. I've gotta establish a stable base on which to *build*.)

I lean back in my chair in order to gain enough *momentum* to overcome the combined force of my weight (~141.51 pounds = ~64.32 kilograms) multiplied by the acceleration due to gravity (~9.80665 m/s^2), which is to say, I must counter the forces which are keeping me seated. Then, I contract both my *quadriceps* muscles, bend my knees and quickly straighten 'em. All the while, I'm going *against* gravity by pushing my heels down against gravity. (Actually, I suppose that'd be **with** gravity.)

Once up, I check one more time to where I'm walkin'. Regardless of my Final Destination (good film), I try to keep my eyes up in a straight gaze. Sooo, I'm not staring down at my unstable feet as they awkwardly step.

When you *normees* walk, y'all maintain a forward, shoulder-height gaze for the most part, right? (AUDIBLE sigh) I just **almost** forgot the proper stance for a comfortable gait.

Per the advice of my Trainer at *rehab*, I really shift my bodyweight via my hips. This tactic has been *instrumental* in easing the temporarily growing pain I had in\my surgically-repaired left knee and left hip **and** right calf.

(*KUDOS* to the gym staff member who recommended the shift!)

For awhile, every time I'd *walk*, I'd internally sing Shania Twain's *'Man, I Feel Like a WOMAN.'* My finally applying the *weight shifts* had made my *walking* completely pain free! Granted, my gait is very *hippy*. But, I'll gladly *take* the completed task **over** the kinetic *beauty* of the trial anyday.

Often after I stand, I'll chuckle as I recall the humorous scene from *Friends*, in which Ross Geller, with two others, is trying to carry a large couch up a thin, winding and circular stairwell. Ross keeps yelling, "Pivot. PIIH-VUHT. PIH-VUUUHHHT!"

I try to begin my treks by stepping with my right foot. So, all my weight's *anchored on* my left leg.

Before each stride, I hafta shift/transfer most of my bodyweight onto the opposite leg from which I'm *striding*. (Sooo, if I'm stepping with my right foot, I lean waaay left.[1]) I am getting better at maintaining a non-*pigeon-toed*, non-*wide-legged* gait.

In early 2014, I'd developed a swinging, inward-tilted left footed stride. I wanna tell y'all that even my lower body thinks like my brain[2] biophysically. Sooo, 'twas creating a wider base, establishing a stronger foundation for stable standing. Lately, I've been *walking* a helluva **lot** at my gym with only a walking cane for support.

(YAY! YYYEEESSSSSSS!)

I love to *walk*!

(Not entirely 'cuz of the kinetic exercise I so desperately covet.)

But, after I *walk*, I get overwhelmed with this feeling of accomplishment!

Plus, I just really enjoy exhausting myself! My 'Theory of Everything' (spectacular movie[3] that kinda/really *hits home* for me):

"If you're gonna GO, go ALL OUT."

---

[1] As I noted in *Volume I*, I really AM "The Man with *TWO* Brains."

[2] *Ibid.*

[3] "Theory of Everything", a biopic about wheelchair-bound, semi-mute genius Ştephen Hawking

I live *ballz-to-the-wall*.

One major rule I have is that I **never** *walk slooowly* to my toilet, when I've *gotta go #2*. If any speed, I *walk* **briskly with** my walker. prior to making this seemingly-outrageous stipulation, I did some research.

It turns out that humans anatomically possess over 50 different **kinds** of *sphincters*. A *sphincter* is a ringed structure that relaxes and contracts to allow the passage of solids and liquids from one bodily section to another. The digestive system, complicated as it is (especially mine), contains several *sphincters*.

As I am a rather immature—at TIMES—**male**, I cannot seem to flatulate without an inevitable laugh, while I *walk*.

Thus, I usually don't smile as I *walk*, 'cuz I'm prolly a lil' *backed up*.

When I *walk*, one of the countless muscles I hafta consider would be my anus. Gross as it may seem, I **lack** complete control over the supposedly-voluntary muscle contraction.

Like Pringles, "Once (I) pop (my anal cavity open), (I) can't stop!"

I have far more control over the relaxing of my *anus* than of its contraction.

Sooo, as I *walk*, my anal *sphincter* subconsciously tightens. Thus, I never *walk* to my toilet to poop. I hitch a ride on my toilet chair.

I'll review just some of the numerous issues I must consider before and as I *walk*:

— TREK Distance

— OBSTACLES to AVOID?

— STOMACH *Settlement*

— TIME of last *MEAL?*

— TIGHTENING of anal *sphincter*

— FOOT Placement

— BIOPHYSICS

— WEIGHT shifts

— ARRIVAL stance

An ongoing issue when I *walk* is that I'm kinda *heavy-footed* with my right-footed stepping. My leg trainers used to always tell me to "be quieter", when I *walk*. Psychologically, I just didn't yet have the confidence to lean much bodyweight on my weaker left leg.

However, o'er the year of 2016, I developed enough confidence and strength in my left leg to make my *walking* **appear** more *even-keeled*.

I prefer taking smaller steps, 'cuz I feel more stable. Psychologically, I can step more affirmatively and confidently when I'm more balanced.

(It's *BASIC* biophysics!)

12.
MULTI-TASKING

MY OWN MOTHER ABHORS THE CONCEPT of *doing multiple things simultaneously*. She insists that you can never devote your full and complete attention to any one task, if you're trying to do several things at once.

Technically/mathematically/**physically**, she's correct. But, since I just happen to have known her for the past ~31.71 years, I know that her antipathy comes mainly from her inability to *quarantine her focus*.

Bein' in a wheelchair with an **extremely** busy life, I've **gotta** multi-task, if I wanna get anything done! I need time-savers! When I'm fillin' out my biweekly payroll, I rapidly mentally make sure the Caregivers' hours sum to 168. ('Cuz that's the # of hours in a week, and they hafta be with me 24/7)

Since I could and do advanced math *in my sleep*, I like to watch television, while I fill out my biweekly payroll.

Now, you're prolly all thinkin' that that's very irresponsible, considering I'm dealin' with others' money. To which I retort:

At that instance, technically, it's still **my** money. And, until I commit some egregious error, I'm gonna continue my unorthodox but self-calming ways. In other words: "KISS my ASS. I do what I want!"

When I design a *Martial Arts* technique, I kinda need the television on. I'll randomly glance at the screen to better visualize a moving body and how it reacts to certain stimuli.

Yes, I have a collegiate degree in *Bioengineering* with a thorough understanding of physics. But, **my** body, which I've been observing for 11,590 days (as of December 31, 2016), is a bit *odd*. So, I need to SEE a typical reaction to an external stimulus.

During my speech therapy, my teacher and I will frequently (at least once a week) play 'Scrabble', while I eat—via mouth—an egg or two or chicken, salmon and/or meatloaf and assorted condiments. distracting myself with *word play* really helps me to relax and to not think so much about swallowing.

Multiple tasks at once: that's how I like to organize my *Martial Arts* classes. O' course it certainly helps that I always have a 'sempai' to help. multiple *stations* increase efficiency, which will increase production, which will increase happiness, which will produce more 'Karateka' (students → *customers.*)

(Ya know, for *Martial Arts* teaching's being **JUST** my NON-paying *occupation*—for which I am an UNPAID *volunteer*, I am surprisingly **BUSINESS**-*savvy*.)

When I work out my *upper body*, I like to stretch and strengthen simultaneously. I like to keep my body guessing'! I've gotta make my body excel in new and uncomfortable settings, in order to improve.

With that thinking, I aim to—however **un**likely the task—strengthen my arms to at least a large extent of the power my legs **used to** have!

I've deliberately *morphed* my *speech therapy* into quite the *commitment*! Contrary to what the course name implies, my **speech** *therapy* is very *all encompassing*.

THANKS to my *teacher*'s SUGGESTIONS, I include various bodily-POSITIONING techniques to improve my INTELLIGIBILITY (PHYSICAL), *REWARD* myself for a great *Scrabble* play with a BITE of chicken (PSYCHOLOGICAL), utilize a SMORGASBORD of different lip movement techniques to *enhance* my ENUNCIATION (PHYSICAL) and feel INSPIRED to write ANOTHER book.*\[1]

---

[1] Look out for '*A.J.'s Applaudable Alliteration And Aria Alterations*' in the NEAR future.

13.
Rarely — But It Does Happen

Y PRACTICING every morning and every night, I stretch my left ankle—my injured side—by rotating it counter clockwise.

B As of November 15, 2016, I could—while lying in bed—rotate my left foot ~130 degrees, in which my upright left foot is perpendicular to the mattress. O' course, this technique is aided by the bed mattress's serving as my anchor/stabilizing weight. I use it as a counterweight, as I push down to turn my foot.

As of December 31, 2016, I can—while seated in my wheelchair—*only* rotate my left foot ~105 degrees counter clockwise. This location difference is important, 'cuz I now lack the "counter push." it's kinda more demonstrative of my ankle flexibility.

With repeated practice and determination, **my** *physical* strength can **overcome my** *neurological* lapses. The key variables are **e***ffort* and *time*.

THIS MULTI-variable Calculus function would IDEALLY equate as such:

As **t** approaches 65, STRENGTH increases at a rate of 1.5 times[1] **e** times **t**.

The *neurological* issues remain constant. My energy (**e**) in joules must be greater than time (**t**) in years after my accident.

Thus, as time increases, so too, must my effort.

(No rest for the weary!)

So, how does my energy (**e**) increase, as i age (**t** increases)?

---

[1] I like to think that I have the physical strength of 3/2 men. (Mentally, I'd decimate ~98.6% of any men.)

Well, 1) as I age, I grow more and more accustomed to the *biophysics* of my extensive injuries. 2) I utilize *trial and error* in my constant *biophysical applications*. 3) That tremendous feeling of accomplishment upon my completion of a task acts as a *motivational barb* to continue my efforts. 4) I'm an anomaly.

All I do—especially now—is *governed by* laws of biophysics.

Thankfully, I understand what my body should do. Sooo, I almost always try to start my *morning jaunts* with a right-footed step. By doing so, my left foot starts as my *anchor* as my *deadweight*.

Well-focused physical strength **can** *overcome* psychological flaws. sometimes, I'll surprise **myself** at the gym. *'Por Ejemplo'*, I was about to *walk* across my gym with my walker. My left leg had been stubbornly *ignoring* my *neural messages* all day.

I wanted to *challenge myself*. Ergo, at the last minute, I asked to switch to the gym's cane. I proceeded to *walk* to various exercise machines all over the gymnasium. I *feared* fatigue. But, my leg muscles and nerves proved otherwise.

Now, I cannot *see* the future. (speaking of which, doesn't *foretelling* have a much more positive connotation than *foreshadowing* or *foreboding*? I mean, just look at the *root words* — *tell* as opposed to *shadow* or *bode*.)

But, I am determined to make significant *physical improvements*, after I've left that rehab facility, and just teach **myself**. Thus far, through ~four years, I've been emphatically and wholeheartedly correct.

(I'm *sticking out my tongue*—like a CHILD—at no one in particular.)

I'd like to start an *underground CAPPIES' Fight Club.*

"The first rule of 'Fight Club' IS …. NO talking about 'Fight Club'."(—'Fight Club') Alas! With NO *word-of-mouth*, I could only **WRITE** *about* it.

My life motto is and would be, *"I don't start fights. I FINISH 'em."*

Ignoring popular *racial stereotypes*, *pre-accident* I **could** dance very well as a *Caucasian male*. Post-accident, I cannot dance at all. That's **not** because of my *weakened leg nerves* but since, as a genius, I have **two** *left brains*.

I use so much *logic*, it's as if I have **two** of that area of my brain. (Ya see, the left portion of the human brain controls *mathematical functions* and *logic*. Plus, it's a pun on my having *two left feet*, 'cuz—sadly—I've become uncoordinated.) So, i'm *offbalanced*. My *accident* **might've** reinforced my already incredible intelligence.

Now, I try to *compensate* for my longtime nystagmus that's mostly in my left eye by deliberately doing the opposite of what I used to always—subconsciously—do.

I used to *heavily* favor my right eye by—without realizing it—*tilting* my head slightly left to *lead with* my (better) right eye.

Now, when I'm *cozied up* in bed, I purposefully lean 'mi cabeza' way right to try to *balance out* my previous asymmetry. My vision has definitely **improved** since my accident. Strange!

14.
I Will Rebuild 'em: BIGGER, STRONGER, FASTER, BETTER

WELL, **I MIGHT NOT GET THE SPEED.** (Although, I was never notably fast in anything pre-accident. so, it wouldn't be that difficult to improve upon it.)

And, in terms of "bigger" for muscles, I've always preferred tone/definition over bulk. Sooo, I'd need more conditioning and endurance. Thus, I'll hafta do more repetitions at a tolerable weight.

The last time—pre-accident—I measured my height, I think I was ~5' 6.5". Now, as of early 2016, I'm ~5' 7.375". Thus, either I had a delayed growth spurt, **or** the metal implants from the accident, in my hip and knee, have somehow made me slightly taller. I'm guessing it's an unknown combination of both. Plus, some unforeseen bone implant fusion may have occurred.

It has been an annoyingly long and arduous process. but, my determination and tenacity have proven that an ultimate *victory*—for me—is very *possible*!

(DARE I say, *"LIKELY"*?)

I **am** becoming more courageous! *With my back up against the wall* in the face of *adversity*, I continue to push onward. I figure that I can't be much lower, literally **and** psychologically. Sooo, why not utilize the few *gifts* I **still** have?!

Since I'm an anomaly, and most of my virtues are *still* **mental**, I'll just continue to try to further develop my *gifts* into full-fledged bragworthy skills!

(E.g. writing, proper grammatical speaking, arm strength, *math magic*, conditioning, pain tolerance,[1] time management, organization.)

With three formal hour-long workouts per week, I'm trying to redevelop my extraordinary metabolism that allowed me to comfortably **stay** within a *five weight class range* (21 pounds → 119, 125, 130, 135, 140) for over eight years of competitive wrestling in my late teens and early twenties.

When I admire my flexed triceps in the mirror, I note the distinctive imagery:

My RIGHT arm is *CHISELED* like the *David* statue.

My LEFT arm looks like it USED to be HERCULEAN

I can't take all the credit for my improving health. A *water-soluble B-vitamin* does help. Ssshhh! *Biotin* acts as a dietary supplement that helps regulate my amino acids and *carbon dioxide* transfer. Additionally, the *biotin* promotes nail and hair growth. Sooo, i know what's to blame for my *growing* bills for manicures, pedicures and haircuts.

(AUDIBLE sigh)

---

[1] Since my accident, my deadened nerves **block** the *messages* between my brain and *pain receptor* cells.

15.
LESS SORROW, MORE ACTION

IT**IS NO USE** *drowning in sorrow*, when I can and should create new tales. Sooo, I've gotta get outta my *comfort zone/wheelchair/house* more to initiate the so-cial/*party* atmosphere. I wouldn't say that I get **bored**, 'cuz I was never allowed to say that in my childhood. My mom would harangue my siblings and me, if we ever uttered that term in her presence!

My mother always said to my siblings and me: "if you're *bored*, then your brain's **not** workin'."

True, that's extreme hyperbole. But, to three young children, 'tis one scary warning! I'd say that my mom's early exaggeration indirectly initiated my creativity. I would always create fun kinetic alternatives to stay busy. Now, there's only so much I can physically do on my **own**.

'Listen' and 'silent' are spelled with the same letters in a different order. (Duh!)

That makes me think of *dramatic art*: "Be *SILENT*. Be *STILL*."

(I knew there was more to the film *She's All That* than *just* a catchy title.)

That's my ongoing goal for my *walking*, to walk more quietly, because I tend to slam my right heel down against the ground. And, I deliberately ignore the second part of my *walking* regimen: I've gotta *swing my hips* like a woman to better weight shift.

I **briefly** tried *feeling sorry for myself*. I've concluded that it's exhausting just **trying** to *drown all my success in tears of sadness and pity*. if I could, I'd kick myself.

I understand that my left hip is very brittle and sore. but, with alotta *R and R* (*rest and* relaxation) in mid to late 2016, it's definitely improving and almost pain**less**! Sooo, now I'm *pushing myself* even hard**er** in my workouts, 'cuz I **know** I can take it! There's no real time boundary for my *allotted* recovery.

Now, this saying is especially poignant: "Rome wasn't built in a day."

Along that same *line of logical/realist* thinking: "Good work takes time."

Accepting this inevitability—eventually—*will be* **good** for my physical reform: I can and will use my *profusion* of alone time to exercise more, write, and design new *Martial Arts* techniques.

Everything in **my** life traces back to its *roots* in romance. I mean, I know I'm good and smart and talented. I just miss having someone—besides myself—to impress. Ya see, I never used to care at all what others thought of me.

(This is A.J. if you like what you see, "Hey, wassup?!" If you don't, "To hell with you. You're missin' out!") Now, I'm *far too concerned with* **others'** *opinions* of **my** *work*!

I'm **not** proud o' that. I used to *give it my all*, then not care. If anyone disrespected my *best*, then I'd just *shrug it off*. Next time will be better. I **was** more concerned about me. Now, I've gotta impress my trainers, my *neuropsychologist*, my caregivers, my mom, etc. it's getting overwhelming.

16.
THINK OF DRAGONFLIES

THE INSECTS' ABILITY TO ADAPT and survive for over *300 million years* serves as a fantastic *pick-me-up*, when I'm struggling. If **that** little bug could overcome all those times of hardship for so long, then certainly I can *reconnect* with my own strength, courage and happiness!

When my muscles do not *process* my *neural messages* timely enough, I merely close my eyes, audibly sigh, devise an alternate tactic and *carry it out*.

In order to **bask** *in my potential glow of* **accomplishment**, I've gotta reorganize my physical *visions*. I used to only rarely go out for social activities, 'cuz I **had** a live-in girlfriend who provided tons of entertainment: intellectually, comically, and physically.

As unlikely as it may seem, I am determined to at least make my abdominal muscles visible again.

(Just as I typed that, I felt compelled to complete three sets of at least 50 sit-ups each.) Plus, I remembered to email my *sempai* about my/our technique video.

If only I could fly like a dragonfly. That would nullify my unreliable leg nerves. It took me *forever and a day* to accept the fact that my leg issues are nerve-related and definitely **not** *muscular*. Once I've (finally) positioned my feet comfortably, I don't tire for awhile, 'cuz I've always had commendable **muscle** *endurance*.

Now, it's become *painfully* clear that there's a distinct, irrefutable difference between muscle pain and nerve fatigue. Plus, there's the *emotional pain* that **hurts** my **heart**. I've **seen** my potential. And, it **hurts** that I can no longer accomplish many of my previous *physical* **wowees** like wrestling takedowns, Karate *jump kicks* or wrestling rolls.

To further clarify, *discomfort* is ~three levels below even the slightest *pain* on the *degree of intensity* scale. Thanks to my 24+ years of *Martial Arts* training, I know how to take alotta physical abuse.

(It STARTS in the MIND.)

But, since *the (dreaded)* **day**, I've grown extremely sensitive to tangible items, like *water temperature* or *food texture.* Now, thanks to my severed nerves, I'm not some *badass,* just **desperate** to impress folks.

Or, AM I?!

17.
JUST PARENTAL SCARE TACTICS?

RENTS LIKE MINE SAY THAT boredom = neurologic inactivity. As a naive, sophomoric pre-teen, I nearly *soiled my pants*, if I even pondered *doldrums*. Therefore, I always like to *be moving*.

Granted, I am by no means some spastic liability of uncontrolled movements! *There's a method to my madness.*

(SINISTER laugh and SNORT)

Hhhmmm, what else do they *say*?

— If you keep the television volume loud, you will eventually go deaf.

I'll be watching television from bed at night, when my bladder *tells* my brain and legs that I've gotta urinate.

So, I'll *walk* to my bathroom[1] with the television still on and loud, and I feel kinda disappointed in myself that I can still hear all of the show from *'mi potty'* ~80 feet and a closed door away! Do I really keep the volume that **loud**?! I **thought** my *hearing* was better than that.

Only slightly loud noises actually hurt my brain—like a headache and not my ears. Yet, my mom and employees frequently describe my hearing as "supersonic."

I *hold such* **high** *standards* for myself. I try to **not** use my *T.B.I.* as an excuse. But,

---

[1] What's the difference between a *bathroom* and a *restroom*?! Well, I own a *bathtub!* Does that factor into the *classification*? What male legitimately goes into a *restroom* just to better *gather his thoughts*?!

sometimes I have no logical choice.

— If you sit too close to the television, you'll eventually go blind.

I have four large, wide screen television sets. But, I enjoy my viewing stance never closer than ~21 feet away. I would not like to constantly tilt 'mi cabeza' from side to side.

Ironically, my ophthalmologist said my vision has actually improved since my accident. Somehow, my cranium's *bouncing on* the highway **settled** my *nystagmus/wandering eyes*, so I can better focus.

— If you repeatedly make a strange look, your face will get stuck like that.

Unfortunately, my *T.B.I.* has left me (EXTERNALLY) rather apathetic. But, I still feel extreme *joy, laughter and sadness*. It's just temporarily impossible to display a heartfelt legitimate smile, a *Laugh Out Loud* and/or tears.

— If you don't **ALWAYS** *pay close attention*, you could confuse your oral thermometer with a rectal one.

(OK, that was ONE time, and I'd rather **NOT** discuss it!)

— If you suffer now, *karma* will **reward** you in the long-run.

(I'm eyeing my watch and tapping my foot.)

It's been 3,054 days (as of November 15, 2016) since I first started physically and neurotically **suffering**. Sooo, supposedly **all** knowing/omniscient 'rents, when's the "long run" **end**?!

18.
DEVELOP NEW LIKES OR CHERISH THE OLD

TANGENT: **I OFTEN** *switch languages* between English and Spanish and Turkish and Japanese and latin-based medical *roots*, because I'm trying to **re**establish that conglomeration of cunning *colloquial cutlery* I once **had**.

I was never exceptionally fluent in multiple languages. But, I **used to** *hold my own* in my *foreign flappings*. Thus, I now find it quite psychologically *rewarding*, when I actually remember the foreign (semi) translations!

I used to like only the sports and games in which I could play, which was practically everything. personally, I see no problems with holding onto the past but still being open to changes and developments for the future. I still very much like wrestling, football, basketball and soccer.

I've even developed an embarrassingly new (ssshhh!) tolerating of (gulp) hockey. (Ya see, I could never ice-skate, nor roller-skate, nor ski. plus, I live in sunny south Florida so, I almost had to not like the sport.)

I hafta still gladly love *Martial Arts*. (I kinda hafta, since it's my occupation! I feel like "job" has a **negative** *connotation*, as if it has to be done for payment.) I "hafta love it, 'cuz I **said so**. The obligation is completely **self**-imposed!

I've always liked Jujitsu a lot. But, since I can't stand at the moment, I've developed a bit of an **obsession** with my current only form of self-defense, which would be *Jujitsu*, 'cuz it's *ground* *fighting*.

Along the same lines, I've increased the joys I get from teaching kids. Ya see, during my ~10+ years of *Martial Arts* teaching, I always taught children.

As much as I do enjoy my time with *younglings*, I've recently *taken a liking* to explaining the *do*s and *don't*s of self-defense to adults. They seem to be more appreciative, 'cuz they just have a more extensive understanding.

I am currently so *out of place* in *hand-to-hand combat* that I doubt a fist would even recognize me as a target! Nonetheless, I **design** self-defense techniques.

Business-wise, I've kinda *stumbled into* becoming an entrepreneur. I **entered graduate school with an *entrepreneurship* concentration.** currently, post-*accident*, I own and manage my own *healthcare* organization.

Thankfully, I've hired a very competent and helpful nurse, who *doubles* as my *SEC-OND-IN-COMMAND.*

(Ever the curious *scientist*, I tried—only for humor—to *bite the hand that feeds [me]*. My nurse giggled.)

Romantically, I still loved my ex-*fiancée*. Throughout my looong *editing* process, she contacted me exactly two times. I was still trying to rekindle our *trampled fires of love and lust*. But, : (she won't even *talk* to me! (AUDIBLE sigh) Sooo, I've reluctantly *moved on*, by awkwardly *hitting on* my trainers and my party guests.

Hobby-wise, I still create Jujitsu techniques. All the time! Aaahhh, the thrill, and feeling of accomplishment I get from designing—from scratch—a legitimate attack and its ensuing/necessary defense is unparalleled!

While typing this, I sadly realized that I'm not nearly as physically involved with activities as I once was. I'd very much like to get more involved with/in sports. But, alas! There's only so much I can do. Sooo, I'll devote nearly all of my waking moments to Jujitsu!

And, re*walking*.

Obviously, most of the intricacies that compose my physical *functioning* hafta be altered! **Unfortunately**, I can no longer (ever?) run. Thus, I can't jump. I cannot safely swim. Sooo, I've gotta alter my forms of *kinetic functioning*.

Instead of exercising and working out only in my spare time at home, I've now joined a (formal) gym to keep building and testing my leg strength two days a week.

Even though my weak legs are my main focus now, I see an *upper body* trainer another day. Sooo, that's three workout days (Monday, Tuesday, Friday) in addition to my two days of *Martial Arts* viewing/teaching (Thursday, Saturday). Ergo, ~28.57% of my days lack a formal/scheduled workout. So, you'd think I'd just reeelax.

Hellz naw! Yes, i **do** have a large amount of free time, thanks to **my** own efficient planning. But, I make sure to frequently *act out* homework.

All I do requires more work and extra energy for/from me than it would from the pro-totypical ambulatory *biped*. Yes, I am constantly either in a chair or bed. But, that's just where I'm most comfortable.

I've noticed that, since my accident somehow improved both my vision and hearing, my focus has inversely changed.

(*As my vision and hearing improved*, my ability to concentrate *decreased*.)

Ya see, pre-accident, i was a little strange.

(And, the AWARD for "**UNDER**-statement of the 21st CENTURY" goes to [DRUMROLL] Altan Kaynatma! For HIS SELF-description of his focus!)

You didn't let me FINISH! I was going to say:

"I was a little strange. (AUDIBLE sigh) Now, I'm really frickin' weird!"

My own mother even calls me **"RIDICULOUS,"** after I *dissect* what she—a speech/language pathologist—says for its *numerical significance*.

For instance, she noted how proud she is that her offspring have been so successful.

So, I *broke down* an IMPORTANT date:

On, March 15, 2003 (3/15/03), just five days after the birth of her *THIRD* child, I earned my *FIRST*-degree black belt ('shodan' OR 'kuro obi') JUST ~*FIVE* minutes from my HOME.

I was surprised to learn of my *two* earned/awarded black belts, which further separated me as having *zero* immediate dual rank peers[1] and *zero* promotion accomplices. I'd hafta graciously thank my *three* main instructors.

---

[1] Except for my teachers

19.
I Miss *TOUCHING*

IN THE **SINGING** words of Olivia Newton-John:
"Let's get PHYSICAL. FIH-ZIH-KUHL!"
I was and am very sports-oriented. I still watch alotta football and soccer. I definitely can**not** play either sport anymore (ever?). But, I watch 'em, so I don't forget the rules.

It's weird, that I cannot remember most facts. But, sports-related info seems to be sooo *embedded in* my off *da wall* mind that I just remember the rules and moves and stats and trivia. I do enjoy greatly representing one of the few instances in which *muscle memory* usurps *neural processing*.

Such has been the same, frustrating, reoccurring case for the last ~8.34 years: my brain thinks one thing. But, my muscles do another. this *internal* **quarreling** *is especially* **frustrating**, when my trainer(s) think that I'm ignoring instructions. The fact that I can't exactly speak to defend myself only *adds* **fuel** *to the* **fire**.

I *come from* a very athletic, contact filled background of Karate, wrestling, Jujitsu, and automobile *accidents*.

(Hahaha! i had to throw in that last bit of self-ridicule, 'cuz it's funny to **me**.)

In addition to my hardcore *organized contact*, I'd practically habitually devise different games to *up* the contact and physicality of my fun/game/*hangout* time. **Less** so now in lieu of my injuries, but I've always been very *pro*-contact.

I've always thought that *two-hand touch football* is very wussy and pointless.

(I mean, if you're gonna *go*, go *all* **out**! who's afraid of some contact?! *grow a pair!*)

With my workouts, I've always preferred my trainers' applying resistance to just lifting dumbbells. 'Tis a matter of a set/in controvertible weight or another person's varying degrees of resistance. If it's too easy, I'll signal to my *upper body* trainer to push harder.

At *my rehab gym* it's a bit of a different story with standardized resistance weights on machines. This is just 'cuz it's an organized business service for/with multiple customers.

So, there I start at a low weight for my legs, then work my way **up** to exhaustion. (This incremental advancing strategically builds my endurance and stamina while **simultaneously** testing my strength. this strategy necessitates added repetitions, as the weight slowly yet surely increases.)

More reps as opposed to more weight develops *muscle* **tone** as opposed to *muscle* **bulk**.

(I'm bowing for designing my own *exercise routine*.)

Romantically/intimately, I very much wanna **surprise** her with random kisses, *snugglefests* and massages. It appears as though I'm *just* **sittin'** *on the job*. But, I've had extensive **surgery** on my left knee! So, it pains me physically to put significant weight/pressure on it!

I.e. supporting my body-weight (~65 kilograms) in my barely-supportive bed.

But, I **try** for that *'A' for effort!*

20.
DON'T *UNDER*-ESTIMATE ME

ESTIMATE me!

(After you've compiled an extensive history of physical/kinetic observations)

If y'all have any statistics of *T.B.I.* victims with anything remotely close to **my** conditions (you can't, 'cuz there are **none!**), then beware of *outliers.*[1]

Most *T.B.I.* victims unfortunately don't display any progress if at all after two years. Most die within a decade.

Well, it's been ~83% of that ten-year allotment, and I'm improving *better* than **ever!**

So, statisticians, you'd better go re-calibrate the *curve*. I'm sorry I'm **not** sorry! I actually like to be the **odd** *man out!* Rather than just unquestioningly *following the crowd,* I prefer to take "the (road) less traveled."

"And, THAT has made ALL the DIFFERENCE."

(—'THE ROAD NOT TAKEN', ROBERT FROST)

Please! Pardon my appearance in a wheelchair, with a speech-generating device. But, I really am quite exceptional *with numbers*. I incorporate 'em into all my actions and *kinetic*

---

[1] An observation that is well outside of the expected range of values in a study or experiment, and which is often discarded from the data set; a person whose abilities, achievements, etc., lie outside the range of statistical probability.

decisions throughout my every day: from the biophysics of my *walking* to the trigonometry of my foot placement to the caloric intake of my *feedings* to the kinetic output of my workouts.

"Don't underestimate me. I know more than I say, I think
more than I speak and I notice more than you realize."
(—MICHAEL FLORES)

I'm unorthodox. I do not *fit the norm*. I'm an *oddball*.

Whenever I'm designing techniques for my *Martial Arts* classes, I make sure to factor in the words of the great Robert Oppenheimer:

"Geniuses *see* the answer **before** the question." I interpreted that as my *knowing* the biophysical response to *kinetic stimuli*.

I've never had *incredible* **physical** strength. I've always prided myself on my awe inspiring **mental** power. Granted, I was never some fickle nerd sitting' on the sideline with his head buried in a book.

i was/**am** an exemplary combination of both *realms*.

So, I *shot in* on a *double leg, took down* (the school) and *finished it* with a *Turk*.[2]

During the course of *my time*, people have (formally) sought **my** input on a variety of topics, from school success (peer counseling) to *brotherhood* (fraternity) to math success (tutoring) to grappling applications (*Martial Arts* Instructor).

I teach what I know.
– ALTAN J. KAYNATMA — TEXTBOOK *SCHOLAR*
ATHLETE

I'm still the only **wrestler** in the looong, storied (81-year) history of *my high school* to

---

[2] Upon my learning that there actually **is** a pinning combination in wrestling called *"the Turk,"* I had to know it. Being naturally *Turkish*, I incorporated the technique into my wrestling *repertoire* constantly.

also be the **valedictorian**.

(*ReEP-ree-ZENTin'* c/o '03, YEAH!)

Y'all: "Yeah, so, A.J.? You're SMART. Whoopee. This volume's supposed to discuss your *physical* **hurdles**."

ME: "Well, EXCUUUSE ME, Ms. Antsy-Pantsy! My MENTAL *STRENGTH creates MORE doable/feasible PHYSICAL* tactics."

P.S. In *the game of* **LIFE**, Altan (A.J.) Kaynatma **IS** an *OUTLIER*.

P.P.S. After *evaluating ALL circumstances*, I'd DEFINITELY say: 'Tis *FAR* **BETTER** to be UNDERestimated and pleasantly surprise observers with GOOD results, than 'tis to be OVERestimated and sadly disappoint 'em with BAD ones.

21.
I Don't Just Create
Conundrums With My Mind

YES, I TURNED THE MEDICAL world all topsy-turvy, when i survived my
death-defying accident.

Yes, I gratefully surprise 'Karateka' with my safe but debilitating *Martial Arts*
techniques.

Yes, I enjoy *balancing my mom's checkbook*—in my head.

But, what of my non-*neurological realm*?!

Why do I speed up my bike rides with my trainer to leave my mom way behind and
complaining? I don't especially care for her dog, and i think my mom's *yelps* are amusing.
And, somehow my surgically-repaired left knee hurts less, when it's pedaling at a quicker
speed.

Why do I always shut my eyes, when I eat by mouth? Closed eyes helps me better
focus and *nullifies* my annoying nystagmus. Additionally, *shut eyes* makes my astigmatism
more tolerable.

Master Yoda voice: "Both I have."

Chewing and swallowing are a lot more **complex** for me—a *Traumatic Brain Injury*
survivor. I'm trying to reestablish some *muscle memory*.

Why do I **insist** on *walking* to my toilet to urinate, even if it's ~3:30 am? Thankfully,
my bladder control is still *top-notch* despite an obvious *drop* in leg strength. I shan't just

sit on my *toilet chair* anymore. Plus, I've gotta continue *working* my muscles. *If* I don't **use** it, I **lose** it.

(Hence, the concept of *muscle **atrophy***)

Why did my previous G.I. *doctor* insist on my *excreting (**solid**) bodily **waste*** at least every three days yet also prescribe *stool softener* medication? I think he seriously under-estimated just how *calamitous* my *innards* **are.**

Why and how do I *combat* said *stool softening meds*? Despite *consuming* only liquid *nutrition*, I frequently *walk* to my manual wheelchair in the morning(s) to *get fed*, while I sit.

After majoring in *bioengineering* in college, I understand *full-well* the biophysics of human anatomy (all 206 bones and ~640 muscles). (AUDIBLE sigh) my nurse supports my opinion that my body's a *riddle crossed with a mystery*, stuffed with an *enigma*, all coated with a *conundrum*.

Ya see, **my** (messed up) digestive system does not *process* anything. Fiber or straw-berries (extra lactulose) or bananas (constipating agents) or protein (muscle developers) don't have any effects on my body.

22.
STILL A MAJOR PART

NOW THAT **I** CAN'T TEMPORARILY PLAY SPORTS (wrestling, *Martial Arts*, football, basketball, cycling, swimming, soccer), I'm just realizing how obsessed with athletics I really was/am!

In lieu of my extensive injuries, I now view—not play—all kinds of sports. But, it sucks, when I see a move and think, "oh, man! I could've/would've done that differently!"

However, I can/do use this hypothetical athletic prowess as motivation to continue my **100% effort**! Despite all the odds, stats and doctors **against** me, I am still progressing albeit **ssslowly** but **surely**. Now, I can only yearn for a **return** to my *athletic peak*.

(SHUCKS!)

Even now, as I *write*, I'm switching my attention between my favorite NCAA wrestling team (University of Minnesota) on my laptop and my favorite NCAA basketball team (University of Wisconsin) on television.

(I still check how my *alma mater*'s doin' in both sports. but, I *accepted* long ago, that I chose academic excellence over athletic prowess in my choosing of *University of Pennsylvania*.)

Every morning, the first thing I do after my morning routine of x number of crunches (my # of necessary sit-ups varies, as my health improves.) is check *ESPN* to monitor all the goings-on from the late games on the west coast.

Each morning and every night, when I have a free ~15 minutes while watching television, I'll do various amounts of reps/sets of crunches. As I'm a very *visual learner*, the moving and talking figures onscreen act as a pleasant distraction from the growing muscle fatigue and *burn* in my abdomen. But, by no means is it pain!

I've experienced enough voluntary exercise *discomfort* (~24.36 years *Martial Arts*, 8 years wrestling, 3 years organized soccer, ~4 years *leg* training, ~5 years *upper body* training, etc.) to know the difference and my *limits*.

23.
MUSCLE MEMORY

EVEN THOUGH I CAN'T YET *perform*/demonstrate ANY of my *Martial Arts'* FORMS (*kata*S), I actually SOMEWHAT **RECALL** SOME of the moves, IF I SLOWLY, PHYSICALLY IMITATE the *Karate's* HAND and UPPER body movements, AS I watch.

The SAME *VISUAL cues* occur/HELP, when I watch WRESTLING,

EITHER/BOTH online and LIVE at my *'Sempai'*'s former *high school* AND at **MY** former *high school*, as the coach AWARDED me with a *Raider* WRESTLING **Staff** shirt.

(MORESO lately, at MY former *high school*/Florida WRESTLING POWERHOUSE, as I've become more *MANEUVERABLE* with my HURT limbs and *grown* more ACCEPTING of my various *HANDICAPS*.)

To a MUCH lessER extent, I get this *cueing muscle memory*, when I watch SOCCER on television. Granted, 'tIS SLIGHTLY different, 'cuz

1) I WAS a BETTER wrestler than *'futbol'er*.

2) It's been MUCH longER, since I played SOCCER (competitively) (~19 years ago) than since I last WRESTLED (~nine years ago).

3) I only watch the U.S. WOMEN's National Soccer Team, 'cuz they're BETTER than the MEN.

At a *Martial Arts* class one Thursday evening in early November of '16, I was VIEWING one of my *Sempai's* TEACHINGS. Toward the BEGINNING of class, while the *Karateka* were STRETCHING, I EXCITEDLY saw my assistant POINT to one student, then hor-izontal *peace sign* to HIS eyes, then point 'em AT the KID, as if to say, "I'm lookin' at you, kid." I KNOW I USED to do THAT *gesturing* as a SEMI-joke with the KIDS. After class, he CONFIRMED I inspired HIS JOKING with the KIDS.

WHEN I play 'BEIRUT'/BEER PONG once in a LONG while with FRIENDS at HOME, my RIGHT fingers, wrist and shoulder just SEEM to *KNOW the drill* of MY award-winning shooting ETIQUETTE/FORM.

(I WON MANY a 'Beirut'-tournament back in my FRATERNITY-days some ~10 to 12 years ago.)

I've GOTTA have a SET ROUTINE for EVERY *REPETITIVE* task. EVENTUALLY, I can and DO ADAPT.

But, my *T.B.I.* has made ALL my activities take longER than they did PREVIOUSLY (ALL communications, urinating, *technique* CREATING, showering, etc.). So, I COM-PENSATE by planning AHEAD for ADDITIONAL time.

24.
SOMETIMES
VISUAL CUES ARE ENOUGH

I **GO IN TO MARTIAL ARTS CLASS TO WATCH** AND comment two or
three times a week.

(Yes, I AM considering my OCCASIONAL *CO-TEACHING* as "WATCHING,"
'cuz it's INCLUSIVE. ASIDE from *issuing INSTRUCTIONS*, I HAFTA VIEW the
STUDENTS' *katas*, techniques and sparring.)

Even PRE-injurIES, I was/AM a VISUAL learner. Even something so SIMPLE to ME,
such as CALCULUS, I'd HAFTA **SEE** the STEPS, BEFORE I can *ACT 'em out*. It's NOT
that I'm cognitively *SLOOOW* by ANY means.

(Such a RIDICULOUS assumption couldN'T be **MORE** *WRONG!*)

Y'all: (EXASPERATED) "'**MORE** *WRONG*'?! Are there *degrees* of "WRONG".
Judges? No. 'Tis NOT expressed in various DEGREES.

ME: "'Too-SHAY!'"

POST-injuries, I frequent a rehabilitation GYM, where I'm generally a very COR-
DIAL and PLEASANT person. During my INTENSE exercising, I noticed one especially
INSPIRING young **person with disabilities** (*handicapped person*). (I'm gonna refer to her
as *Special K.*)

I do NOT KNOW her **back** story for her injury, and I'm NOT gonna **PRESUME** to
KNOW it. But, she *APPEARS FAR **WORSE** than* I am. Yet, *I push myself a LIL' HARDER*

EVERY time I witness her exercising in anything CLOSE to the *STANDING position*. She *pushes THROUGH* any *OBSTACLES to get 'da job DONE*. (AUDIBLE sigh and BIG smile) 'Tis truly GREAT to see!

Yes, I DO have incredibly ACUTE hearing. But, **COMPREHENDING** instructions and **APPLYING** 'em are **FAR from** the *SAME*!

'Por Ejemplo', I KNOW HOW to play HOCKEY. But, THAT certainly does NOT mean I CAN skate!

HOWEVER, NOW more than EVER, I HAFTA operate on a *TRIAL and ERROR* basis. MY INJURED—but STILL STELLAR—brain NEEDS to LEARN by EXPERI-ENCE. I may LOOK at something and THINK, "Yeah, I can DO that. No problem." But, MY FAULTY/SUB-par/UNreliable muscular NERVES TEND to have **CON-TRADICTORY** *opinionS*.

So, I calculate the BIOPHYSICS, devise a LOGICAL—and FEASIBLE—procedure, determine the PROBABILITY of SUCCESS, estimate the *BIO trigonometry* and *SET in MOTION* my findings.

I've ALWAYS *found* COMEDIC television AND/OR film to be MUCH more RE-LAXING and ENTERTAINING than MUSIC. Yet, post-injury, I have developed a pen-chant for writing SONG parodies.

WHY? 'Cuz I like to humorously relay **MY** tales, so others can SOMEHOW relate to 'em.

SONGS are MUCH shortER than SCRIPTS. So, THAT way I can ENJOY the AMAZING feeling of *ACCOMPLISHMENT* **MULTIPLE** times! Also, I am MUCH too SCATTERBRAINED and RANDOM to write a FULL, ENTIRE, LOOONG script.

Recently, I was playing the CARD game *cribbage* against my mom. (There's ALOTTA **mental** MATH. So, I FREQUENTLY win.) As I extended my LEAD, I *noted* a quantific *ODDITY* or *play on* **WORDS**:

TEN cards NOT 52 = 1 *DECA*cards as opposed to 1 DECK O' cards

RECENTLY, I started wearing SUNGLASSES, ONLY when I BIKE around m' 'hood. MAINLY, it's 'cuz my *ACCIDENT* made my EYES extremely SENSITIVE to the BRIGHT sunlight.

But, also SSSHHH! They COVER the TEARS, when I frequently CRY.

Legitimately, **THAT** was an ATTEMPTED JOKE. Medically, I caN'T *produce* **TEARS**.

25.
I'm Rather *STREAKY*

MY **T.B.I.** **FURTHER ESTABLISHED** my psychological *need for* routine and task repetition. As a *mathematical nut*, I've long sought **order** and **precision**. By meticulously following a steadfast convention of twice-a-day teeth-brushing, I have not had a dental cavity in 11,590 days—as of december 31, 2016. (Translation: my *life*)

By nerdily following a dweeb-like ever-studious standard, I *survived* ~1,379 days of high school with *nothing **less** than* all **a**s for 24 classes and 96 report cards and a 4.9451 cumulative *grade point average.*

(Hahaha! legitimately, my "study" habits were less than *exemplary.* as for school, I'd just read or hear it once, and I'd *store it in my memory file forever.* then, I'd just need to see the situation to apply it for future use.)

Over ~1,461 days of *high school* wrestling, i never once *missed a weight* during weigh-ins. Pre-Penn, I wrestled at 119 pounds, 119, 125 then 135. I shan't discuss my college wrestling weights, 'cuz I'm not sure how much **alcohol** imbibing may have *influenced* my *extracurricular activities.*

26.
IF YOU DON'T USE IT, YOU LOSE IT

WITH THE OVERWHELMING SEVERITY of my *Traumatic Brain Injury*, I feared *losing* my **many** gifts. As a direct result, I *joined* a rehab gym to regain (some of) my leg strength.

I started a *math tutoring service* to avoid **needing to** count on my fingers and toes. I still attend *Martial Arts* class twice a week to *use the kids'* movements as *memory liaisons* between my eyes and muscles.

I still teach Jujitsu to ensure I don't *lose* that knowledge of *ground combat* I've long had.

I was relieved, when I remembered how to *be intimate* with my now ex-girlfriend. (I'd even joke!) Since I have **not** *used my external genitalia* for *sextracurricular activities* in ~5.66 years, I am kinda **worried** that society may have initiated alotta **changes** to *intimacy*. Now, am I *inadequate*?!

With the (temporary) *loss of* my legs, I've kinda **had to** become very reliant upon my now stronger *upper body*.

I frequently watch *folk style* and/or *freestyle* wrestling on television[1] and/or *YouTube* just to remind myself of how kinetically and physically ***badass*** I once was.

---

[1] Rather than just sayin' "TV" and *takin' the easy way out*, I'll always say **"television"** to practice my speech.

27.
MAKING NEW *MEMORIES* FOR MY MUSCLES

SINCE I'VE KINDA lost the majority of my (long-term) neural/mental memory, I've gotta create **new** thoughts and ideals.

I've had countless setbacks/low points/troughs since/**because** of my accident. But, as an ardent **optimist**, I've tried to put a positive spin on any and all bummers. For instance, while working out and walking a lot at my gym during halloween season of '16, my right knee gave out. Tragically, I fell. But, I had the quick thinking and muscle memory to trunk rotate and *break fall*. Since then, I've miraculously been speaking much clearer. Why?! How?!

Well, my theory is that since my *inner drive* and self-confidence are so, so, sooo high, that I continue my efforts to *fruition* or *recognition* or *accomplishment*. As my editor noted, "success *breeds* success."

(As a legitimate *biomedical engineer*, I'd say I suffer from a bit of *low-grade*, long-term semi-amnesia. Or, it's just a typical consequence of a *Traumatic* **Brain Injury**.

I'm *LEANING toward* Option **B**.)

As a long-time athlete, I know the **necessity** of practice, repetition and instinct **and** insightful analysis. I did **not** become an excellent two-time black belt (well, formally, two. but, I was training for my third. I'm very close. I used to teach, 'cuz i'm that good.) by just attending class once in a while and not *systemizing Martial Arts* as a habit. I avoided NBA-great Allen Iverson's grandiose *stance* of

"JUST *PRACTICE!*"

The trick is to instinctively combine analytical insight with keen instincts repeatedly in **practice**! I'm not sure if, it's a fear of physical harm to my legs or *tube area* or, if it's an *attitudinal malaise* toward finding competition that's *holding me back* from actually employing *my ground knowledge.*

In any case, I am overly CAUTIOUS before all I do.

HHHMMM, so what ARE my CONSISTENT/DAILY activities?!

— Athletic STAT checking

— BOOK writing

— Showering

— Brushing my teeth (TWICE)

— ALOTTA crunches

— Lip and Tongue movement

— ALOTTA INDOOR *WALKING*

— (*Martial Arts*) Technique Checking

I can't remember. : (

But, I imagine that 'twas like a John Woo film with my *releasing twelve doves from penile captivity.*

28.
I CAN'T ARGUE WITH SCIENCE

SO, I RECENTLY (POST-ACCIDENT) took a non-technical neural test to determine which neural hemisphere is more *dominant*:

Apparently, I'm ~75% *left brain* dominant.

But, **HOW?!**

I landed—on the highway—on my left side, but the impact was not so destructive that it got through my gorgeous *locks* of blond hair.

I'm **still** analytic, rational, organized and mathematically and digitally oriented, very *symbolic*, objective and order seeking.

I'm **still** less emotional, less *musically inclined*, less *artsy fartsy* (that's a **clinical** term. I checked.) and a lot less memory reliant.

"**How?!**" Y'all earnestly inquire, knowing that said characteristics are *organized* in the left *neural hemisphere*. Well, seeing as the brain is an internal organ, 'twas thankfully **not** exposed to the violent trauma of my left shoulder, left hip and left knee which were all brutally mangled and surgically repaired.[1]

(You would **NOT** want me *EXPOSIN'* myself! 'Twas NOT the time for *NAKED driving*.)

Sooo, externally, my left side is near *worthless*. But, neurologically, I'm **potentially** better than I was.

(How the hell could I get *better* at math?!

---

[1] Somewhat

Well, in terms of memory and actual writing, I'm *lower than shit*. But, my *mental quantifying* is *through the roof*.)

I had to *compensate* for my non-writing (pre-accident, I never wrote anything. I was all memory and numbers.) By increasing my *mental workload*. In addition to my additional *processing*, I bought a 3-foot whiteboard and markers, so my caregivers could write my daily schedule.

29.
THE GLASS IS HALF-FULL

JUST 'CUZ **I** HAVE **A** series of (physical) *disabilities* does not mean that I cannot *redevelop* a portion of my once impressive physical prowess.

Often, I just need the proper motivation. As *strong as* my legs and arms **were**, now I've just further *strengthened* my already enigmatic psyche.

'Por Ejemplo', when I'm sitting in my motorized wheelchair, and I have a *horribly uncomfortable* wedgie, I unbuckle my seatbelt, push-down my footrests and use my **legs** to thrust my pelvis up/off the chair to slide my right hand underneath *m' bum* and yank my briefs out o' my ass.

My *accident* did severely minimize the amount I could open my left hand. But, with constant finger-stretching, *formally* in workouts and *relaxed* in bed, I'm limiting the resulting minimalized hand movement range.

After I only got through 75% of the pushups I was demonstrating to my Karate class (only 24 of 32), just a week later I adjusted my pushup stance to show 'em 33!

I might *look like* I'm just sittin' around in my wheelchair, but—in my head—I'm quite *busy*. If I acted out all of my thoughts, I'd be exhausted!

It'd be as-if I were to run 30 marathons! That'd be 786 miles! (It's 30 marathons — 30 x 26.2.)

In late 2016, I crashed a **stationary** bike at my gym. At my gym, the machine tipped over, while I was pedaling on it. Sooo, I bought an actual, leg-powered, outdoors-bicycle to further develop my quad power, my stamina and my orientation around my own neighborhood.

30.
OTHER APPLICATIONS

ONE OF THE INFINITE LESSONS I've learned in my ~24.32+ years of studying and training in *Martial Arts* is the *'B's and 'S'es.*

Now, said letters stood for the *focus points* students should focus on when *demonstrating* their *'kata'*: Beauty, Balance, Breathing and Strength, Speed, Stamina.

Personally, I've never been *"pretty."* But, I'd like to **think** that my *presentation design* was *appealing to the eye.* Now more than ever, I hafta focus on maintaining my *balance*, both metaphorically/karma-wise and literally/biomechanics-wise.

My *speech therapist*—bless her soul—is helping me reestablish my commendable breath-control. Now, I'll probably never regain all of my once herculean strength ('cuz the majority of one's lower body strength comes from one's hips).

I have likely developed a mild form of *gluteal amnesia.* 'Tis a sad case. But, (AUDIBLE sigh) *'tis a cross I* **must** *bear.*

Currently, my muscles lack the speed I once had. But, my *neural velocity* is *through the roof!* As, I continue my three (FORMAL) weekly workouts, I'm noticing that my endurance is DEFINITELY INCREASING!

DAMNIT! My hyper-active but under-utilized *amygdala* wishes I would've told my ex-girlfriend how to better incorporate Beauty, Balance, Breathing, Strength, Speed, and Stamina (The *Bs and Ss* are the six MAIN focus points a *'Karateka'* should emphasize when demonstrating his or her *'kata'[1].*) into *OUR LIVES TOGETHER.* She would've laughed.

In hindsight, 'twas particularly helpful that I **was** so obsessed with non-biking kinetic activities, 'cuz **now** it's great! It's my favorite activity to do at my neuromuscular-rehab gym.

My continued biking at home has *heightened* my endurance of the resulting discomfort in my surgically-repaired left knee.

---

[1] Japanese for *'prearranged fighting movements'*

31.
MY WAY OR THE HIGHWAY

THIS **T.B.I.** **HAS DEFINITELY** *thrown me for a loop* in terms of *setting the bar.* previously, I was so **used to** my *establishing a high precedent*, then comparing and contrasting others' mistrials.

Now, I must first witness how a task is done. Then, I mimic the procedure with my personal adaptations and variations.

Too many people just *brush* **my** *thoughts* **aside**, 'cuz of my *T.B.I.* So, I feel particularly proud—almost vindicated—when someone tells me I can't, then I dooo! I'm ever so self-conscious of being a jerk.

So, I've been very *upfront* and *warning-full* for the few times I've **had to** fire an employee. I.e. yes, I know I generally take longer to do just about everything. but, that's no excuse for giving me a 28-minute shower directly following a 34-minute shower, twice ignoring my repeated instructions.

A number of my assorted *leg trainers* at my gym have told me to "take bigger steps" when I'm *walking*. (AUDIBLE sigh) After countless *walking trials* at home, I deduced that I was not **yet** ready to lengthen my gait. I psychologically *feared* feeling so unstable. Sooo, for now, I'll continue with my small, stable steps.

Several different times my trainer or my *caregiver* will instruct me one way, but I'll do it another. Every single time *my* way ends up bein' fine. I take *a minute* to gauge my personal biophysics to work out an alternative option that's better adapted to **my** unique physical *dimensions*.

In the end, it *always* comes down to the question:

Who knows my body better than i?!

(THAT was RHETORICAL.)

Rather than taking the time to try to explain my reasoning to others nonverbally via my DynaVox, I'll spare myself the **wasted** energy and frustration by just acting out **my** plans. I'd rather y'all just smile and nod, and let the cards fall as they may.

Currently, I'm in fight or flight mode. Since I currently can't flee the scene quickly, I have no **choice**, but to dedicate **110%** to my rehabilitation.

32.
THE ENDS JUSTIFY THE MEANS

IN THE LOOONG RUN, my muscle contentment (from my legs) *ultimately will dwarf* all the nerve damage I still have. Unfortunately, there's only so much I **can** do to stimulate my *hippocampus* to regenerate nerve cells.

I thought this *rebuilding* process was just a matter of time that my fantastically odd body would compensate, regrow then start anew. I was really *lookin' forward* to that!

But, upon further research, it turns out that the *hippocampus* **re**grows neurons less frequently and less easily as I had hoped and thought.

: (

Regardless! I have a history of **defying** odds. That's kinda what I **do**.

Getting back to my ongoing *battle* against my mostly *physically* **destructive** *Traumatic Brain Injury:*

By always *having to* compensate for my lack of leg strength, I've greatly improved my already strong arms. As my hip strength weight shifting **improves**, so too will my upper body power. An important concept I learned during my 24+ years in *Martial Arts:* all (physical) *POWUH* originates in the *hara*.

The '*HARA*' is near one's belly button, ~two inches inside the skin, near the stomach. '*HARA*' is Japanese for 'sea of energy'. To the *casual observer*, it may seem *coincidental* that, as a fetus, you were fed through a nearby *tube*. The abdominal region—believed to be the body's *energy center* for its life processes—controls various types of pressure. Said *forces* may or may not exert themselves on the abdomen in 'shiatsu' to stimulate the flow of energy through the 'hara'.

'Tis no coincidence that that 'hara' location is the site of my g/peg-tube: it acts as the transportation liaison for vitamins and energy-builders between my nurse and my stomach.

I always factor-in physics, before I start my walks. I picture where I'm goin' and how. I suck it up, before I walk back to bed after a successful urination into my toilet.

As awkward as a right footed lead step is, I realize that my left leg has to get used to supporting my ~64.76 kilogram frame half the time.

(Repeatedly alternating the anatomic responsibility with my right leg is just how the wonder of *walking* works!)

Ok, ENOUGH with the SARCASM.

in order to better my steady gait over the test of time, i've gotta repeatedly push my limits. I must know what works and doesn't work for me, 'cuz "to each, his own".

33.

"THE UNIVERSE IS GOVERNED BY THE LAWS OF *SCIENCE.*"

—DR. STEPHEN HAWKING

I SHOULD AND DO UNDERSTAND *bodily kinetics*. After all, I did successfully major in *biophysics*.

Okay, technically, that was a lie. 'Twas *Biomedical Engineering*. It's just that most of my study topics involved the *laws* and *rules of biokinetics*.

Ok, that too was a fib. Technically, my degree is in *bioengineering*. It's just that most of my studies were *medically*-related, specifically to humans.

Since my actual major is a very broad subject, encompassing many *fields*, I tend to vary its *name* per my *audience*.

I hafta incorporate the *Laws of Biokinetics* into all of my decision-making. Pre-accident, I kinda *took my legs for granted*—not really realizing just how much they do. Now, I know what I've gotta change in my body. (I SHRUG.) Regardless of required time, my pride will NOT let me stop.

That's mainly why I tend to require extra time for all of my doings: I need and use that time for *prep* and angular analysis.

I'll sacrifice **time** for **efficiency**. I'll gladly take those extra minutes to devise a more *energetically* **conservative** plan. After I stand to urinate into my *revised* toilet, I'll *fight the* *urge* to step first with my left foot with my stronger right leg as the *anchor* to weight shift onto my left hip and step initially with my right foot.

(In order to LIFT and MOVE a leg, one's bodily WEIGHT and GRAVITY **MUST be** on the OTHER leg.)

When my caregiver puts on and takes off my shoes, I make sure to lift and hold both legs up to *test* my *leg* **endurance**. But, occasionally, I'll *value* strength **over** endurance. I understand and incorporate *leverage*, whenever I push down with my right leg to easier push up with my left leg.

I'll try to do as many tasks as I can with my left side, 'cuz it's my weaker side, and it needs *work*. Over *extensive time*, it **will** improve.

Could I eventually have **two** *good sides*?!

Ideally, I'd be a *dodecagon* with twelve *good sides*.

(Sumthin' to *WORK* for)

34.
MY HINDSIGHT > MY FORESIGHT

I thought my *muscle memory* was better than my *mental memory*. but, I *thought* **wrong**. Contrary to popular thought, *having sex* is not *like riding a bike* in terms of memory: I *fell off* twice!

(That was a joke *attempt*.)

After watching some *high school* wrestling nowadays, I realized that much of the scoring technique has changed!

During some housing reconstruction on *stuff* the previous owner **neglected**, I had to *change my mind* once or twice—based on *aesthetic* **appeal**. I *called for* the installation of two *lifts*—over my bed and over my bathtub. I thought, incorrectly, that I would require much assistance in my *transportation*. Foolishly, I underestimated my own strength and determination.

(In hindsight, I can't help but wonder: *have I ever* **met me**?!)

35.
Nutrition Input

TO ELIMINATE ANY ACCIDENTAL CONFUSION, lemme clarify just how **my** body *builds strength*:

— I *eat* by way of a *gastric tube* that's surgically-*attached to* my inner stomach and *protrudes out from* my gut. (My main nurse describes said *tube* as "a cross between a *g-tube* and a *peg-tube*".)

— I shower just fine (daily). I just can't *immerse* it like in my -*OOL* (Notice that there's NO 'P' in it.) or pool.

— As I've already stated, I *consume* **four** *meals* per weekend-day and **five** *meals* per weekday. I need a greater caloric intake—and thus more energy—on the days I have a workout or a bike ride.

My *nutritional meds* mostly consist of *muscle relaxers, calcium, fiber and extra lactulose.*

To remain *somewhat healthy*, I cannot lie *face down*. Such an awkward position would put ~142 pounds (my approximate body weight) of direct pressure on that less than one square inch of *bodily opening*. (That's my *G-tube*.)

(That'd be over ~*142 psi*. **Approximately**)

AFTERTHOUGHTS

DESPITE MY NOW-KNOWING OF MY *hippocampus*'s slow inactivity, I am determined to press onward with maximum focused effort, 'cuz that's just what I do: give my 110% effort all the time.

Even with my *Traumatic Brain Injury*, I dare ANYONE to CHALLENGE me to a *Trivial Pursuit* in ANY topic!

(No. No. NOPE! I realize that every one has his or her *area of expertise*. sooo, mine shall be *Biophysical Applications in Martial Arts*.)

Although, I've long been very proud of my multifarious *areas of expertise*, just now I can *highlight* my other virtues and further develop my already commendable qualities.

As a (HUMOROUS) Halloween costume, I'm considering wearing all white while carrying two **empty** suitcases. When someone asks me about my *getup*, my response will be:

"I'm *travelling LIGHT*."

My subconscious to myself: "You have been weighed (~63.67 kilograms).[1] You have been measured (~170.18 centimeters). And, you have been found *wanting*... some leg nerve **strength**."

I use the *METRIC system*, 'cuz I'm HALF-Turkish. TECHNICALLY, I'm ONLY ~5% European, as ONLY my father was 100% Turkish, and ~one TENTH of Turkey (the COUNTRY) *falls IN* Europe (the CONTINENT).

---

[1] My exact weight varies slightly, as my daily activities and *waste excretions* change.

Qualitatively ranking my desires, I'd say I really *crave* walking and swimming. But, I *yearn for* talking and tasting and kissing.

Quantitatively, I yearn for my *one and only*! I thought I'd already found her. But fuckin' ay!

Don't be fooled by the length of my *volumes*. Originally, I thought I'd write three separate books. But, one book of three sections just *made more sense*!

(*Size isn't everything*!)

Plus, my physical progress will take the looongest and be the most gradual. As I *see* my body every day (as of December 31, 2016, I've only had to *admire* that handsome post-accident *mug* for 3,100 days.

Since birth, I've admired my own (masculine) *beauty* for 11,590 consecutive days. I'm not gonna notice **every** little detail and variation.

There's likely not gonna be a gargantuan difference in my day-to-day self-observations. Despite my *underlying reasoning*'s always rooting in science, my everyday life *centers around* maximizing **fun!**

I shall never quit in my attempts to walk and talk again. In the inspiring words of legendary scholar and fellow *invalid* Stephen Hawking:

"However difficult life may seem, there is always something you can do, and succeed at."

ESSENTIALLY, I've got NUTHIN' with which to **PUSH** me. (AUDIBLE sigh)

"But, sometimes NUTHIN' can be a pretty COOL hand."
(—LUKE, 'COOL HAND LUKE')

A few months ago, I *struck **gold*** during one *upper body* workout: I did **66** consecutive painless pushups *sans* break. (I don't remember ever doing that many pushups *in one sitting* pre-accident!)

After much practice (two days per week for ~two months), I *raised the bar* to **85** *consecutive painless pushups sans break* but slowed down in the last ~8, 'cuz of fatigue.

ME: "Over?! Was it 'over', when the Germans (ERRONEOUSLY) declared that they invented 'yogurt'?!"

My Illustrator: "'Germans'?! But, isn't the word, *'yoğurt*, Turkish? And, isn't he Turkish?!"

My mom: "Yes. But, SSSHHH! He's *on a ROLL!*"

ME: "**Nothin'** is 'over', 'til I admit defeat! Dude, when's the last time that happened?"

Illustrator: "Uuummm. Never?"

ME: "'*CORRECTamundo.*'"

It finally occurred to me, during my *editing*, that my injuries are **not** *quite* physical *handicaps*. But, they're more neurological, or nerve-related.

I can still build (even MORE) muscle. It's just that sometimes my muscles just do NOT *process* my *neural messages* in sufficient time.

So, rather than to *disregard* ALL I've just said, please just *keep that in mind*.

'Tis a fantastic feeling, when I still set (physical) personal bests even after my debilitating *accident!*

MUCH thanks to those **ALL** around me! Specifically, with this book: my editor(s), my illustrator, my foreword writers, my trainers, my legs.

So, I was sittin' o'er my toilet, just waitin' for my *anus to explode* (TRUE story!), when I got to *thinkin'* **MUSICALLY** (How ODD!):

"Gettin' BETTER"
"Dealin' with a T.B.I. can be quite exclusive.
I know too well.
I try so hard, everyday
To gain some respect.
No notable results yet.
After a decade, I'm writin' books as a way to vent.
WALK and TALK are my ultimate goals.
Somehow, I did not forget my Biophysics,
Which I apply in my workouts.
Get. Gettin' better.
It's gradual progress. It's not obvious to outsiders.
Get. Gettin' better.
It's gradual progress. It's not obvious to outsiders.
NOT too late to improve.
Just gotta find my legs' groove.
Ev'rything's gotta have ORDER! Math's IN music.
I'm gettin' better, doubters.

Gettin better. YEAH!
I'm gettin' better, doubters.
Gettin better. YEAH!
Dealin' with a T.B.I. can be quite exclusive.
I know too well.
There are plenty o' times I get ridiculously lonely.
Just suck it up and push through.
Lately, I'm SEEIN' improvements and FEELIN' more!
I won't give up.
Now I've gotta be quite a BIT more obvious,
Because you ALL can't see my thoughts.
Get. Gettin' better.
It's gradual progress. It's not obvious to outsiders.
Get. Gettin' better.
It's gradual progress. It's not obvious to outsiders.
NOT too late to improve.
Just gotta find my legs' groove.
Ev'rything's gotta have ORDER! Math's IN music.
I'm gettin' better, doubters.
Gettin better. YEAH!
I'm gettin' better, doubters.
Gettin better. YEAH!
I'm gettin' better, doubters.
Gettin better. YEAH!
I'm gettin' better, doubters.
Gettin better. YEAH!
I'm gettin' better, doubters.
Gettin better. YEAH!
I'm gettin' better, doubters.
Gettin better. YEAH!"

KEY

* = 'Tis a STATISTICAL term for a *unit's* NOT *following* the *PATTERN*.

** = The words in *ITALICS* are WRESTLING terms. Yes, there IS an ACTUAL move called *the TURK*. I HAD to MASTER it, 'cuz ... YEAH.

(Biogenetically, I AM half-*TURK*ish.)

*** = My EXACT weight VARIES SLIGHTLY, as my daily activities and *WASTE* excretions CHANGE.

A NOTE FROM THE AUTHOR

A **LONG, LONG** TIME AGO (~a DECADE), I **WAS** very psychologically SOUND and socially ADEPT.

But, THAT was a LONG time AGO.

NOW, I'm **BURDENED** *with* this TRAGICALLY debilitating *Traumatic Brain Injury*.

(I SHRUG my shoulders.)

C'est la vie. **SHIT** happens. (I, AGAIN, shrug.)

My *late* father sings a snippet from the 'Kansas' song *IN my head*: "Carry ON, my WAYWARD SUUUHHHN. There'll be PEACE, when YOU are **DDDUUUHHHN**."

I used to be creative enough to have fun in ANY situation EVEN at an insurance seminar.

Now, I hafta keep telling myself:

"If you want be a party animal, you have to learn to live in the jungle."

—*Weird Science*

In OTHER words, to be more social, I've gotta become COMFORTABLE with being *UN*comfortable.

In order to *build* myself a STABLE and SUCCESSFUL *future*, I hafta *acknowledge and incorporate* my **PAST**.

What a *PHENOMENAL PAST*, for the most part, 'twas!

I don't have an ego, I just **LOVE** how awesome I AM.

I'm a people person, very personable. I absolutely insist on enjoying life. Not so task-oriented. Not a work horse. If you're looking for a Clydesdale, I'm probably **NOT** your man. 'Tis like, I don't **LIVE** to **WORK**, it's more the other way around. I **WORK** to **LIVE**. As a self-proclaimed *math* **NUT**, I take a **LIL'** bit of extra time to devise the most energetically efficient *solution* possible.

Can one man, *preaching* of his triumphs over injustice and ADVERSITY, *make a* **DIFFERENCE**?!

To **truly live**, THAT **will** be a great *ADVENTURE*!

OVERALL, do not judge my story solely by the chapter or VOLUME at which you just happened to START. Please read all three volumes in my autobiographical series about SUCCESSFULLY rehabbing a *Traumatic Brain Injury.*

Only THEN, could YOU, an unbiased observer, supply a legitimate response to MY REHAB.

Regarding MY *Volume III*: WOW, it's a **BIG** one! You know that.

My hyperactive yet underutilized *amygdala*—in charge of my LIBIDO—YEARNS to YELL, "THAT's what SHE said!"

But, my LOGIC producing *neocortex* claims that *he*/it is ALWAYS searching for inappropriate *PUNS.*

(OR, are they double entendres?!)

I try to relate my goings on to MOVIES to TRY to make my tales slightly more UNDERSTANDABLE. Also, I caN'T HELP but *see parallels*, as I've LONG had a cinematic mind.

(I can't help HOW **MY brain** *OPERATES*!)

Hear me now, believe me later. And, LISTEN to me in ~two weeks: WORK on this *T.B.I.* is a 24 hours/day, 7 days/week, ~52.14 weeks/year **JOB**!

I am by NO means equal to any of y'all, 'cuz of my *T.B.I.* But, instead of just *brushing me off* as *INFERIOR*, what IF I'm somehow better than you *NORMEES*?! (I hafta put extra effort into ALL I do.)

(It's a BIT of a *mind F*CK*.)

As I continue my *FIGHT*, I've realized that it's kinda like my getting a new pair of underwear: I need a LIL' *support*, yet a LIL' *FREEDOM*.

A lot has CHANGED. A lot had to CHANGE! So, you shouldN'T expect from me what I embodied in the past. For that part of me NO longer *exists*.

My current *battle* against this CATASTROPHIC *Traumatic Brain Injury* is my *dare to be great* situation. And, I shaN'T be denied!

Currently, I'm a RIDDLE crossed with a QUANDARY then multiplied by a BEWIL-DERING ENIGMA raised to the exponent of an INTRICACY.

Sooo, please do not *BULLSHIT* me with your *faux empathy!*

SPOILER ALERT!

I'm gonna be ALRIGHT.

Dream **BIG**. Work **HARD**. Play **OFTEN**. Laugh **a LOT!**

Yes, my **MENTAL** section is significantly largeR than my **PHYSICAL** section, partly because I reevaluated just how much I cared to share and partly because **MY** physical injurIES and improvements are better witnessed than explained. Furthermore, my **MENTAL** accomplishments are slightly more impressive than my physical *KICKASSedry*.

P.S. There's a rumor goin' 'round that I'm makin' phenomenal progress, and it appears I shan't be DENIED!

P.P.S. I started that *rumor!*

P.P.P.S. (Regarding MY recovery/rehab:)

It isN'T OVER.

1.
WHAT A *BATTLE!*

I **WAS A GREAT MAN.** My laundry list of both MENTAL and ATHLETIC accomplishments was quite distinguishable. Looking back now, I shaN'T LIE. It impresses even me, 'cuz I caN'T remember all the little details of my positively eventful *term of existence*.

But, rather than sitting in bed, SLACK jawed and DUMB founded in disbelief, I shall remain *cool about it*. Especially now, I rarely display much emotion. Instead, I prefer to appear *calm, cool and collected* throughout any/ALL circumstances—good or bad.

I'd really like to add to my *résumé* of moral/physical accomplishments, most importantly, a *VICTORY OVER* my *Traumatic Brain Injury*. (Specifically, I have a "Diffuse Axonal Brain injury". Ya know that saying, "A little DAB will do ya"? That's *CRAP!*)

So, on the dreaded afternoon of July 6, 2008, I had my HORRENDOUS car accident that left me comatose and with a *Traumatic Brain Injury*.

My injuries were so serious that my *T.B.I.* was initially classified as a 3 on the Glasgow Coma Scale. (That's a <u>neurological</u> <u>scale</u> that gives *laypeople* a reliable and objective way of recording the conscious state of a person.) There are 3 categories worth 5 points each, for a total of 15 points, with *Eye, Verbal and Motor* components. So, comatose A.J. earned the lowest possible scientific score a LIVING person could gain.

So, how am I still alive?!

That's a DAMN good question. I'm glad you asked. It's called *TENACITY*.

On my as of yet imaginary tombstone, it'll read,

"Here lies *Altan Javit Kaynatma 1.0* → *LOST but NEVER Forgotten*"

My writing may not seem agreeable to you, but, it's just **MY** (the author's) interpretation of a particular event. However, just to be clear, I **DO** have a *Traumatic Brain Injury* and a heavily biased *sense of JUDGMENT*. But I'm pretty sure the *American Constitution* (CLEARLY) grants me my "freedom of SPEECH."

The consequences of boredom for such a mentally capable person are RESENTMENT and ANGER. So, rather than becoming too morose and despondent over my tragic impairments, I write what I can remember. Rather than dragging others **DOWN** with my tales of sorrow and anguish, I prefer to pull people **UP** with comedy and inspiration. Consequently, my writing not only emboldens y'ALL. But, it acts as a vent for me to release my frustrations. I prefer to encourage rather than to discourage.

In either case, I've GOTTA have courage.

It's by NO means an excuse! It's merely an explanation. But, repeated *put DOWN*s of *A.J. 2.0* (POST-*accident*) have left *A.J. 3.0* (POST-*breakup*) very defensive of his thoughts and opinions. So, he shan't be DENIED!

'Tis THIS tactic of *apparent* emotional apathy that fools people into THINKING I just remain blasé about everything. But, NO, siree! I still have numerous *passions* (ROMANCE, *INTIMACY*, friendship, sports, comedy, fitness, *Martial Arts*). I just struggle to outwardly display my excitement over too many things.

I'm pretty sure that, yes, I *lost* the ability to *smell rain*. SMELL **RAIN**.

Thankfully, I did so well in Academia, I think my credit score actually went *UP*! So, I could just relax, buy lots of motorized help, and be LAZY.

Nonetheless, I must march onward.

Personally, I am much more about the *reaction* than the *action*. That's how I *spar* in *Martial Arts*. I *weather the storm* of an attack, then I develop a *block and counter*.

How WEIRD is it that I actually *feel smarter* (in maybe TWO areas) NOW post- accident (computation and logic)?!

I'm reactivating infinite neural synapses.

If I were sneakier, I would better manipulate society's misunderstanding to benefit my psychological state. But, I am better than that. Plus, I'm neither that selfish nor sinister.

IS it **WRONG** that I'm contemplating *dating MYSELF*? My *clinching line* would be:

"If my brain *operated* as YOURS does, I'd never shut up!"

My *Matrix of leadership and inspiration* is NOT just found. it's earned!

I NEED a woman to *snap me out* of this DEPRESSING metaphor of *CHOKING SADNESS* that has gradually become my life. (Hopefully, this lady will NOT *back out* of a potential engagement. That hurts!)

People will do some *CRAZY* things. But, when it's for love, maybe it's not so *CRAZY*. (Me, especially)

I can't help but be a HOPE *FULL* romantic! Some people say that *nothing lasts forever.* But, I'd like to disagree. O' course, 'tis very circumstantial: For positive outcomes, I believe optimism CAN remain constant. For negative results, change is a (gradual) process, hence the word *PROGRESS = POSITIVE/FORWARD movement.*

An actual *"JOB"* with a **401k** REQUIREMENT? Why the HELL would I wanna run/walk 401 kilometers?! That's about 249.17 miles. I'd bet that those first 248 miles are relatively *easy.* But, those *last* ~1.17 miles must be **HELL** *on Earth!*

My ever present *journey to neurologic aptitude* has been a LONELY and ARDUOUS process. (AUDIBLE sigh) Pre-injuries, I felt that I was separated, and peers tended to shy away from me. I'm guessing 'cuz of my OVERBEARING brilliance. NOW, I'm shunned, 'cuz my physical disabilities promote social awkwardness.

I mustn't ever be intimidated! Showing *FEAR* is just a display of **WEAKNESS**. Just 'cuz I'm wheelchair bound does not mean that my whole body is weakER. Just 'cuz I have a *Traumatic BRAIN Injury* does not mean that I can't still be an AMAZING nerd. I'm PROUD to help others! I'm a math tutor. I'm a *Martial Arts and Wrestling* technique Designer. The *greatest* knowledge comes from the least expected origins.

I shan't lie: Right before my *TRI weekly* visit (every third Tuesday) with my *NeuroPsychoTherapist* to CALM my nerves, I felt as if my brain just withstood a *SHITstorm.* Sooo, it's in utter disarray!

FYI: I use **humor** often as a coping mechanism to combat my voluminous tales of SORROW. Also, I shan't lie: I've *found* that I tell jokes as a means of deflecting my insecurities.

SENSE is something one may or may not possess, when one has a CHOICE. One could either make a GOOD or a BAD decision, according to inherent *JUDGING.* Conversely, *Sense* only exists, when *Choice* is present. Since many of my daily decisions DISallow options, I often lack options. As a direct result, I lack *Sense* and therefore shaN'T be *Judged.*

I hafta *shrug* ASIDE my MANY *limitations* and *live in the* NOW, while simultaneously being MINDFUL of *TOMORROW.* I hafta treat TODAY as a *GIFT.* That's why 'tis referred to as the *PRESENT.*

I am oh so GRATEFUL to my meticulous neurosurgeons and grateful FOR my own *powerful* mental *strength* for ensuring I HAVE a *present state* at ALL!

Yet another oddity about me is that I maintain a strict limit that I can only die ONCE per lifetime! Sooo, I *reached my MAXIMUM* on July 6, 2008.

I like that my *Martial Arts* Professor has informally accepted me as *the Motivational Speaker* for the kids' and sometimes the adults" class. Every month or so, I present an ~eight minute *talk* on my speech generating *Dynavox* about OVERCOMING *odds* or *mental strength* (Oh, SWEET IRONY!) or *exceeding potential.*

Only through intense pain and prolonged suffering can we truly learn the boundaries of our respective limits.

I am determined to POSITIVELY change my life circumstances by *utilizing* some of my still remaining mental and psychological *virtues/strengths* (ALL encompassing determination, business organization, *Martial Arts* creativity, social kindness, stock market understanding, FULLY *capable* arms—not hands or legs— and helpful employees).

As I **am** a bit of an intellectual and athletic **ANOMALY**, I think of my SEMI/QUASI/FAUX biographical film *Weird Science.*

It's about two super smart kids (We'll call 'em *Altan* and *A.J.*), who are *sorely* underappreciated by the female sex. So they use their incredible intelligence to *CREATE* innumerable opportunities for *intimacy.*

Despite my countless PHYSICAL limitations, I always aim FOR the BEST.

Conversely, a healthy life *guide* is to HOPE *for* the BEST. PREPARE *for* the WORST. But, do not *SETTLE for* good enough.

Life's ROUGH and TOUGH. Get a *helmet.*

(Translation: continue to *take* CHANCES. But, know the likelihood of success.)

Alas, *sanity* is not a choice. Nor, is it OBJECTIVE. It truly IS open to interpretation.

I NEEEEED *positive reinforcement!* (It's the *T.B.I.*)

I very much believe that since *my devastatingly debilitating accident*, my deduction and self-analysis have efficaciously become more acute.

(NOT to BRAG, but Yeah.)

Sister Mary Clarence, of *Sister Act 2: Back in the Habit*, to ME:

"IF you wanna *GO somewhere*, IF you wanna *BE somebody*, you've gotta *wake UP* and *pay ATTENTION!*"

To exemplify my support of her singing, I tend to sleep ONLY ~0.2292 days (= ~5.5 hours) per night.

I supplement my constant psychological PREP by maintaining a *steady diet* of *"eatin' LIGHTNIN' and crappin' THUNDER"*(*Rocky II*). 'Tis a stupendous feeling of accomplishment for my *inconsistent* and *unreliable* digestive system when I begin my day with a SOLID to SEMI-solid *bowel deposit*. That shows that my stomach and gastric juices still *work!*

Throughout the first ~3.36 YEARS of my **long**-term rehabilitation, I thought (**IN-CORRECTLY**) that I was developing tolerance and patience. '*Au CONTRAIRE!*' That living NIGHTMARE merely and tested my WEAK *restraint*. Ergo, I learned nothing new. My poise and rigor simply became more apparent.

NOW, I'm a BIT of a procrastinator with an obscenely large ego: Someday I'm gonna be AMAZING.

Initially after my JUDICIAL *turn of* **FORTUNE**, I wanted REVENGE. But, *REA-SONING* soon *nestled into* my mind:

Vengeance won't settle my heart at ease. It'll be a TEMPORARY FIX. But, long-term, I need bigger success to settle my nerves. Whether I'm motivated by spite or by self-improvement, this is a realization I must determine and accept EVENTUALLY.

Yeah, I think I'm entitled to *toot my OWN horn*.

Throughout my *battle WITH*, and my IMPENDING *victory OVER*, my *Traumatic Brain Injury* (*T.B.I.*), I've learned that *fighting* and eventually beating a *T.B.I.* doesn't *build* character. It *REVEALS* it.

'Tis NOT that I'm learning much ACADEMICALLY anymore. It's more that I am learning the EXTENT of my mental and my physical limitations. Therein I can solve for any necessary compensation and further detail an extensive rehab regimen.

I apply my extensive *BioPHYSICS* knowledge for the *HOWs* and *WHYs* of my many (limited) movements. (IS it selfish **or** intuitive that I'm now *analyzing* my own movements and noting the BIOPHYSICAL *gain* or *loss?*)

I became a math tutor for mathematics and a MOTIVATIONAL Speaker for *Martial Arts* classes. PLUS, I'm still a teacher at my dojo. MY *EXPLANATIONS* are exponentially tougher for me, 'cuz I've gotta TYPE my messages into my *DynaVox.* I'm STILL workin' on—via my *SPEECH Therapy*—varying the tone of my voice so that I can be understood by others.

Since I kinda **HAFTA** frequently rely on my LOGIC and DEDUCTIVE reasoning, my existence as an *ANOMALY* has become more and MORE evident. Despite the MENTAL damage the NAME of MY injury (*Traumatic BRAIN Injury*) SUGGESTS, my limitations are MAINLY PHYSICAL. Sooo MANY THINK—INcorrectly—that, JUST 'cuz the *injury DESCRIPTION/diagnosis* is severe brain TRAUMA, that I'm a *menace to society*.

I love to teach! But, I make sure to only *share my* KNOWLEDGE, WHEN I am 100% sure of the topic.

(E.g. *Martial Arts*, MATH, co-teaching math and science at *N.R.S.F.*, SPORTS info, etc.)

I shaN'T lie: As a direct result of my UNeventful stay at *the rehab facility*, I DID develop some LOW-grade *depression* from being surrounded by all the concentrated sadness.

Having a *Traumatic Brain Injury* is a LOT like being an ORPHAN to society: They **CARE** *about* your *development* but NOT **REALLY.**

ALAS! **No** one is UNIVERSALLY LIKED. My common *toast* at SOCIAL gatherings: "CHEERS to ALL o' those who wish me **WELL!**

... And, those who doN'T can go to **HELL!**"

Since my *life*-**THREATENING** accident, I've actually done fairly well financially. Using my fondness for *NUMERICAL* hijinks, I calculated that I'm now making ~14 cents per minute before expenses.

JEEZ! I have so much TIME and so little to do!

SCRATCH that. *REVERSE* it.

I am really, REALLY enjoying all the *freedom* I have to tutor, entertain, and teach *Martial Arts.*

Since I kinda hafta frequently rely on my logic and my deductive reasoning, my *T.B.I.*

has—from an extreme/*glass is half FULL* perspective—*heightened* my extremely broad in-tellect. Though my *MULTI*tasking ability *has* SUFFERED, my *FOCUSING* ability has be-come enhanced.

At a recent party, a NEW girl expressed to ME that "it is amazing how much you've learned!" Flattered, I responded by stating, "Actually, it can be rather **EXHAUSTING**, 'cuz I'm re-*cultivating my mind*."

"Oh, so you're kinda like an *idiot savant*."

Flabbergasted, I retorted, "Well, I think that *'SAVANT'* is rather INSULTING!" (She chuckled.)

A major *turn on* for me is making the opposite gender GIGGLE.

(IF I can DO that with *MATH*, then that's a bonus.)

My NeuroPsychoTherapist to me: "There's a tremendous difference between *knowing* the path and *walking* it."

My response: (chuckle) "Clever pun. or, are you teasing me, 'cuz I cannot YET *WALK*?"

The long-distance *trek* of life is a **MARATHON**: You're NOT gonna *win it*, if you doN'T *give it 110% effort 100% of the time.*

I did the math. It works.

The *journey of LIFE* is filled with trials and tribulations. I will **ERR** CONSTANTLY, but **LEARN** always. Hence, society accepted the common experimental procedure of **TRIAL** *and* **ERROR**. From THAT respect, the art of HUMOR seems to favor precision over accuracy, 'cuz it requires MULTIPLE attempts.

I NOW prefer **PRECISION** in my EVERYDAY tasks, 'cuz I *AIM* to REPEAT the SAME procedure over and over and OVER again. 'Tis as if I were in grade school design-ing my science projects: I'm doing my big *BIOPHYSICS final* on:

Full recovery from a Traumatic Brain Injury.

I am now more concerned with *REPETITION* than with *CORRECTITUDE.*

I'm in my 30s now. Sooo, I've gotta start making smarter decisions.

"Ya know, you could be a LOVING husband and CARING father and JUST have *POOR judgment*."

(*Irrational Man*)

I know this *ALL* too **WELL**. : (

But, I am determined to meet an understanding, patient, and sympathetic woman who'll *look PAST* my occasional erroneous acumen. For I **KNOW** that I am a morally and ethically **GOOD** person. I just sometimes view situations apathetically, thanks to my *Traumatic Brain Injury.*

CURRENTLY though, my life is *GOOOOOOOD*. THAT's with a CAPITAL **G**, which stands for *GREAT!* Ya see, I **COULD** be sad and get depressed over my significantly limited current physical and social lifestyles. BUT, my *OPTIMISTIC life view* and *inner DRIVE for self-BETTERMENT* does NOT let me quit EVER!

Now that I've GOT *MATERIAL possessions,* I've *concluded that* I'm personally prouder of that wonderfully mesmerizing feeling of accomplishment than any *monetary recognition.*

So, in a way, I'd kinda rather be **UNDER**estimated than **OVER**, 'cuz I enjoy delivering those feelings of *awe and surprise* rather than *sorrow and disappointment.*

At the given moment, I am **NOT** psychologically **UN**clear, **NOT** dramatically befuddled, **NOT** thoroughly nonplussed. I am very **LUCID** in merely stating an IRREFUTABLE **FACT**:

My stay at the rehab facility provided me TIME to REFLECT and to REeducate **MYSELF** on PATIENCE and BIOPHYSICS. Also, I believe I have improved more in the seven years since I left the facility than I did during my early days there.

'Gustavit victoria super optimum tempus.'

(Latin for 'Victory tastes the best over time.')

KEY

* = The ONLY exception I can recall would be my co-teacher of a generic class for a LARGE group of *T.B.I.* patients more severely mentally damaged than myself. said teacher is beautiful!

(I'll just refer to said tantalizing teacher as "Leslie K.")

** = 'Tis a RIDICULOUS tactic I learned in my fraternity days. I'd jam my right index finger down my throat to INDUCE vomiting. This procedure *clears my stomach* for more alcohol imbibing.

2.

THE BELONGING YOU SEEK STANDS NOT BEHIND YOU BUT IN FRONT OF YOU

CURRENTLY, **I LIVE IN A DREAM WORLD**. But, I shaN'T let my VIVID imagination limit what I can and **WILL** make *REALITY*.

From my unique *growth*, I know what it's like to have people's always thinking (a lot) less of me.

I'm different. SUCH is I.

DREAM your **DREAMS**. But, *DESIGN* your **REALITY**.

HHHMMM. Interesting *diction* or *word choice*. Ya see, I am set on transforming my *dreams* of walking and talking into my *reality*. Thus, I've GOTTA *DESIGN* my *DREAMS*. With as *strong* as my mind still is, I can **SEMI/PARTIALLY** foreshadow* my own LIT-ERAL/SLEEP induced *IMAGERY*'s becoming my own *reality*.

UNfortunately, it's humans' NATURAL inclination to FEAR and shy AWAY from what they doN'T know and understand. I've LONG been an INTELLECTUAL *enigma*. Now, I am a Medical Mystery of PHysical Fortitude. Alliteration aside. EXCUUUUUSE **ME** for habitually proving doubters **WRONG!**

(I'm sorry, I'm not *sorry*.)

A turbulent and horrific death on a *hustle bustle* highway would **NOT** be MY *Final*

Destination!

(INTRIGUING movie!)

For any given situation, I hope for the **BEST**, but prepare for the **WORST**, while I EXPECT kind of a *run o' the mill* performance. THAT way I'm RARELY disappointed in myself. Some may interpret my REASONING as *setting myself up for* inevitable disappointment. But, NNNOOOOO. I've learned to shrug off the **BAD**, and better cherish the **GOOD**.

I always try to see the humor in any situation. I like to think of the GENIUS words of COMEDIAN Anthony Jeselnik:

"Ya know **NOT** *laughing* is just **LAUGHING** *but for* WUSSES."

HALF joking aside, I'm making such admirable progress with my standing and walking that I'll probably be OFFICIALLY noted as an astounding medical and inspirational ANOMALY.

No, that sounds like I'm unsure of myself. DROP the "probably."

EVEN as the SURREPTITIOUS *OPTIMIST* that I AM, you doN'T **HAFTA** be POSITIVE **ALL** the time.

Shit **DOES** TEND to happen. Mistakes are INEVITABLE.

UNFORTUNATELY, it's taken a DEVASTATING *Traumatic Brain Injury* for me to REALIZE that it's the SEMI-occasional ERROR that makes me *HUMAN*. Last time I CHECKED, THAT's what I AM kinda.

It's how we REACT to certain STIMULI that TRULY determines each of our respective CHARACTER.

(I **WAS**/AM a *SUCCESSFUL* REACTive fighter in my Karate sparring. 'Tis ODD that my Jujitsu fighting is far MORE PROactive.)

From my recent research, I found a particularly FRUSTRATING fact: The human brain does NOT *lose memories* JUST the *ability to* ACCESS them. Also (AUDIBLE sigh), an instrumental *sense* used in *memory* RETRIEVAL is **OLFACTORY**, which I LACK.

"It's perfectly OKAY to feel SAD, ANGRY, ANNOYED, FRUSTRATED, SCARED or ANXIOUS. Having FEEL-INGS does NOT make you a NEGATIVE person. It makes you HUMAN."

(—Lori Deschene)

I **STILL** FEEL ALL of the ABOVE emotions. NOW, I just TEND to INADVERT-
ENTLY *INTERNALIZE*.

I HATE the morally QUESTIONABLE *souls/psyches* of MOST **people**. Yet, I LOVE
gatherings! And, I despise IRONY!

As I'm TRYING to be more social, I've THANKFULLY grown more accustomed to
my physical and linguistic awkwardness. I like to think of the cinematic COMEDY,
'Weird Science', before guests arrive for one of my *par-TAYS*:

"If you want be a party animal, you have to learn to live in the jungle."

(In my case, the "JUNGLE" would be my WHEELCHAIR.)

Along the SAME lines, I saw my MAIN doctor on a Friday, the day before I hosted a
PAHTEE, just as my semiannual checkup.

As ONE of the PARTY attendants was to be a buddy I hadN'T seen in ~14 years, I
was NATURALLY rather enthused.

Thus, after checking my blood pressure on his *sphygmomanometer*, the doc remarked:

"(A.J.), you're going to have a heart attack by the time you're forty if you don't learn
to RELAX."

I canNOT *evolve* as a MAN until I can admit my mistakes. I'm NOT gonna *mature* in
a SYMBIOTICALLY affectionate, relationship, 'til I can better *see* my own faults.

KEY

* = 'Tis certainly NOT *foreBODING*, 'cuz *BODE* has a **NEGATIVE** connotation

** = 'Tis a PUN of/on *PATHETIC*, 'cuz I am BOTH pitiful AND affecting feelings

3.
MUTUAL LOVE IS TOUGH TO FIND

I'M A **SAPIOHETEROSEXUAL MAN** = I'm ATTRACTED to INTEL-
LIGENT WOMEN.

I'm by **NO** means *ugly*. I've just always been kinda humble. So, I'll just say I'm *beauty CHALLENGED*. Thus, I seek an affectionate partner so *BLESSED* that she has enough beauty for both of us.

It's complicated. All this LOVE stuff is complicated. And, that's good. 'Cuz if it's too simple you've got no reason to try, and if you've got no reason to try, you don't.

OBVIOUSLY, **MY** romantic life requires **ALOTTA** WORK. And, I'm tryin'! I've EVEN ventured to *hit ON* one, two, FOUR different (FEMALE) trainers. In addition to my *GYM trials*, I've recently reconnected with my former co-teacher from my LONG-term rehab facility. (THANK YOU, *The Book of Faces!*)

(*Facebook*)

She's like *WHOA!* So, PERHAPS I shouldn't worry SO MUCH about **MY RO-MANCE**, 'cuz when I didn't focus ON **MY** romantic INTERESTS, *JACKPOT!*

Slow DOWN, A.J.! Don't JINX yourself*!

I wanna believe in the *BEST case scenario*.

(Oh, WAIT! I only HALF believe IN *superstitions*! ACTUALLY, I **DO** BELIEVE in **MY** *SUPER*ness. So, I BELIEVE in ONLY ~42% of *SUPER*stition. 5 *letters out of 12*)

I TRY to justify everything mathematically, since everything has an explanation. If I cannot verify something quantitatively, then I won't do it, and I'll doubt myself. This self-judging depression explains why my psyche is still so fragile and needs a third-party helper.

I'm HUNGRY for a 'GYRO' **OVERFLOWING** with the *secret sauce* of OPTIMISM. (THAT was BOTH corny and lame! I APOLOGIZE!) I am hungry for a 'GYRO' though, with ALOTTA *'yoğurt soslu'* and tomatoes with a BIG side of pilaf.

Someday, IDEALLY, I'll get married on a *quantitatively HARMONIOUS* day, like one in which the month number is equal to the sum of the *squares of the set day's digits.* (month = square of day + square of day)

I.e. 1/1, 2/11, 5/12, 5/21, 10/13, 10/31

And, my fiancée will agree to it, 'cuz she'll LOVE my little *eccentricities.*

UNfortunately OR FORTUNATELY, I'm one o' those people who can be hurt (emotionally) by someone MULTIPLE times, yet STILL believes there is a good side to every person.

The GREATEST thing(S) one can learn are to love and to be loved!

PERHAPS those who have been *hurt* the MOST (ME—emotionally) possess the *greatest potential* to *heal.*

(Obviously, I just *bleed OPTIMISM*, which is a FANTASTIC *ailment!*)

A woman doesN'T HAFTA be *PERFECT* to be EXACTLY what I NEED.

Romantically, **PRE**-*accident*, I **WAS** a *Protector*. Now, with my *debilitated* PHYSICAL *state* but my *invigorated* PSYCHE, I'm more of a *Provider.*

KNOW your *ROLE.*

KEY

* = After ~a MONTH of ONLINE *courting*, it turns out that she DID choose a different, closeR guy SHUCKS!

4.
CINEMATICALLY, I'D BE *THE PURSUIT OF HAPPYNESS*

MY **INTERNAL** D**RIVE** **DEMANDS** THAT
I shan't be DENIED!
I can't STAND when ANYONE **IGNORANTLY** claims
"(He/She) KNOW(S) how (I) FEEL."

ME: "Is this mike *ON*?! Uuuummm. NO, you doN'T."

I'm KINDA/LITERALLY like 'The Man with TWO Brains' in that EVERY action in MY life has a *DUALITY of PURPOSE and ACTION*, in that ALMOST every deed FINISHES with a DIFFERENT outcome from the INTENDED result.

But, the film's a COMEDY. So, I can USUALLY just *LAUGH it OFF* like a "WILD and **CRAZY** guy!"

—HILARIOUS ongoing skit on OLD school 'SNL' with Steve Martin and Dan Ackroyd

AND/OR, my LIFE with a *T.B.I.* is KINDA like the brilliant film *Along Came a Spider* in that "'it is a book that will NEVER '(END).'" By that, I am hoping that **MY** *tactics* and **MY** *scheming* will *OUTlive me.* **MY** unique thoughts will just become *THE WAY.*

Along those SAME lines: "You *DO* what you **ARE.**" I AM an AWE INSPIRING, TEMPORARILY *PHYSICALLY* disabled, MATHEMATICAL GENIUS who DOUBLES as a *Martial Arts* SAGE.

Thus, I AM a habitual BLOGGER of anything INSPIRATIONAL, my *fightS FOR handicap* RIGHTS, my NUMERICAL analysis of most EVERYTHING and my *Jujitsu* triumphs.

MY first ~23.24 YEARS *aboard Earth* COULD be COMPARED to the INTRI-GUING film *The Man Who Knew Infinity*. 'Tis the *INSPIRING* yet *HEARTBREAKING* tale of a FOREIGN young man—LIKE 23 year old HALF TURKISH **me**—who OVER-COMES CONSTANT **DOUBTS** and *FROWNS* from *Society* to *REshape* others' THINKING.

The protagonist SUFFERED and technically *OVERCAME* a MAJOR MEDICAL in-jury—like 23-year-old **me**—to ULTIMATELY *TRIUMPH*.

IF I were to *break DOWN* the MUCH heralded *Star Wars* sagas, it'd be:

(ALL below titles are based on the ACTUAL film titles and SYLLABLE #.)

I: 'Brain Wars: Mathematical GENIUS'

II: 'Brain Wars: Attack of the DOUBT'

III: 'Brain Wars: Revenge of *KARMA*'

(MY injurIES — July 6, 2008)

IV: 'Brain Wars: A STRONG Hope'

V: 'Brain Wars: *Brain TRAUMA* Strikes BACK'

VI: 'Brain Wars: Return of the WISDOM'

VII: 'Brain Wars: The *SKILLZ Awaken*'

VIII: 'Brain Wars: The First Success'

(Yet UNNAMED) IX: 'Brain Wars: Hear Me *ROAR*'

RELUCTANTLY, I've realized that MY TRIUMPHANT *WALK of my ULTIMATE* vic-tory over my *T.B.I.* **WILL** be a *LONELY* one. But, IF I **LET** it, IT **CAN** make me the STRONGEST I've EVER been. I've just GOTTA *put a POSITIVE spin on* ANY and ALL social INTERACTIONS.

By "triumph OVER", I mean my eventual *victory over* Society's ignorance of *Trau-matic Brain Injuries*. UNfortunately, I'll always have a *T.B.I.* But, I'm working to minimize Society's IGNORANCE of the/my condition.

I likeD to THINK, PRE-accident, that my potential was *LIMITLESS*. POST-accident, I found the television show *Limitless*, which is AWESOME. *SURFING through* some movie channels, I soon discovered that there's ALSO a *Limitless* film, which is ILLUSTRI-OUS.

I'd LIKE to START my OWN 'Fight Club'. That'd be APPROPRIATE for ME, 'cuz 1) I've earned TWO 'Shodan' ranks in two DIFFERENT styles of 'Okinawan' Karate and one HIGH ranking BROWN belt in Jujitsu. 2) I STILL LOOOVE to TEACH. 3) I doN'T have MUCH anymore. So, it's psychologically NECESSARY to HIGHLIGHT my *VIR-TUES*.

"It's only after we've lost EVERYTHING, that we're FREE to do ANYTHING."
(—TYLER DURDEN, 'FIGHT CLUB')

P.S. *Jujitsu* is GROUND *fighting* for those of us in wheelchairs.
To any and ALL visitors of ME:

"What you might see now is ordinary glass, I promise you will soon remain to see a diamond.
—SRINIVASA RAMANUJAN (PROTAGONIST), THE MAN WHO KNEW INFINITY

('Por Ejemplo', I wrote a SONG to describe SOME of my PHYSICAL *battles)*
(MODEL tune for MY revision that ALSO kinda APPLIES to MY rehab:
('Fresh Prince' theme song; just REPLACE "Bel Air" with "Davie."")

*Anomaly in a Chair**
"Nooow, I'll tell y'all what it's LIKE
To be a genius with a messed up PSYCHE.
So, I'd like to tell my STORY,
Just sit right THERE.
I'll tell y'all the tales of an anomaly in a CHAIR.
From Karate class, I was drivin' HOME,
Just kicked some ass, so I had a 'big DOME'.

Four other teachers tried to take me DOWN,
But, I danced around 'em like I was wearin' a GOWN.
Suddenly, my tire shredded and began to ex PLODE,
And, I was ejected out onto the ROAD.
I slipped into 2 comas, so I got SCARED:
I thought, 'HOW will I function, always SITTIN' in a CHAIR?!'
I TRIED and 'pushed' my legs day after DAY.
Ya see I'm DETERMINED, for in this chair I woN'T STAY!
I started to STAND. Then, I started to WALK.
These were BOTH with a walker, as my legs TEND to just
LOCK.
Aching left HIP makes it ROUGH.
But, where's the CHALLENGE, if it aiN'T TOUGH?!
I've GOTTA keep tellin' myself that I CAN BEAT IT.
'Yes, I WILL BEAT IT.'
But, WAIT. What about when I'm TIRED and DREARY?
This aiN'T a LUXURY cruise! NO rest for the WEARY!
BUMMER, ah CRUD!
HOW can I GET from HERE to THERE?!
I'll just HAFTA be an anomaly in a CHAIR.
Well, I GUESS it's alright that I'm a 'HANDICAPPED MEM-
BER'.
But, my PAST was so ADMIRABLE. 'REMEMBER'?!
Will I EVER WALK alone 'AGAIN'?!
I NEED 'PATIENCE'.
ALL my progress is GRADUAL over a LOOONG stretch of
TIME.
I closed my EYES to BETTER CONCENTRATE.
I glance at my watch OFTEN, 'cuz my REbuilt LEG nerves
ARE very LATE.
Ah, I mustN'T RUSH 'em. My LIFE is QUITE RARE.
LATER, I'll say, 'NAH. DoN'T NEED IT.
WHO WANTS a CHAIR?!'
I've straightened my LEFT foot. so it's NOT 'pigeon TOED'.
Now I just need my LEG nerves to 'WAKE up STRONG'
I looked DOWN at my LEGS
and exhaled this PROUD AIR,
As I think how I 'WUZ' this ANOMALY in a CHAIR."

In a WAY, my MIND is a raging torrent, FLOODED with rivulets of THOUGHTS cascading into a waterfall of CREATIVE alternatives.

THINK ABOUT IT: We never earn respect just by winning. We earn respect by fighting back, by being MENTALLY TOUGH and giving it everything we've got.

President Eisenhower put it well: "It's not about the size of the DOG in the fight; it's about the size of the FIGHT in the dog."

Romantically, I've discovered (SADLY) that humans (specifically—in MY case—WOMEN) *follow* their HEARTS and AFFECTION, NOT their MINDS and LOGIC.

> *"There are no proofs nor underlying laws that can determine the outcome of matters of the heart. Of that I'm sure."*
>
> **(—G.H. HARDY/ADVISOR, 'THE MAN WHO KNEW INFINITY')**

KEY

* = NEXT, I'll be writing a BOOK of SONG revisions.

5.
I Am Full of
Mistakes and Imperfections

THUS, I AM **REAL**.
WITHIN the *REAL* designation, I PROUDLY boast that I am only *HEMIDEM-ISEMIQUAVER[1]* esquely I**R***RATIONAL*.
(Thus, I'm ONLY 1/64th INcompetent.)
WHEN I am feeling RATIONAL (YES, I can CONTROL my thinking ONE way or the OTHER.), I'll USUALLY SETTLE on a UNIQUE and RAREFIED number—such as *73'.*[2] When I am feeling **IR** rational, I TEND to DRIFT toward the *transcendental* numbers, such as *pi* (= ~3.1415926535897 SADLY, THAT's as FAR as I CAN remember. DoN'T JUDGE me!)
(SINGLE tear)
WHY IS it that, of ALL *MEMORY stimuli*, I can *register* NUMBERS the BEST— over *NAMES*, over *STORIES*, over *PICTURES*, SLIGHTLY over *FACES*.

---

[1] 1/64th musical note

[2] "73 is the 21st prime number. Its mirror, 37, is the 12th and its mirror, 21, is the product of multiplying 7 and 3. In binary *talk*, 73 is a palindrome, 1001001, which backwards is 1001001."—'The Big Bang Theory'
"The difference of 7 and 3, when raised to the power of 3, summed to the square of 3 equals 73."—ME

ALSO, I'm MATURE enough to RECOGNIZE my FAULTS.

ALL of MY thinking is QUANTITATIVELY based.

(I have ONLY ~65% of my TWO hands FULLY operational, ~17% of my TWO legs FULLY operational and ~56% of my OWN mind FULLY operational.)

I'm DETERMINED enough to ARDENTLY WORK to IMPROVE upon those *WEAKNESSES* in TIME. CURRENTLY, my PSYCHE is NOT YET STABLE and SE-CURE enough to INTENSELY *tackle* SOME of my MANY *WEAKNESSES*. Those will go on my *EVENTUAL To DO List.*

NOW, I've gotta CONTINUE to HIGHLIGHT my STRENGTHs, in HOPES of *CHARMING* a LOVELY *fawn* (HUMAN!) with my GINORMOUS

Adam's apple.

(MAYBE I'll SURPRISE her with my incredible intellect, WOW-ing wisdom and/or HILARIOUS Humor After An Amazing And Appealing Alliteration Appetizer!)

I KNOW what I MUST do to OVERCOME my *T.B.I.!*

There WILL be/ARE COUNTLESS *battles* between my OMNIPOTENT—yet VERY UNGODly—brain and my *ignorant* muscles by way of my *ailing* yet *stubborn* nerves. BI-OLOGICAL **WARS** are NOT *won* by doing everything RIGHT.

SAID **WARS ARE** won by NOT getting overwhelmed by doing a few things WRONG. That takes mental toughness, steady composure and lucid INNER soliloquies.

EVEN at age ~31.68, I'm STILL learning about MYSELF. I was noting COMPOUND words, like *SOMEthing, INside, LIFEtime,* when I thought of a GREAT self-applicable adjective:

FLAWSOME — I embrace my FLAWS, but remain AWESOME nonetheless.

ALAS! *The POISON is the REMEDY.* I must **LIVE** and **LEARN.** I've come to AC-CEPT that I'll, LIKELY, never FULLY/COMPLETELY recover from my *Traumatic Brain Injury.* Thus, I've also ACCEPTED that I HAFTA learn more about my OWN *BIOPHYS-ICS,* RESPONSIBILITY and GENEROSITY. Thus far, I've concluded that my logic, reasoning and overall deduction are thoroughly labyrinthian.

I've been WONDERFULLY entertained, as I've learned how MY very HIGH *Intelligence Quotient* belies a dangerously LOW *Emotional Quotient* from the BRILLIANT TV show, 'Scorpion.' I **THOUGHT** my *LITTLE to ZERO EMPATHY* was a DIRECT and UN-FORTUNATE consequence of my *Traumatic Brain Injury.*

BUT! It NOW appears that my *T.B.I.* MAY have kinda *STREAMLINED my pursuit of KNOWLEDGE* by *blocking OUT* ALL unwanted AND/OR unnecessary FEELINGS.

I HAVE had a SOMEWHAT *UP and DOWN* PRE-accident life.

('Twas MOSTLY *PEAKS* as opposed to *TROUGHS*.)

Even though my memory of MANY events SUCKS, I'll still OCCASIONALLY) *live in the PAST.*

NEVER be DEFINED by your PAST. 'Twas MERELY a *LESSON*, NOT a *LIFE* sen-*tence.* Yes, I WAS in a HORRIFIC car accident that CATASTROPHICALLY and SE-VERELY injured my brain, legs AND nerves. But, now I've LEARNED MANY Auto-motive AND Biophysical applications, e.g. BETTER driving safety rules, WHEN and WHERE to CHECK tire expiration, PROPER treatment for the *people with DISabilities*, Weight DISPLACEMENT via the HIPS, *MINIMUM pressure yields MAXIMUM OUT-PUT*, and MULTIPLE ACCESS points IN/TO/OF the STOMACH.

Note to SELF: It's not enough to JUST apologize. You hafta forgive YOURSELF.

To my FUTURE (POTENTIAL) ROMANTIC interests AND to ANYONE: *SCREW* "FORGIVE and FORGET"! How 'bout *ACCEPT and TRY your BEST?!*

(AUDIBLE sigh) I shan't be just ANOTHER *WHEELCHAIR bound CRIPPLE.*

Ya see, these injuries serve MORE as *BUILDING blocks* or *STEPPING stones* along my journey to ULTIMATE SUCCESS.

Actually, **my** NeuroPsychoTherapist abhors when I use the term "cripple" in my self-descriptions. But, sometimes, 'tis necessary. And accurate. I.e. If I'm composing one of my humorous song parodies, and I need a word to rhyme with the **ripple** effect of my (temporary) leg *loss*, I shan't use *nipple*!

ALTHOUGH, the COMBINATION of my MANLY *UPPER body* and my PREF-ERENCE for *form FITTING* shirts COULD/does kinda CHAFE my *"NIPPLE"*(S). PLUS, THAT's FUNNY!

As a *MATH man*, I've concluded that one should "beware the Ides of March"(—Shake-speare), 'cuz the day represents *the END of Pi Day (3/14).*

DESPITE my occasional *setBACK*, I MUST maintain my RESOLVE and *SPUNK!* Af-ter I REgain my INTELLIGIBLE voice, I am DETERMINED to make just ONE onion CRY.

6.
GO WITH YOUR GUT

SOMETIMES, **WHAT YOU KNOW** DIFFERS from what you LEARN. I'd *learned* umpteen biophysical principles over my 9+ academic YEARS in *advanced academia* (high school, undergraduate and beyond).

But, MANY of SAID hypotheses have proven to be just THAT—UN*proven* THEORIES FOR/to ME.

I.e. I GREATLY struggle to weight SHIFT on my LEFT hip.

(I've developed SEVERE arthritis in my LEFT hip.)

: (

Since it's been SOOO LONG, since I walked withOUT an AIDE, I've almost FORGOTTEN how to SAFELY/painLESSly *AMBULATE*. So, I ALTERED my *STANCE* on Biophysical *WALKING* **SAFETY**.

OR, were those *WALKING* theories just SEEMINGLY *FALSE*, 'cuz I'm a PHYSICAL (and MENTAL) ANOMALY?!

Regarding MY *recovery*, I'd say *Candy* **CZAR** Willy Wonka summed it up BEST, when he stated, "You should NEVER, ever *DOUBT* what NO ONE is SURE *ABOUT*."

"'*EDUCATION*' is **NOT** 'the LEARNING of **FACTS**', but 'the TRAINING of the MIND to **THINK**."

(—attributed to Albert Einstein)

Can I get an "AMEN!"? I ALWAYS remember THIS, when I design *Martial Arts* classES:

A *GOOD* teacher *SHOWS* students *HOW* and *WHERE* to *LOOK,* **NOT** *WHAT to SEE.* As a 'SENSEI', the 'Karateka' MAXIMIZE my feeling of CONTENTMENT, when, after I FIRST MENTION the issue, the KIDS recognize their OWN errorS, and correct THEMSELVES.

As MUCH as I **LOVE** TEACHING, ULTIMATELY, I WANNA **TEACH** FUTURE TEACHERS. Hopefully, one day my PRESENCE IN the DOJO will be MORE an OPTIONAL bonus than a NO nonsense NECESSITY.

I'm a *PEOPLE person,* very personable. I absolutely INSIST on enjoying life. Not so task oriented. Not a work horse. If you're looking for a Clydesdale, I'm probably **NOT** your man.

Especially NOW, post-injurIES, I doN'T LIVE to *WORK.* It's more the other way around. I WORK to *LIVE.* I HAFTA stay BUSY and keep my mind occupied. Otherwise it'll *DRIFT* into UNwanted THOUGHTS of disgrace, sorrow and bewilderment.

Besides, aren't we ALL *lookin' out for OURSELVES deep down?* Yes, we **ARE.** It's *psychological EGOISM.* As a human, it's just *INGRAINED in my deoxyribonucleic acid (DNA)* as a kind of evolutionary advantageous adaptation. I don't know. I'm not a scientist. I just have that **SCIENTIFIC,** analytic way of thinking.

"Yesterday I was **CLEVER**, so I WANTED to CHANGE the **WORLD.** Today I am **WISE**, so I am CHANGING **MYSELF**."—Rumi

In MY case, *YESTERDAY* refers to my PRE-accident days (April 8, 1985-July 5, 2008). While, *TODAY* envelopes July 7, 2008 to the PRESENT moment.

July 6th, 2008 is/was my **SEPARATING** milestone, 'cuz 'twas the day of my HORRIFIC accident. Sooo, in MATHEMATICAL lexicon, THAT date would KINDA be **MY** *Life MEDIAN.*

(ACTUALLY, TECHNICALLY, 'twould be my *Life MEAN.* MATHEMATICALLY, my **ACTUAL** *Life MEDIAN* would be my 5,795th day ALIVE on Earth—February 18th, 2001 my brother's 14th birthday.)

(FYI: THOSE #s were calculated with the PREMISE of MY life = April 8, 1985 to December 31, 2016.)

I've lived TWO very DIFFERENT but both SUCCESSFUL (to DIFFERENT degrees) lives. So, I've kinda HAD to FREQUENTLY ADAPT to my CHANGING environment.

DESPITE my NON-speedy *WORK*, I WILL eventually determine the CORRECT answer.

Regarding my deduction:

It's like NOVOCAINE: Just give it TIME. It ALWAYS works.

My logical and insightful reasoning is MUCH like my MATHEMATICAL testing in academia.

I'd RARELY FINISH anywhere CLOSE to FIRST chronologically. But, I'd FREQUENTLY EARN the TOP grade.

Thus, I CHOOSE to **NOT** BOMBARD my meticulous MIND with MANY contemptible thoughts. By *DISTANCING* myself from NEGATIVE thoughts, I **DECREASE** my potential ANXIETY.

Since I'm very much an anomaly, my actions are frequently UNusual. I choose not to worry about how different I am what's "NORMAL".

> *"'ANXIETY' is the DIZZINESS of FREEDOM."*
> —**SOREN KIERKEGAARD**, '*THE CONCEPT OF ANXIETY: A SIMPLE PSYCHOLOGICALLY ORIENTING DELIBERATION ON THE DOGMATIC ISSUE OF HEREDITARY SIN*'

Even PRE-injury, I've NEVER gotten SO DIZZY that I felt NAUSEATED. WHENEVER I leave the house, I make SURE to leave a NOTE JUST in case.

(My mom—who HAS a KEY—worries a LOT.)

I ALWAYS leave the SAME message:

"Gone CRAZY.

Back SOON."

NEW > Old

I didn't want to throw IN the towel regarding my EX-fiancée. But, since she REFUSES to SEE or even TALK to me, I'm kinda FORCED to move ON. For my OWN SANITY, I SHOULD try my LOVE luck ELSEWHERE.

BUT, my LOYAL HEART just DENIES my MIND and my MOUTH from even attempting NEW ROMANTIC escapades.

(Since I **BELIEVE** in NEITHER *LUCK* NOR *COINCIDENCE*, I HAFTA WORK for any/ALL NEW *ROMANTIC* connections.)

I **EXCEL** at *NUMBER* of things! But, *getting* **OVER** my LONGTIME belle has, UNFORTUNATELY, **NOT** been one of 'em.

'Tis ALOTTA **EXTRA** WORK to OVERCOME my *INSECURITIES* and UN*successful ROMANTIC* **ATTEMPTS**, and KEEP my head held HIGH.

(The two moves SEEM **CONTRADICTORY**. But, REGRETTABLY, I apparently know next to NOTHING about *LOVE*.)

ACCLAIMED writer Henry Miller said that the *BEST* way to *get OVER* a woman is to *turn her into* **LITERATURE**. Sooo, I'm TRYING to *VENT*.

SSSSSHHHHH!

*"The SECRET to CHANGE is to FOCUS **ALL** of your ENERGY NOT on FIGHTING the OLD, but on BUILD-ING the NEW."*
(—SOCRATES)

Can't I do BOTH?!

(NEED I REMIND y'all of my TALENT for *MULTItasking*?!)

More specifically, I feel especially encouraged **every instant** I need to urinate! First off, just the fact(s) that my urinary system still **works**, and I don't need a catheter is awesome!

Mainly, though, I *loooove* the fact(s) that—as of ~my 25th birthday—I could *walk*, with a walker assist **and a** caregiver nearby, to my *handicap accessible* toilet, lean onto the handrails, stand and urinate kinda like a semi-functioning **man**.

Since *my accident* somehow really stimulated my *libido*, my ONCE commendable social *APLOMB* has deteriorated to constant AWKWARDNESS.

Shit Does Tend to Just Happen

IF I were to SUM up ALL I've LEARNED about 'MULTI Variable CALCULUS' into ONE BROAD/GENERAL/INSTRUCTIVE sentence, it'd be:

ALWAYS account for variable *CHANGE*.

> *"I think the saddest people always try their hardest to make people happy, because they know what it's like to feel absolutely worthless, and they don't want anyone else to feel like that."*
> **—ROBIN WILLIAMS**

(I wholeheartedly **agree** with the comedic legend!)

I wouldn't wish my current situation on my worst enemy!

In the middle of chaos, there **is** opportunity.

When you're as *low* as you *have been/can get/*as i am now, there's really nowhere to go but *up*.

(Metaphorically and for **me**, literally)

I may be an asshole at times. But, I do not/will not treat people badly. I treat them accordingly.

What goes around comes around, like the flu. As an obviously devout advocate of karma, I'm desperately trying to *drown myself* in *cascades of* **positive** *qi*. I've had entirely too much of a bad aura **fully** encompassing my last ~8.56 years, that there's gotta be some kind of **terrific** comin' to *balance* out all the **awful**!

I'm *far too* scientific to **care to** *dabble in* the theological realm of strictly *faith* and *beliefs*.

Then again, *sitting alone* is infinitely better than *standing around* people who don't value you. Thus, I've gotta surround myself with positive, optimistic and creative people.

I *feed off* the energy given off by my peers around me. I shan't lie: my *peer pressure* influences me more so now than it did *in my previous life*. Pre-accident, I **was** very independent and stubborn. I'm still very *thick skulled*. I'm just nowhere near as self-sufficient.

(AUDIBLE sigh[1])

As the Chapter title (LITERALLY) SUGGESTS, *FECAL BOWEL OUTPUT* occurs on OCCASION. It's GREAT that my MIND can SEMI-*control* my **REGULARITY**. (PARDON the *lavatorial* PUN.)

I never *get the urge to go '#2'* with visitors here, 'cuz I feel it would be ridiculously rude to leave guests to entertain themselves! So, but, I occasionally *clench my anus too tight for too long*. If I wait at least three uneventful days between

Bowel BOMBS/*Fecal* FESTIVITIES/Excretory EXPLOSIONS/

Poop PARTIES/*Shitshow* SHENANIGANS, then my nurse(s) will recommend my *ingesting* some medicated *bowel* **stimulant** to try to initiate some *excretory action*.[2]

No, I am **not** some nasty weirdo, just 'cuz regardless of how **cruddy** things are goin' (like now), I always **walk out** of *'mi baño'*, after I *drop a repugnant* **deuce**! I'm just happy, 'cuz my much maligned digestive system actually *performed* **accordingly**! Sooo, why not **further** my joy with a steady/triumphant jaunt back to *work*?!

---

[1] I realize I type "AUDIBLE sigh" often. but, it's more as a *dialectic tool of* **emphasis** in my writing. I tried *sighing* the other day, and 'twas surprisingly difficult! DAAAMMMN! My gastro intestinal *innards* are really **askew**!

[2] Many of my tasks/movements are executed *automatically*. I mean, I've brushed my teeth for so long, that it's not something I hafta really concentrate to do. I've developed commendable muscle memory, 'cuz of my affinity for *trial and error* and repetition.

7.
WHY DON'T MORE PEOPLE *FLOCK TO* ME?!

DESPITE MY NUMEROUS SETBACKS of incalculable suffering, i remain chipper and upbeat, cheery and optimistic, receptive and generous, kind and helpful, funny and social.

I like a wide spectrum of assorted topics from *math and science* to *movies and sports* to *swimming and Beirut* to *stories and jokes*. I'm a (really) smart dude. But, I don't have the slightest *clue* as to why no one will talk to me.

I have an *inkling* that I, unknowingly, *scare* folks **away**. People are naturally scared of what they don't understand. Contrary to what the cocky dolts claim, no one *could* "know how (I) feel"! That may be my biggest *pet peeve*: faux empathy.

For instance, when I close my eyes to better concentrate on biologically *sending* neurological *impulses* to my legs to move, but nothing happens. So, I'll slam my fist in frustration. Then, an observer says, "Aaawww. I know how you feel." In my head, I'm sarcastically thinkin', "Uuummm. No, you don't."

There's a ***ginormous*** difference *feeling with* someone (empathy) and just *feeling for* someone (sympathy). Approximately 99.8643% of y'all **can** communicate your sorrow to me. While a ridiculously **small** amount (~0.1357%) **can** express your shared/identical hardships.

When I was *pledge master* of my fraternity way back in the spring of 2007, a *pledge* complimented me by telling me:

"Your voice is so calming yet convincing, that I interpret it as a unique *blend* of Bono and Moses." *The jury's still out* on whether the guy was just trying to **avoid** more beer. (Regardless, I gave him a *high five*, and I finished his *tasty beverage*.)

A major frustration of (only) mine is an inability to *voice my thoughts*. Yes, I'm very much **trying** to improve my *speaking*. I just need **patience** and an impressive *handle* of verbiage, as I tend to unintentionally *speak* via letter board *over my companion's head*. But, I'm WORKIN' on my INTELLIGIBILITY, ENUNCIATION and TONE VARIANCE. (THANKS, SPEECH Therapy.)

And, regarding my *stilted* language, i try to *cater to my audience*. I try to *smart it up*, when I'm *shootin' the sh*t* with my mom or with my speech therapist. I use little known big words (like *exsiccate*[1] or *concrimination*[2]) with them to impress and amuse 'em.

This necessary *voluminous* vocabulary somewhat explains my delayed messages and seeming hesitation.

With such a plentitude of *free time* now, I devote my energy to what I do best: **enlighten** and **amaze**.

---

[1] to ROUSE someone from SLEEP
[2] JOINT accusation

8.
WHICH IS IT?!

IN ALMOST **EVERY** ONE OF **MY** *predicaments*, there are MULTIPLE options for HOW I can resolve[1] the situation. USUALLY, I'll almost instantly HAFTA make a *RAPID fire* decision, and *live WITH* the CONSEQUENCES and REPERCUS-SIONS.

Ergo, I've kinda *TRAINED* my mind and my body to *accept CHANGE* while remaining *open to* ADAPTATION. I make ALOTTA **IMPORTANT** decisions that affect ALOTTA **IMPORTANT** people (7 employEEs as Business OWNER, ~20 students as *Martial Arts* INSTRUCTOR, 1,000+ viewers as inspirational BLOGGER). So, I try to *steady MY ship* through the **TUMULTUOUS** *winds* and **UN**stable *waters* of LIFE.

CONVENIENTLY, I earned the *MILE Swim* merit badge at Boy Scout summer camp in North Carolina. I doN'T recall the exact # of laps I swam in an OLYMPIC sized pool OUTDOORS. BUT I have an *INKLING*, 'twas either 72 or 76 laps.

(Or, MAYBE 78?!)

Since my *Traumatic Brain Injury* WIPED OUT most of my MEMORY,

my FAVORITE boy band is

'One DEMENTIA'.

(Ha ha HA! The group name SOUNDS like the ACTUAL music group, *'One DIREC-TION'.*)

---

[1] (PHONETICALLLY:) *resolve*, meaning 'to come to a DECISION about; to DETER-MINE'. 'Tis NOT *re solve*, meaning 'to compute AGAIN'.

73 > 1729 (?!)

WHY? HOW? 73 is the 21st prime number. Its *mirror*, 37, is the 12th prime. ITS *mirror*, 21, is the product of multiplying 7 and 3. In binary 73 is a palindrome, 1001001, which backwards is 1001001.

While 1,729 is ONLY the smallest number expressible as the sum of two cubes in two different ways, known as "the Hardy–Ramanujan number".

$$(1729 = 1^3 + 12^3 = 9^3 + 10^3 .)$$

Do I ALWAYS listen to everything my *leg trainerS say*, OR do I accept the **FACT** that I AM an **ANOMALY** of the PHYSICAL and MENTAL nature(S)?!

I'm goin' with Choice *B*.

Each and every morning, I *WALK* to my (MAIN) bathroom to *relieve my bladder* after ~1/28th of the WEEK (6 NIGHTLY SLEEPING HOURS/168 WEEKLY HOURS)

(It's MAYBE been ~*a quarter CENTURY or SO*, since I last *WET myself*. While *WALKING*, I GAUGE how *RESTED* I'm feelin', in order to *GUESSTIMATE* **WHEN** I should get UP to *OFFICIALLY* START my day. (It's ALWAYS sometime BETWEEN ~7 am and 10 am.)

(UNofficially/PRIOR to my day *BEGINNING*, I've ALREADY checked my schedule, my email, my SPORTS teamS and *EATEN* **TWO** meals.)

As I AM BOTH a **NIGHT OWL** and a **MORNING GUY**, I **COULD** get UP relatively EARLY. BUT, after inspecting my day's PLANS, I'll usually REST *in BED* for as LOOOONG as POSSIBLE (USUALLY 'til ~10:00 am), before my *WALK* to 'mi cepillo de dientes' ('brush my teeth').

MY days may SEEM UNeventful, 'cuz I caN'T DO much on my OWN, and I still TIRE WAY too QUICKLY. My stamina WAS EMBARRASSINGLY LOW POST-accident at FIRST. But, THAT (MINIMAL) self-*awareness* may JUST be present, 'cuz I've LOOOOONNNGGG *held such HHHIIIIIGGGHHH standards for MYSELF*—PHYSICALLY AND MENTALLY—that NOW I'm just NOT USED to *SETTLING* for LESS than the BEST.

CHANGE is TOUGH but DOABLE. 'Tis practically INEVITABLE. (EXCEPT for natural *anti-gravity*)

After both my Internet and cable *shut OFF* one day, I realized that I *write* everyday as my OWN attempt to REgain memories. Since *my DREADED accident*, I need ORDER, *ROUTINE* and *REPETITION*. Thank goodness I'm so, so, SSSOOOOOOO *LEFT* *brained*: POST *July 6, 2008*, I can still do **MY** *thing*—exemplary advanced mathematics. And, that gives me tremendous joy.

IF I were more *RIGHT* *brained* in my interests, and I liked music (at ALL), then I'd be unbearably MISERABLE that I can no longer play the piano or the saxophone ('cuz of my *MAIMED* hands).

'Tis NOT often. But, you've gotta be READY! Ya see, *when LIFE gives you something* *that makes you feel AFRAID, you HAFTA recognize it as an opportunity .to be brave!*

There's monumental difference between (CHOOSING to be) SMART and (CHOOSING to be) SCARED.

Be ALL you CAN be!

Ya Know, Just 'cuz I Am Super Smart (Most of the Time), Doesn't Mean I Can't Act Stupidly (Some of the Time)

Yes, I DID have a very DISTINCT and ADMIRABLE youth—both ACADEMICALLY and ATHLETICALLY. BUT, I STILL do NOT incorporate ALL the *lessons* I've *LEARNED* into each and **EVERY** task I have.

Even though I AM *QUICK* witted, THAT would take *FOREVER* *and a day*. 'Twas a *painful* realization some ~five years ago, that MUCH of my academic AND athletic BRILLIANCE *stems from* my MEMORY—NEURAL and *MUSCULAR*.

Well, since CURRENTLY my memory recollection kinda sorta *sucks*, I HAFTA rely ON my muscles a LOT. Since my RANGE of MOTION is STILL rather DESPICABLE, my *WORK* here CAN be LIMITED. Thus, I COMBINE the two *IMAGES* to *CREATE* a form of *Paralyzed* but *Active Neurological Dance Always*. Sooo, my UPPER body Trainer will occasionally yell to/at me:

"Do the *PANDA!*"

It's PARAMOUNT in my personal agenda to do as much as I can SANS Caregiver.

ONE of the MAIN reasons WHY I doN'T go OUT as MUCH as I **SHOULD** is I *WORRY* that MY *SITUATION* with my *EVER PRESENT* and *HELPING* Caregiver acts as a ***THIRD*** *wheel*.

That MAY PARTIALLY be WHY I'm STILL *SINGLE* and **LONELY**.

No. No. No. NO! I've GOTTA take RESPONSIBILITY for my **OWN** actions or LACK thereof.

Now that I REALLY THINK about it, I do NOT consider myself to be THAT competitive. I just have a **STRONG** DESIRE to be the BEST.

(AUDIBLE sigh) *Bein' a* ***HERO*** is THANKFULLY **NOT** a FULL time job. Hell, it's **NOT** even a *JOB*, 'cuz to ME, just the term *JOB* has a slightly NEGATIVE connotation. And, what's BAD about *bein' ADMIRABLE and INSPIRATIONAL*?!

CONVERSELY, since *bein' HERO-esque* is more a HOBBY, I doN'T get paid FOR *my Recovery WORK*. That's more for me.

9.

Visual Clues Tend to Trigger Memories

'VE LONG TAKEN **GREAT PRIDE** in my 24+ YEARS of *Martial Arts* RANKS, WINNINGS, LESSONS and TECHNIQUES. But, I NOW feel maybe MORE **ACCOMPLISHMENT**, when I WATCH a (CHILD) *'Karateka'* CORRECT himSELF/herSELF.

It's NOT like I am NO longer NECESSARY to TEACH! I think I'm MORE of a *TEAM player* NOW with MUCH **NEEDED** HELP, than I WAS PRE-accident. It's just now, my *DynaVox* assisted words are more helpful for the students than are my strikes or kicks. I can no longer *lead by EXAMPLE.* Thus, I can only hope that my *diction* on my speech generating device (*DynaVox*) is powerful enough to ring **TRUE** for the *Karateka*.

I mean, BACK in my PRIME, I didN'T **FORMALLY** have an **ASSISTANT** Instructor (*'Sempai'*). NOW, I have TWO.

Well, they're still NOT *FORMALLY* **MY** *assistant*S. Based on our LOOOONG history of working TOGETHER PRE-accident, they just HELP me *out of the GOODNESS of their HEARTS.* (PRE-accident, I kinda SEMI-coached 'em into becoming the WRES-TLING phenoms they ARE.)

So, ANYWAY, I'll FREQUENTLY **WATCH** the KIDS in class *perform* a "PRE-ar-ranged SET of FIGHTING movements, or *'kata',* and notice a LOGICAL, INTUITIVE tendency. I'll think, as a smile of great PRIDE *CREEPS* across my face: "Heeey, I

TAUGHT that to *him*."

I'll occasionally visit my old high school to watch the WRESTLING matches. FIRST off, I've always gone with a BUDDY, 'cuz I'm SOCIAL and KNOWLEDGEABLE of ALL the rules.

(I've gone to FOUR matches with SEVEN friends in TWO seasons.)

SECOND, it's ENCOURAGING to see three of MY ol' WRESTLING teammates are now ASSISTANT coaches. And, MY ASSISTANT coach is now the HEAD coach. Wow, *(CHUCKLE)*, it sure IS reassuring, when the Coach is YELLING ANNOYING— but HELPFUL—*TIPS* to OTHERS.

:)

I'm happy that I'm, at least, CLOSE to good technique. If I were a *LOST cause*, then Coach would just sit back, and shake his head in silence.

Also, I'm a QUICK learner. Thus, I watch ALOTTA SPORTS PARTIALLY to TRY to *VISUALLY stimulate* my **muscle MEMORY**.

(I doNT ALWAYS *PHYSICALLY MIMIC* the movements, 'cuz my IMAGINATION's so VIVID. But, it HELPS.)

When friends tell stories of OTHER people, I'll LISTEN INTENTLY. But, to be PO-LITE, I'll MAINLY just kinda *SMILE and NOD*. With **PEOPLE**, I've gotta SEE LITER-ALLY the subject, 'cuz SADLY that's ALL my LIMITED brain will ALLOW. I am entirely too *visual* a *learner*, an *observer*.

Seemingly Indestructible Barriers

I've encountered COUNTLESS OBSTACLES, from VERBAL (doubt, criticism, and put downs) to PHYSICAL (muscle atrophy, lost flexibility, and brittle left hip) to NEURO-LOGICAL (BRAIN to Muscle MIScommunicationS, temperature hypersensitivity and a LACK of empathy) to PSYCHOLOGICAL (CONFIDENCE LACK in TRYING NEW things, SUBpar MEMORY, and CONSTANT FRUSTRATION at my FALL from COORDINATION GRACE).

On TOP of THESE TWELVE VAGUE, but SPECIFIC, INTERNAL *hurdles*, I also have the AUDITORY SLEIGHT of a *LACK of SPEECH COGENCY*, which only ADDS to my *GERMINATING* frustration!

I **DO** unfortunately become LESS speedy and MORE critical and SELECTIVE with my DICTION/*word choice*, when I DO speak.

Nonetheless, I am NOT and NEVER have been one to back down from a *fight*.

I couldN'T HELP but NOTICE that withIN my twelve LISTED (BELIEVE me, there are MORE!) *weaknesses*, CLOSE to ZERO are MENTAL!

(OTHER than my SUBpar memory)

THAT just further *ILLUMINATES* my *uniqueness* as a *Traumatic BRAIN Injury* SUF-FERER: ~86.47% of my MEASURABLE injurIES are NOT *MENTAL/COGNITIVE*.

I Like to Think My Shit Don't Stink

ACTUALLY, as a METAPHORIC interpretation, I kinda HAFTA be SOMEWHAT COCKY. So MANY BAD events have occurred within my last ~8.48 YEARS that I kinda HAFTA *adopt* a SEEMINGLY COCKY persona to *push me THROUGH* to the *semi-HIDDEN REWARDS*.

Y'all might MISTAKENLY THINK it's OVER confidence, ONLY if you didN'T KNOW me at ALL.

In a more LITERAL sense, my *excretory OUTPUT* actually sometimes DOES *stink*. Furthermore, I can infrequently smell my nurse's subtle, good perfume. Slightly more regularly, I detect the scent of my *Arctic Fresh* antiperspirant.

My NASAL nerves ARE (FINALLY) startin' to REdistinguish certain *WAFTS*:

My *FECAL excretions/BOWEL deposits/POOP parties* are actually MORE discernible the MORE SOLID they are.

I am NOT *FULL of MYSELF*. I just LOOOVE how AWESOME I AM!

HONESTLY/CLINICALLY/BIOMEDICALLY/PSYCHOLOGICALLY, I NEED to MAINTAIN a HIIIGH level of CONFIDENCE in ORDER to WITHSTAND and even-tually OVERCOME my CONSTANT *OBSTACLES*!

In lieu of my JUDICIOUSLY/*RIGHTFULLY* awarded, MONUMENTAL MATERIAL wealth, I'm givin' BACK to the community.

I co-TEACH kids *Martial Arts* classES.

I've DONATED chairs and paintings to the LESS fortunate.

Granted, I AM *singing' my OWN praises*, 'cuz 'tis *I*. But, SUMTHIN's GOTTA be done FOR those who STRUGGLE to *VOICE their RESPECTIVE thoughts*! I *write* partially to demonstrate the potential of said "UNDERprivileged."

I've Gotta Get Me More O' That

Since PHILOSOPHY is, essentially, JUST Verbal MASTURBATION, am I some sort of a *SICK*, PERVERTED VOYEUR?! (I SHUDDER.)

Well, MAYBE I'm JUST *SICK*. **MAYBE.**

I FEEL that I am REASONABLY/LEGITIMATELY/RESPECTABLY CREATIVE, **PARTICULARLY** SINCE my INFAMOUS accident. Since I caN'T TEMPORARILY **WALK** around, I MUST devise OTHER modes of transportation, communication and entertainment. I decided I **NEEDED** a form of LONG-distance TRAVEL to and from my various commitments (*Martial Arts* class, GYM trips, BANK trips, MOVIES, groceries, DATES).

(SNICKER CACKLE)

THANKS for FINDING and *EQUIPPING* my VAN, Uncle Randy!

My BEST buddy of 28+ YEARS created a *letter board* to allow me to **COMMUNI-CATE** my THOUGHTS, REQUESTS and **NEEEEDS.** (GENIUS!)

(His name is Grant Christopher Engel— he is my Illustrator and my *Yoda*)

For ~9 hour a week DAY and ~12 hours a weekEND day, I'm *STIMULATING my CU-RIOSITY and JOY and ATHLETIC MEMORY* by researching random STOCKS and FRIENDS' activities and SPORTS *goings on* online.

However, I'd GLADLY **JUST** *twiddle my THUMBS,* IF I could FIND a FEMALE compatriot! As I was researching cooking info for one of my OTHER bookS, I read that the typical life cycle of a **taste bud** is anywhere from 10 days to two weeks. Then, they **DO** grow **back.** So, that's encouraging. I have taste buds. They're very few now. They're sparingly found. But, they're there.

OCCASIONALLY/FREQUENTLY (2 days a WEEK), in speech therapy, I will practice ingesting small bits of food. I'll actually SENSE the chicken OR fish (SALMON) I EAT via MOUTH **AND** assorted CONDIMENTS I try in addition to the cinnamon rich pudding or applesauce.

(I *SENSE*—NOT **QUITE** *TASTE,* but my THROAT or NASAL passage *FEELS* it—the *SWEETNESS* of the KETCHUP, the *SALTINESS* of the *French's* MUSTARD and the *SOURNESS* of the *Grey Poupon* MUSTARD.)

10.
LOSERS QUIT WHEN THEY FAIL

WINNERS FAIL until they succeed.

(hence the term, *trial and error*)

I've *tried* countless times to open my left hand fully ~every other day for the past ~three+ years.

(Actually, it **can** be *counted*. 'Tis 558 times)

I'm makin' progress.

My "hard times" began continuously on July 6, 2008. That has made me "strong"er. In turn, I've adapted to my (current) *physical status* to better "contrive good times." I've grown to accept my *handicapped status*, and I try to rejoice with peers regardless. However, I've realized that *all good* must come in **moderation**.

Thus, I deliberately **limit** my "good times" to maintain my *good karma* and 'cuz I am **not** a "weak man." bad drivers are the "weak men" who "construct (more) hard times." thus, I shouldn't *go buck wild*.

I am no longer *mobile* enough to kinetically *maneuver around* various problems. However, I have become less stubborn and more accepting of my occasional *incorrectitude*. Therefore, I've developed a different perspective when *confronting* my various problems.

With patience and pride, I continue to *give 110%* in/to all I do. Despite my frequent *misfires, i* continue to *hold my head up high. Rome wasn't built in day.* I accepted the fact looong ago, that unfortunately, I **am** very physically handicapped. But, why can't I im-**prove**?!

All my medical *doctors* said, "(I)'ll never be more than a nonfunctioning *vegetable* let alone that I'd *live*." But, that pessimism does not mean I should *hold any truth to that* opinion as **ironclad**. I've been habitually proving *naysayers* dead **wrong** for the past 23+ years.[1] So, why stop now?! If anything, I'd have thought that now's the time to start *playin' by my own rules*!

Technically, I'm the *Chief Operating Officer, Chief Financial Officer, Production Manager, Chief Executive Officer* and Founder of MY **OWN** SUCCESSFUL business—a Home HealthCare and Therapeutic facility.

I proudly and responsibly *wear many hats*!

Since, regrettably, I do not go out and socialize as much as I would like, I do need a *marketing manager* preferably a female.

I work harder than mickey mantle's liver did the night his Yankees won the '51 world series.

(Mantle was a NOTABLE *BOOZE hound*.)

---

[1] Ever since I was correctly multiplying two digit numbers—in my head (Sooo, ~age 8)

11.
I'm Still Experimenting

T

IS MAINLY in/along the biophysical *realm*, as i am supremely confident in my *mental* logic and *cognitive reasoning*. 'Por Ejemplo', at least three different times a day, I'll gauge my biokinetics, stand alongside my walker, *walk to* my toilet to stand and urinate into my toilet.

While standing, I'll attempt to *drip/drop* **two** *wads of saliva* (spit wads) into the toilet water, before I start *streamin'*. In order to do so, I've gotta begin my *trek* at the first signal of necessary oncoming urination.

(if worse comes to worst and I don't *evacuate my bladder*, then i got some good *walking* practice in there.)

I try to *walk* as much as I can—before fatiguing at home.

As one of my *resolutions* for 2017, I *decided* that I'd like to go out to see at least four different movies in 2017.

(I'm counting my seeing *rogue one* in late December of '16 as one.)

To periodically *test* my nasal nerves, I sniff my deodorant, before I apply it.

(What would *arctic chill* smell like? Can I say it *"smells* **cold**"?! Is that legitimate?!)

'Twas very encouraging, when I *nasally detected* a smell change from my *bowel excre-tions* to my *lavatory air* **freshener**. Granted, I could only identify a *nasal difference* not specify the *scent*. It's tough to explain. Somehow, the two tingle differently along my nasal hairs.

But, hey! It's a *start*.

To periodically *test* my taste buds, I close my eyes and try to taste the food in my mouth during *speech* therapy. I try to will my taste buds into *action*! I'm only semi-tasting the chicken **or** salmon. But, as a pleasant surprise, I'm really gettin' alotta *condiment taste!*

(Sweet ketchup, *zippy French's* mustard, salty *'Grey Poupon'* mustard and lemon, tangy Italian dressing)

Order of easiness to detect *taste*—from easiest to toughest:

'Grey Poupon' mustard, Italian salad dressing, ketchup, French's mustard

Plus, I'll further *examine* my taste by—only some mornings—swallowing some of my excess saliva, while I brush my teeth.

Inevitably, I swallow a minute amount of toothpaste with my saliva.

(I do not know/recall the exact *taste* of *peppermint*. But, I did feel this tingly sensation of kinda *bitterness* on the back middle of my tongue.)

Sometimes (read: "often") I like to display my *gift(s)* as *ice breakers*. When I'm in an uncomfortable situation (like at a social gathering of strangers), I'll resort to an *area* that is more *within **my** realm* (like comedy or math).

'Por Ejemplo', as my dentist *cleaned* and *inspected* my teeth, I exclaimed, "isn't it **great** that in my (I stroke my *goatee*, as I calculated.) 11,590 days alive, I've never had a cavity?"

She giggled and countered by remarking that "(I) have *shown* three of four 'wisdom teeth', and there's no sign of #4. Soooo, you're not quite as wise as you could be!"

I chuckled, 'til I understood the *playful jab* and then frowned.

If you're at ~68 degrees Fahrenheit (20 degrees Celsius), and you're somehow traveling ~343 meters per second (~1125 ft/sec = ~767 miles/hr to Americans) (that's the speed of sound), and you try to scream in terror, could anyone hear you?

I would. Since my *accident*, i can just *sense* **fear**. My phenomenal hearing detects heavier breathing. My improved vision *reads anxiety in your eyes*. My astounding quantification calculates your *numbers of worry*. Thus, my phenomenal deduction reasons your *disquietude*.

My *cocktail* of various *(medicinal) vitamins and nutritional supplements* stimulates my hair growth and nail growth. Plus, there's one **drug** of *extra lactulose*, as needed.

I recently decided, post-*accident*, to try to learn *"hexadecimal language"*. To test myself, i researched the translation to convert the words,

"My name is Altan Javit Kaynatma."

It's the following:

"4d 79 20 6e 61 6d 65 20 69 73 20 41 6c 74 61 6e 20 4a 61 76 69 74 20 4b 61 79 6e 61 74 6d 61 2e."

(I can kinda follow the symbolic reasoning. I prefer letters.)

Did Curiosity Kill the Cat?

Since I am not a fan of neither felines **nor** *life termination*, I'll focus more on the incessant questioning and overall uncertainty. That's kinda what I now **do**.

Gone is my *know it all* attitude and extreme confidence. Instead, I've realized just how little I really know *sans* my previously near photographic *memory*.[1]

: (

If it's any consolation, my logic and reasoning have actually increased. Since my mind naturally operates in mathematical/scientific terms:

As my *muscle memory* **de**creases, my *neural compensation* increases. Thus, my *biophysical self-awareness* increases, which, in turn, amplifies my *emotional stability*.

(The two senses are *inversely* proportional.)

(It *is somewhat* of a "consolation"! Somewhat)

In simplified terms, oddly enough:

My *psychological happiness* **can be** indirectly related to my *muscular familiarity* but directly related to my self-*learning*.

Explanation:

I can **find** some emotional contentedness in my new/unfamiliar *physical ventures*, 'cuz I'm learning more about my own *physical* potential and limits.

Conversely:

My *psychological* happiness **can be** *directly* related to my *muscle retention*, 'cuz I **can be** pleasantly surprised by/with this new *kinetic success*.

Obviously, I'm **always** *testing* new hypotheses as to my *physical* potential. Undoubt-

---

[1] ACTUALLY, I **HAD** more of an *EIDETIC* memory. "Eidetic" relates to detailed visual imagery used to comprehend. But, the FACT that ONLY ~2 **to 10%** of CHILDREN aged 6 to 12 display symptoms of an *EIDETIC* memory again highlights my sophomoric thinking as a 23-year-old adult.

edly, there **will be** numerous unsuccessful trials along my journey. But, please don't consider me a failure.

My Mesmerizing Mind of Mastering Mathematical Magic Summing With My Surreptitious Scientific Supremacy (Sorta)

Alliteration aside.

Subconsciously, everything, to me, can be quantified. Not to brag, but I *see* the fifth root of 3,125.[2]

I know not how or why my mathematical puppetry has remained so prevalent and *tip top* in my much **injured** mind! I mean, I *have an inkling* that the areas in which I was most comfortable remain as virtues—only to a lesser extent. I can now only visualize Martial Arts.

But, that hypothetical pleasantry *soothes* my ever worrying nerves. Despite my currently not being **able to** neither spar nor wrestle, I still recall tons of techniques, moves, and principles.

I've LONG been a *MATHemagician*—from nerd to prodigy to wizard to MIRACULOUS **SUPER** DWEEB.

Thankfully, the thought of **pretending** to **not** be a *quantitative whiz* never crossed my mind! I relish bein' *that guy*—ANNOYING numbers guru who yearns to correct anyone!

Ambivalence

Y'all couldN'T tell just by *studying* my facial features, but I'm constantly torn between *JOYOUS PRIDE* and *MELANCHOLY LONELINESS*. I'm amazingly PROUD of MY death defying recovery. Yet, I'm deeply saddened that I STILL **LACK** a FEMALE compatriot with whom to share my happiness.

I'm ALSO both frustratingly peeved yet optimistically hopeful, that I can and will develop some external emotional expression. I am sad, for example, when someone accuses me of "NOT caring", SIMPLY because I doN'T shed a tear after hearing her heart breaking story of misfortune.

Even though I LOVE co-teaching—or even just viewing class—at my dojo, my insides

---

[2] = 5

burn with the DESIRE to demonstrate my TEACHINGS. However, I DO experience a WONDERFUL feeling of accomplishment, when I witness young *'Karatekas'* applying my techniques into their sparring.

Plus, it's great that MY *'SempaiS'* (2) are very competent.

My close chums almost always ask me, if it's okay that they eat in front of me.

BLESS their hearts!

I've trained my mind and my heart and even my discombobulated stomach to allow and even ENCOURAGE their eating near me. I like to *live VICARIOUSLY* through their mouths.

When standing BEFORE I start walking, I'm usually torn *between* WHICH leg I should step with first: LEFT foot, 'cuz my RIGHT foot is LOT more stable as a *body AN-CHOR* OR RIGHT foot, 'cuz my RIGHT foot is a stronger step?

12.
DON'T BE FOOLED BY APPEARANCES

SOME OBJECTS **MAY** be more than what they seem.
At first glance, I may APPEAR completely helpless, 'cuz I'm in a wheelchair, and use a *letter board* and speak via electronic device (DynaVox).

'Au *CONTRAIRE!*' I'm *WALKING* with a walker or cane more and MORE. I ONLY use a *letter board* to increase MY *Intelligibility/Time Efficiency* AND to maximize my ENERGY output.

(I tend to tire rather quickly.)

But, my endurance is improving admirably!

Don't *JUDGE* a *BOOK* by its *COVER*.

There's a fine line between insubordination and evolution. I LOOK decrepit. So, don't mistake my struggleS for independence as misbehavior. Let A.J. 3.0 evolve mentally, physically and psychologically.

PRE-accident, I was more academically, athletically and romantically *STABLE* than ~96.07%[1] of my peers. POST-accident, I've *SLIPPED* to ONLY ~77.61%.[2]

---

[1] My age at time of accident *x* # of students *below me* in graduating class of '03 *x* my (informal) # of black belts *x* length of romantic relationship in years (at the time) / 27,000 (just 'cuz I am so, so, sssooooo random)

[2] My age at time of writing this *x* lowest % above average *x* (informal) # of black belts

(I'm TELLIN' you: so much of my intelligence came from my spectacular memory! Now that THAT's GONE, I'll just HAFTA settle for my STILL spot-ON LOGICAL reasoning.)

Must I alter my clothing and accessories?! I hesitate, but ultimately, drop the thought, for not all heroes wear capes.

I've JOYOUSLY accepted my (NEW?) occupation as Doubt Disprover. I get a GREAT feeling of JUSTIFICATION, when a HATER finally recognizes MY correctitude.

Journey or Destination?

Post-accident, I've been constantly torn as to WHICH is the **MORE** VALUABLE of the two: the journey or the destination?

MY analysis is very **DEPENDENT** upon the activity I'm doin' THEN:

— ROMANCE → DESTINATION

(Since I'm currently SINGLE, I'm referring to the NOW. Once I'm IN a relationship, then it's all about the JOURNEY.)

- Martial Arts class → JOURNEY
- NEURAL state SINCE T.B.I. → DESTINATION
- PHYSICAL state SINCE T.B.I. → JOURNEY
- POOL usage → DESTINATION
- SOCIALIZING → JOURNEY
- ROMANTIC partner → DESTINATION
- Ensuing ROMANCE → JOURNEY
- Marriage → DESTINATION

As a result of my various trials and tribulations, I've learned that 'tis **FAR**, far better— psychologically—to ENcourage rather than to DIScourage.

---

involved in my Martial Arts' lessons x length of romantic relationship in years (at the time) / 27,000

13.
I AM A
DRAMATIC INTERPRETATION OF...

MANY, **DIFFERENT** FILMS, as I have a rather *ECLECTiC taste* in film. Actually, I have a pretty WIDESPREAD appreciation in MANY *areas:* SPORTS, *Martial Arts,* Math SUB-topics, Food (to EAT **PRE**-accident), Ingredients (to COOK **POST**-accident).

Off the TOP of my head, I'd HAFTA say that **MY** story could DEFINITELY be APPLIED to...

(Use your imagination.)

(I'm just a WRESTLING fanatic, 'cuz of ALL the DETERMINATION, CREATIVITY, Inner STRENGTH and *HEART* the sport REQUIRES.)

PLUS, I was OBSESSED w/an oldER/*more MATURE* woman—my LONGtime EX-belle.

JUST because (I) STUMBLED and *lost (my) way,* doesN'T mean that (I'm) *lost* FOREVER.

14.

I'VE STILL GOT ALOTTA
(FEASIBLE/ATTAINABLE) GOALS

I **TRIED** FURTHERING MY **EDUCATION:** goin' for my *M.B.A.* in graduate school in early to mid 2016. Before my accident, I had attended several classes and done well. Seven years after my accident, I returned to the university to resume my graduate studies with accommodations.

But, psychologically and emotionally, I was not ready to *deal with* numerous obstacles and misunderstandings.

I am still *training in and teaching kids Martial Arts.* I feel a much *greater sense of pride* and *accomplishment* from teaching other students than from gaining my ranks. It'd be *graaavy,* if I could somehow *test for* my *Jujitsu* black belt.

How rare is it for one student to have three different black belts in three different styles of *Martial Arts?!* Well, technically, i currently have a *'shodan'* (1st degree black belt) in okinawan *shoreii ryu Karate,* a *'nidan'* (2nd degree black belt) and a very high brown belt in *'shinto ryu Jujitsu'.*

Veeerrry rare! I **know** for sure of one other person—my (primary) teacher—to possess such a laudable distinction.

Despite my twice a week *teaching,* public *commenting, creating* techniques and *learning,* I dare **not** ask for *rank,* 'cuz that *presumption* is just **not** *done!*

I really want to profit at least an additional 100% on my stock investments.

(Sooo, if I invest $500 in *the market*, I'd like to *come out* with at least $1000.)

I want numerical proof that I **still** know business tendencies.

I've gotta get back *on the* (romantic/*intimate*) *horse!* I *lost out* on a *good* nine years of my early 20s to early 30s (the sexual prime of my life) to this damn *T.B.I.!* Plus, I've gotta find a wife!

(I get too, too, too damn lonely!)

If I were to cleverly/jokingly start an organization, I'd *found* BROZEPH—as an OFFSHOOT of *HICCUPS.*

(*B*rainy

Yet *R*ambunctious

and *O*ptimistically

*Z*any

and *E*nergetic

*P*hysically

*H*andicapped

...

*H*andicapped

*I*ntelligentsia

Who're *C*urrently

*C*rippled

*U*nder

*P*hysical

*S*tress)

We/I CURRENTLY have only ONE *member.* But, we/I ALWAYS accept *APPLICA-TIONS.*

15.
IF ONLY THERE WERE A FAST FORWARD BUTTON... ON MY LIFE

UP UNTIL JULY **6**, *2008*, my life had **been** rather kickass. But, that was then, and this is now.

On one hand, my past 3,100 days (July 6, 2008-december 31, 2016) have been worse than **miserable**! I *lost* my legs, my voice, my fiancée, ~86.38% of my friends, a fraction of my unbridled self-confidence.

On the other hand, 'tis how I **react to** the setbacks that determines how **successful** I am. As a direct result of said *catastrophic*, life ruining, nearly *life ending* car crash, I have developed quite a few admirable *qualities*:

— I have newfound respect and admiration for the determination, *strength* and resolve that wheelchair *dependent* folks *hafta* have!

— Out of necessity, my mental *processing* is phenomenal! (*i juggle* coordinating my workers' schedules, organizing my daily activity schedule, responsibly monitoring the stock market, *balancing my MOM's checkbook* and designing *Martial Arts* techniques ALL in my head!)

— I've DEVELOPED a BETTER understanding of the *principles of Jujitsu*.

— I've LEARNED 'tis VERY unhealthy to *base MUCH of MY HAPPINESS upon SPORTS outcomes.*

— I've been INSPIRED to *write MY UNorthodox TALES*!

- I've *STRENGTHENED* the PRIDE and JOY I feel when TEACHING!
- I've *SHARPENED* my Business MANAGEMENT skills.
- I've *WIDENED my SCOPE* of BIOKINETIC applications of my studies.
- I've *DEEPENED* my SYMPATHY for how TIME consuming NON-home jobs are.

16.
WHAT MAKES ME TICK

INSPIRED **BY A RECENT** RE-viewing of the CLASSIC film *Dead Poets Society*, I'd declare that the *Four PILLARS* of **A.J.'s** integrity are *CONSISTENCY, PRIDE, RESPECT* and *TENACITY.*

I've gotta (**repeatedly**) correctly select *the path of least resistance* in order to better conserve my limited energy. Since I don't like change, I'll determine an ideal procedure for any *everyday task* through *trial and error, store* the *step by step* in my notably **still** commendable *muscle memory, file* it in my varying *levels* of *need to know*, then reapply on a *consistent* basis.

I've gotta take great *pride* in/of all I've accomplished. Yes, most of my injuries are *physical*, so I'm an *anomaly*. But, it is a *Traumatic Brain Injury*. So, I'm bound to experience some **mental** disabilities.

(I have almost exclusively stored 'em in my *memory files*.)

Thus, I really enjoy ol' friends' visits, 'cuz they tell stories of *yesteryear* in hopes of possibly *triggering* some sort of memory.

I've gotta show tremendous *respect* for my friends, family, peers, teachers, students and employees.

I've gotta remain *tenacious*, as I *weather* my **ups** and (seemingly constant) **downs**.

I personally measure **success** by how one reacts to the tough times.

I very much enjoy eating *meatloaf*—by mouth now. But, back when I could taste, I was not a fan of the non*specificity* of the term. (although I loved my mom's *ham*loaf.)

So, I *took a short, informal thinking test* for fun and curiosity ~8.48 years after my accident. It revealed/concluded that I'm "~75% left brained and ~25% right brained". So, apparently, I'm "analytic, rational, objective, symbolic, mathematical, digital and orderly"

With trace amounts of

"instinct, art, emotion, imagination, creativity and music."

The following week, my *NeuroPsychoTherapist* tested my personality and thinking, yielding (*not so oddly*) similar results.

She rightly wanted to concentrate on decelerating my harsh reactions, increasing my patience and participating in fun group activity.

My response after her test analysis:

"Doc, we have vastly **different** interpretations of 'fun': you encourage me to go out, and audit a film class at a local college. I remark that I'd rather stay home, and create math problems or parody songs or design Jujitsu techniques. You roll your eyes, and chuckle. To each his own."

Game. Set. MATCH. Kaynatma.

17.
DO *AS I SAY*... AND KINDA *AS I DO*

I **THINK RATHER HIGHLY OF MYSELF**. But, there's an *astronomical* differ-ence between *extreme confidence* and *annoying cockiness*. I possess (alotta) the former. I must be careful to not appear overly *confident*, as **over** confidence can *breed* an un-impressed or blasé attitude, which would likely cause people to *overlook me further*.

My *sickly* good hearing allows me to rarely *miss* a *beat* in active conversation not in musical lyrics. Admittedly, I had zero musical inclination whatsoever before my accident. Only afterwards did I discover my penchant for lyrical construction and love of poetry.

I am very, very, **very** *left brain minded/oriented*. I focus my thinking almost entirely on *language, logic, critical analysis, numbers and reasoning*.

My *weakened* nerves prevent me from feeling **most** low *levels* of pain. Sooo, there are really only two *degrees* of my discomfort: *zero/none* or *nine/ooowww*! There ain't much of a *middle ground*.

(Not to seem too *hardass*, but I just **don't feel** much pain anymore. I've had broken bones and botched surgeries pre-accident. But, one of my many injuries must've been a severed pain receptor to my brain, 'cuz I rarely feel any minute discomfort.)

Often times, I'll be greatly uncomfortable. But, my pride and inner *push* do not **let** me stop *trying*!

It's kind of a *package deal*:

With an unrelenting **zeal**, comes inevitable *degrees* of fatigue.

18.
GOTTA DRESS TO IMPRESS

EACH MORNING, I MAKE SURE to select my outfit to match my day's activities. Sooo, if I'm goin' to the gym, I'll wear a loose fitting shirt and my tighter shoes (to prevent my left ankle from *rolling*).

If I'm having *speech therapy*, I'll wear a shirt with a *linguistic* pun on it. If I'm goin' to Karate class, I'll wear a black t-shirt[1] under my '*gi*' ('*Karate uniform*') to match my belt.

Dress for the job you want, not for the job you have. My *Martial Arts* professor actually asked me to wear my '*gi*' to class, 'cuz I'm "a teacher, who must be **respected**". When I first returned to class since my accident, I'd dressed *casual* in a t-shirt and shorts.

But, NOW, I KNOW better. It's as if I were *Eric Cartman* from the TV show *South Park*, as my '*gi*' YELLED, "RIHSPEK my *AU-THOR-IH-TAY*!" I *want* to again be a well-respected '*shodan*' on the teaching staff. Since i can't make my '*obi*' ('*belt*') black**er**, I'll settle for *dressing the part*.

Not ALL *HEROES* wear CAPES.

Since I typically don't speak cogently, I like to wear shirts with goofy messages on 'em. I like to express my (comedic) thoughts via my *garb*.

For instance, one GREAT shirt I have says/reads:

---

[1] I then wear my black shirt to sleep. Since I'll too often forget what new day it is '*en la mañana*', I'll see that black shirt, *put 2 and 2 together* and conclude that the day before was Thursday.

"I'm sorry, if I looked like I was paying attention. I was probably thinking about chugging a beer."

I own another shirt that says/reads:

"Now, it's a party!"

(There's a picture of 10 "*Beirut*" beer pong cups)

(I wore **THAT** to my 32nd BIRTHDAY festivities. 'Twas APPROPRIATE.)

NEURAL > CRANIAL

As strong as I am still mentally, (AUDIBLE sigh), I can**not** *will* activities from/by just my nerves.

C'est la vie.

Actually, no! According to stats, *T.B.I.* Victims demonstrate almost all progress within the first three years. Yet, my nerves *play by their own rules.* **After** I left the rehab facility, I *gained* the *neural strength* and the psychological confidence to actually *walk* to my toilet to urinate. Previously, I'd sit in my bed to use a handheld urinal.

Now, my nerves have *strengthened enough* to allow my *trudging* the ~59 steps from bed to toilet, regardless of time.

(I've awoken to courageously *stumble to 'mi Juan'* at ~3:38 am)

My brain and body were very fatigued. But, my (urinary and gastral) nerves will **not** allow me to just lie there and *hold it.*

Often, I cannot remember all/any of the moves in a '*kata*'. Yet, there are sometimes *little twinges* in my legs, as I watch kids spar.

(Yay!)

As brilliant as I am, I cannot explain how or why my nerves and/or muscles **remember** stuff that my brain does **not.**

'*Por Ejemplo*', when I hear the name of the '*kata*' I'm about to watch, I'll try to mentally recreate the *form*—like **who** is attacking me next, **what** *weapon's he using*, **where** is the next attacker, **when** can I safely get away and **why** I'm blocking here. But, unfortunately, (sigh) my *mental imagery* proves unsuccessful. But, my muscle memory *kicks in*, as I attempt to emulate the arm movements.

19.
PSYCHOLOGICAL > PHYSICAL

OFTENTIMES, I'LL FEEL BETTER and more **accomplished** than I can express.

: (

So, I just silently romp in my lonely solitude. (AUDIBLE sigh)

If only y'all could tolerate and comprehend the maniacal and seemingly whimsical soirées goin' on *up in my ol' ticker*. True, sometimes I wanna display my excitement or enjoyment or sadness. But, my *T.B.I.* Said "**not** up in **here!**"

However, occasionally, I'll state things—usually via electronic mail—that i later do not realize I *said*. Unfortunately, 'tis as if I have totally **different** personalities. I'm sincerely sorry to all affected! : (

But, 'tis just that my *T.B.I.* And hyperactive *amygdala*—temporarily—*overcame* my reasoning.

Not only does my stimulated *amygdala* increase my libido activity, but it decreases my patience and increases my rage.

Looking on the bright side, as i try to do, these emotionless facial expressions kinda force me to talk with my mouth, and to try to smile or laugh or cry. I'm gettin' there:

— I WILL smile on occasion.

— I don't really *LOL* (Laugh Out Loud). There's more of an ATTEMPT to smile, followed by some laborious attempts to produce an audible chuckle. My diaphragm does not cooperate with my spontaneous glee. However, the effort involved in making a genuine laughing sound kinda NEGATES the implied happiness I intend.

TRYING to laugh is—inevitably—making me smile more.

:)

It's just that, if I appear fatigued and distracted, then the laughing gesture seems *all for naught.*

During my *shodan* test for promotion, I dislocated my right shoulder. Rather than quitting the sparring section like a **wuss**, I elected to withstand the immense, searing physical pain, to endure the visible shoulder awkwardness for three plus **hours** and to gain the honor and respect as a new *instructor*!

My *Martial Arts* professor asked me on four separate occasions to write and deliver a speech to the kids' class. One was about *overcoming* adversity, and the other described *sparring strategy.* *Professor* liked my *sparring* thoughts so much, that he asked me to repeat the speech for the adults' class.

My inspirational words (summarized):

(#1 –Overcoming Adversity:)

"Life *throws* us many **curveballs**! But, it's how we react to life's changes that determines our *strengths* and our *weaknesses.*

Now, I've always been a defensive fighter. I like to wait for your mistakes. Then, counter and capitalize on 'em. According to sir Isaac Newton, "For every action, there is an equal and opposite re action."

When sparring, I just liked to take the *level* of my *reactions* and *counters* to a greater extent. With hard work, determination and perseverance, y'all can do **anything** y'all set your minds to, as long as y'all conserve and monitor your energy. It's a basic biological/psychological/mathematical equation:

Hope + Determination *leads to* Perseverance, which, when habitually repeated = Eventual Success.

Unfortunately, my endurance is nowhere near as good as it once was. I'm not sure **why**?! (Head nod to motionless legs in wheelchair.) I kid. I kid! (chuckle)

Let's use my many obstacles as examples of *triumphing over adversity*:

Way back when, students at the dojo could not enter the adults' class until at least age

16. But, I worked hard **always**. And, I guess my commitment was evident, because *professor* invited me into the adults' class when I was just 12.

So, always take responsibility for your actions like an adult, and be respectful and grateful to those who help you over your respective hurdles.

Junior year of high school, I was goofin' around and (I make air quotes with my fingers.) "preppin" for a wrestling match, when I fell awkwardly on my right hand. Apparently, the forearm break was pretty serious, as I needed surgery. Well, the surgeon accidently sliced my right ulnar nerve, permanently preventing my ever fully opening my right hand.

I raise my right hand, and semi-move my *mangled* right fingers. Yet, I worked hard to recover and make do. Through determination, perseverance, and a *never say die* attitude, just 11 months later, I had my best wrestling season ever! Why? How?! 'cuz I learned to adapt to my surroundings, and work with what I've got.

Now, on to the next, most obvious *obstacle* (I nod my head downward toward the belt around my waist):

I was driving home from a *black belt workout*, when my tire exploded and shredded. So, I was ejected out of my vehicle.

Anyway, a bunch of medical *doctors* said

'(I) shouldn't even be alive, let alone functioning!' with my '*never say die*' attitude, i persevered. And, I'm still progressing!

WHY? 'Cuz I NEVER *give UP*! JUST 'cuz someone stumbles or loses his WAY, does NOT mean he's lost forever. You've GOTTA maintain HOPE. 'HOPE' is a good thing maybe the best of things.

(#2 –Sparring Strategy:)

Actually, **that** speech involves alotta Japanese and *inside jokes* with the kids. So, I'll spare you the confusion. Just know that *professor* so liked **my** speeches, that he asked me to repeat 'em to the adults' class.

My third and fourth speeches were again autobiographical and meant to be inspiring.

As questionable as my judgement is, 'tis a fantastic feeling when a peer states his/her agreement with something I say!

Usually, my *neuralpsychotherapist* implies her agreement.

I wholeheartedly apologize **if** my tales *tugged at your heart strings and moistened your tear ducts.* 'twas **not** my intention to prompt a *pity party.* I am way too happy an OPTI-MIST to deliberately induce sadness unless YOU first physically attack ME!

20.
GOOD MANNERS ARE JUST INGRAINED IN MY SOUL

THANKS, 'rents!
(Again, *NURTURE >> NATURE*.)
I greatly appreciate ALL the HELP I get with EVERYTHING from everyone with a soul!

In *Martial Arts* class, I get tons o' respect, teaching assistance, admiration and cordiality from my professor, my *'sempai*'s, my students and their parents. So, I try to return the favor twice over. In social situations, I still like to amuse my peers with my rare recollection of television and/or film quotes pertinent to our conversation topic.

In (my) familial company, they've tolerated my shenanigans and ballyhoo for over ~31.68 years. Sooo, I'll look the other way at their minor irresponsibility. With my friends, they may invite me out. Sooo, I'll host a party for them. With my *Martial Arts* peers, I volunteered to coach and *assist* them in their studies and teachings. So, now they are quick to *return the favor.*

(Thank you, karma!)

I instinctively thank anyone who cares enough to help me, if he or she sees me struggling. I.e. One of my caregivers jokingly responded to my (verbal) "Thanks" by stating,

"It's just my job. (Ha ha) I tell you what: every time you thank me for NUTHIN', that's five dollars."

So, I jokingly retorted,
"How 'bout I just sign your paycheck?"
(He chuckled and conceded the argument.)
TIME is NOT *Absolute.*

"Understanding TIME is ESSENTIAL to understanding RELATIVITY."
(—ALBERT EINSTEIN)

Since I've become significantly injured, EVERYTHING seems to have *SSSLLLOOOOOOOWWWEEEDDD down.* Therefore, I need many activities or friends or movies or sports to keep my exceptional mind busy. Otherwise I tend to focus on my negatives.

21.
WHEN THE DAYS ARRIVE, I SHAN'T LIE TO MY KIDS

'LL BE SURE to get my children to *look up* to me. I mean, *'rents* tend to tell their kids anything to shut *'em up*! But, since I know not when—**not** *if*—my **vocal** cords will *re*activate, I'm content with letting my actions speak lessons about pride, determination and tenacity.

I abhor *fakers*, who claim to have some kind of *god-like* control over too many things! We can only affect the situations that we directly experience first-hand. Sometimes, it's fewer occasions than even that.

(i.e. I can't *speed up* my neural **re**generation! I mean, I can **try** to **prevent** most debilitating incidents. But, "*NOT SLOW down*" is NOT synonymous with "*SPEED up!*")

You Can Be (Almost) Anything You Want!

You've just GOTTA **START** by *putting your MIND to it*!

No matter how physically daunting tasks may seem at first, you've gotta **cement** *yourself in* the proper positive mindset!

I **think** there's some o' that thinking in the coach's *pump up* demand of "*get your head in the game!*"

If you tell yourself you're gonna *lose*, then, psychologically, you're just *beatin' yourself*.

I'm very complicated case: I've got so many **why**s, so many **when**s, so many **what**-

have-yous.

To any and ALL visitors, y'ALL would follow *STEP by STEP LEARNING Sessions* with ME:

1. Watch.
2. Watch.
3. Watch.
4. Graduate to OBSERVE.
5. Take DETAILED notes.

Faith in Yourself Is All You Need

I'm certainly not always correct—especially post-accident. But, it definitely feels good psychologically when someone makes the mistake of questioning **my** thoughts in one of my *areas of expertise* (math, biophysics, *Martial Arts*).

Yes, I have a *Traumatic Brain Injury*. But, I still possess knowledge in my *comfort zones*. I am confident enough to volunteer to mentally *balance my mom's checkbook*—repeatedly.

I recently began *taking* a Zyrtec medication to prevent my *production* of so much saliva. After frequently viewing my *Martial Arts* techniques, my *professor* actually asked me to tape an instructional did of **my** *Karate and wrestling and Jujitsu* techniques.

I'm regrettably aware that my appearance doesn't look like much. So, I've gotta try extra hard to prove that I'm **more than what I seem**.

Bodily Transformations

During my initial rehab after my accident, I'd frequently close my eyes while awake, 'cuz my eye muscles would tire quickly. It didn't help that the staff at the rehab facility I was at **sucked** at their jobs. So, I'd frequently hafta busy **myself**.

After I began my self-*therapy* at home, particularly after I started my physical *work* at my leg gym (*NeuroFit 360*), I realized that I now shut my eyes, when I am really concentrating, like during the last few reps of my last set of squats.

This *physical to psychological transformation* has been *confirmed* by my (current) *speech therapist,* who observed that I close my eyes every time I take a bite of chicken or salmon or *scrambled eggs*. I also noted—with said *"speech therapist"*—that I shut my eyes, whenever I actually talk and/or while I chew food.

Then, there's my **supposed** left leg extension. I thought that the surgically added metal in my left kneecap made my left leg slightly longer. But, after my *arms trainer* measured each of my legs per my request, I concluded that my *seemingly* uneven gait is 'cuz I still favor my right leg.

If I *followed the **norm*** of society's *interpretations*, I'd hafta *kick my own **ass***! I was and am both a jock and a nerd. Sooo, my still *functioning* after such a violent and traumatic incident was "because of (my) *mental strength*"(—my neuro doctor/surgeon). Thus, my post-accident life is my dramatic interpretation of the film *revenge of the nerds*.

Considering I *manage* a successful business of seven employees, teach a *Martial Arts* class and occasionally host big social gatherings, I'm very, very, very happy with my being *the **odd** man out*. Thus, I'm a *civilian marine*: "the few. The proud."

Unfortunately, I have not (yet?!) Biogenetically grown **eyes** in the **back** of my **head**. So, I still hafta occasionally look down, as I *walk* only backwards but, this visual vice is merely a lowered glance, as my *psychologic battle* with anatomic physics has directly improved my peripheral vision. Comparatively, *sporadic* head lowerings are way less potentially detrimental than an unexpected downward topple over my dragging feet.

As time *passes*, life does not get **any** easier. Above all, you just get stronger. According to **my** circumstances, **my** life got immeasurably more difficult and more lonesome after my dreaded accident. Yet, I've flourished, 'cuz I've strengthened my arms, my psyche and my sense of responsibility.

GOOD versus BAD

As part of my extensive Psychological Therapy, 'tis paramount that I can identify and highlight my virtues. Additionally, I've gotta recognize and minimize my vices. 'tis very unhealthy to just dwell on all the negatives in my (somewhat) recent life.

PROs
- MATH
- *MARTIAL ARTS*
- CINEMATIC QUOTES

- SPORTS TRIVIA
- ATHLETICISM
- BIOKINETIC APPLICATIONS
- GENEROSITY
- KINDNESS
- RESPONSIBILITY
- BUSINESS MANAGEMENT

CONs

- EX-FLEXIBILITY
- NECESSARY GLASSES
- LACK of PATIENCE
- LACK of EMPATHY
- *ZERO* ROMANTIC LIFE
- NEGATIVE effect SPORT results CAN have on MY mood

22.
IS IT BETTER TO BE FEARED OR RESPECTED?

WELL, 'TIS VERY CIRCUMSTANTIAL. It really depends on what you're doing, 'cuz that'll affect *in what light you're seen.*
PRE-accident:

— As a *Martial Arts* STUDENT, I welcomed FEAR.
— As a *Martial Arts* TEACHER, I sought RESPECT.
— As a WRESTLER, I caused FEAR.
— As an ACADEMIC student, I encouraged RESPECT.
— As the *New Member Educator/Pledge master* of my *Sigma Alpha Epsilon* fraternity, I MAY have instilled SOME FEAR in the hearts of the *little BEASTS.*
— As the LONGTIME *Eminent Chaplain*/FUNNY Man of my fraternity, earned RESPECT.
— As an active SOCIALITE, 'twas a combination of BOTH.

POST-accident:
— As a Jujitsu SPECIALIST, I promote FEAR.
— As a hopeless ROMANTIC, I strive for RESPECT.
— As a perpetual HALLOWEENIE, I AIM for FEAR.

— As an aspiring AUTHOR, I'm promoting RESPECT.

— As an ADMIRABLE host at social LIAISONS, I UNintentionally inject FEAR.

— As an APPROACHABLE compadre for my friends, I TRY for RESPECT.

— As an unorthodox business manager, 'tis an ACCIDENTAL combination of BOTH.

Fate Rarely Strikes at a Moment of Our Choosing

If my accident and resulting injuries were inevitable (uuummm, no.), that catastrophe could not have occurred at a *less choice* time.

I was respectfully coordinating petroleum drop-offs at work. I was commendably teaching *Martial Arts* to kids. I was understanding and thriving in graduate school. I was mutually *loving* my soon to be *fiancée*. I was financially stable and independent.

then, *all **hell** broke loose*. personally, I believe that you create your own *destiny*. Sooo, I must've done *sumthin'* tremendously **good** to offset the horrifically **bad** karma of my disastrous accident! since then, I've been *dismissed from* my *petrol patrolling*, argumentatively *kicked out* of school and tragically and inexplicably dumped by my **ex**-lover! on the plus side, I have *turned my terrible misfortune* into a quite a few **highlights**:

— I've become a very SUCCESSFUL *Health Care Provider* OWNER and MANAGER

— I've restarted and **UPPED** my *Martial Arts* TEACHING and LECTURING.

— I'm designing my OWN *Jujitsu* INSTRUCTIONAL DVD.

— I've REestablished my stock **KNOW HOW** to RIDICULOUSLY **PROFIT** in the STOCK market.

— I've been *PRODDED into* becoming a WRITER in lieu of ALL my *FREE time* and INSPIRING tale of OVERCOMING *hardship*.

However, as much economic success as I *produce*, I'd trade it all in a **second** for romantic **bliss** again.

Occupational Hierarchy

A few of my employees address me as *"boss"*. Now, technically, I **am**, but I don't need or even welcome such an *awkward* title. but, the implied respect from all old**er** employees is nice.

All of my *Martial Arts* students refer to me as *"'Sensei' A.J."* this title feels more necessary out of habit, I guess. I taught 2 to 3 days a week for ~5.25 years prior to my accident.

Personally, I'm very anti formality, as I'm on a *first name basis* with my *Martial Arts* peers, my *therapists* and my trainers. I respect and appreciate all the help I get with everything **not** math related. I know that *iron sharpens iron*. So, I tend to only associate with *good* people.

Live Your Life to Leave a Legacy

Pre-accident my life was (I shrug.) Rather unintriguing. 'twas definitely **not** *humdrum*, but 'twas certainly attainable by ~0.197%* of competent individuals. Rather than *following the crowd* and **staying in line**, I almost always seek to start my **own** *path*. If others decide to *follow*, then so **be** *it*: I'll **lead** by **example**.

Again, one determines another's **success** by *measuring his reactions to life's inevitable disappointments*.

1. My arm surgeon *botched* the surgery on my right forearm by *clipping my ulnar* nerve my junior year of high school. Sooo, my senior year was my best wrestling season with only ~72% of a good right **hand**.

2. My *social awkwardness* of being an **8th grader** in high school put me *out of my element* in academia in 1998. Sooo, I **aced** honors geometry class all year.

3. My family's *economic status* was ~average pre-accident. Sooo, I only applied to one college. I *got in* and *excelled* at *ivy league* penn for four years.

4. I *suffered* a near death experience and resulting *Traumatic Brain Injury* in mid 2008. Sooo, I survived, functioned and even prospered enough to *write* an inspirational autobiography.

Sooo, AM I *"SUCCESSFUL"*?!

23.
BEAUTY IS IN THE EYE(S) OF THE BEHOLDER

A **ND, VICE VERSA.**
It's tough to remain objective, when I'm evaluating my own accomplishments. Only I truly know the intense concentration, strength and flexibility required in order to accomplish any of my daily tasks. But, just to get some alternative perspective, *my doors* are *always* **open** to guests!

As much as I *fear* it, I like to think of (my) *humor* like the *late* comedic legend Robin Williams did:

"(LAUGHTER) is like an **ENEMA** for the **SOUL**."

What may SEEM like a very MINOR task of

INSTANTLY calculating the CORRECT *Scrabble* score after EIGHT rounds

OR

STARTING your *WALKING* with a **RIGHT** footed step

OR

SCRATCHING an itch on your LEFT ankle

OR

Efficiently OPERATING and FUNDING a SEVEN employee MEDICAL business. But, 'tis really ALOTTA **COMMENDABLE** work. for ANY **ONE** person let alone a *Traumatic Brain Injury* victim!

I always consider that, when I'm *scrutinizing* the kids' forms in Karate class. As an observer, I've had several discussions with parents about their child's energetic or emotional disorder. None of 'em are *visible*! But, if you *take a minute* to talk to the kid, you can better understand his or her **hardship**.

24.
"HEROES GET REMEMBERED. BUT, LEGENDS NEVER DIE."

— BABE RUTH, *THE SANDLOT*

I VERY MUCH WANT my name to **never** die metaphorically! I AM The Sultan of (SWAY), The (Tyrant of Trivia) The King of (Coefficients), The Colossus of (Quantitative CLARITY), The (MATH Slambino).

During my *fraternity career*, the younger guys built a table and painted on it was its name:

A.J. Kaynatma Table of Competitive drinking. After my graduating, the *Penn 'Theta'* Chapter of *'Sigma Alpha Epsilon'* renamed an entire room:

A.J. Kaynatma Arena for Alcohol Abuse.

(Obviously, I left **MY** mark on the esteemed *Ivy League* institution.)

My mom to ME: "What do you think of your popularity?"

ME: "I think it's a TERRIFIC *CONCEPT!*"

Re-assurance of Importance

In the movie *Deep Impact*, orders are given that ~*one eighth* of the designated survivors are to be engineers or doctors. since I'm kinda **both** (*Biomedical Engineering* major), I realize just how *coveted* **my mind** is.

(whew!)

It's especially encouraging, when I *talk with* an ol' friend whom I haven't seen in too long. I share my harrowing tales. then, I'm bombarded with exclamations of "wow" and jeez!"

Speaking Like Master Yoda
of *Star Wars* I am

Nearing the end of this unyielding but noteworthy journey I am. Eventually *emerge* so different I **will** with only my name unchanged. Know the vigorous *journey* on which I have been on you do **not**. To hear your *faux* empathy I do not want.

Achieve success, nevertheless, determined to I am. An unorthodox *path* to greatness, I have. *Take it,* I will. Very encouraging, my gym sessions are. Inspire me to **learn** more, my '*Karateka*' do. Much thanks to my *Martial Arts* professor I owe. Of *restabilizing my psyche* a creditable job my NeuroPsychoTherapist is doing. For a female comrade with whom to share my pending joy, I yearn.

Approval, popularity, a Jedi craves **not** these things.

For knowledge and *dih fence* **never** for attacks a **true** *Jedi* uses *the force.*

ME to my (younger) brother: "'When gone am I, the LAST of the (MALE Kaynatmas) you will be' to *carry ON* our name."

25.
I'M NOT *BITTER...*

(Aaahhh, *sarcasm*! Is it?!)

I most certainly do **not** regret my ~five year *relationship* with **Satan's female counterpart**. But, I do take back any and all apologies I felt.

Since she **never** had the metaphoric *ballz* or **decency** to explain her **dumbassedry**, I'll forever refer to her as *my ex, that crazy ass* **bitch**. Perhaps I'm being rather sophomoric for not taking responsibility for *driving her to* **madness**. But, since I've received zero responses to my infinite inquiries as to why she *left*, I'm puttin' all the onus for my psychological *crappiness* on her! I've looong been an academic anomaly with commendable athletic talents. But, her unforeseen and still unexplained *dumpage of me* has completely discombobulated my otherwise *stellar* state of mind.

(AUDIBLE SIGH) She was—no, is—a *nine point six* with extreme psychological *baggage*. I am a *seven point two* with money. *Do the math on that love connection.* But, even with a *"Traumatic Brain Injury"*, 'tis comforting to know that I am way smarter than she shall ever be.

With my HIGH *IQ* (Intellectual Quotient) and LOW **EQ** (Emotional Quotient), 'cuz of *Traumatic Brain Injury* caused lack of empathy, I genuinely fear dying alone.

26.
FEEL PRIDE NOT SHAME

"Instead of being ASHAMED of what you've been through, be PROUD of what you've OVERCOME."
(—DR. PHIL)

IT'S **GOTTA BE** a *SIGN*!

But, WHAT does it MEAN?!

During a *BREAK* from my EXTENSIVE editing, I sought to RELAX my INDE-FATIGABLE mind. 'Twas the EVE of an INFAMOUS historical date—*The IDES of March*. To be more specific, 'twas *Pi Day (3/14)*. 'Twas a Tuesday. So, I'd ALREADY completed my early *SPEECH Therapy*, finished my *UPPER body* workout, practiced PUSHUPS, gone BIKING and took my EARLY shower.

Sooo, I decided to play some *Minesweeper*. 'Twas the "EXPERT" level. So, there were (16 spaces LONG by 30 spaces WIDE =) 480 TOTAL *squares*. Well, I BEAT said *level* in FOUR minutes and TWENTY-FIVE seconds... FOUR consecutive times. Usually, I'd be kinda EMBARRASSED by such a SLOOOOOW time. HOWEVER, I quickly *CRUNCHED the NUMBERS* on my statistics that afternoon, and I was PLEASANTLY surprised to find:

On 3/14, at 1:59 pm EST, I'd beaten *Minesweeper* in 4:05 minutes 4 consecutive times.

Now, the *AVERAGE mind* would JUST see that as CONSISTENT. But, there's so much MORE.

MY stats:

3/14, 1:59 pm, 265 seconds, 4 times.

As a pertinent COMPARISON,

MATHEMATICAL *pi* = ~3.1415926535897.

Since I believe that *COINCIDENCE does NOT exist*, and that *LOGIC and REASON-ING dwarf "LUCK"*, I am FORCED to CONCLUDE that

I am EXCESSIVELY/EXCEEDINGLY/SUPERLATIVELY *MATHEMATICALLY in-clined*.

ALAS!

> *"I'll live NORMAL someday, but I have to do something first."*
> —UFC Women's Strawweight CHAMP Jo-
> anna Jedrzejczyk

That Feeling of Accomplishment

I don't have much—emotionally, psychologically or physically. So, I do experience this mesmerizing *aura* of extreme accomplishment, whenever I have a long *walk* completely with out any *pigeon-toed* steps! It's like the *middle ground* between *~eight cups o' coffee and low-grade cocaine*.

I may not often display my emotions 'cuz I can't, but they're in there somewhere. (I have a *BRAIN/NEURAL* injury **NOT** a HEART/CARDIAL injury.)

Pre-injuries, I kinda *took for granted* just how physically exhausting, emotionally *painful* and just psychologically **tough** *learning* can be. Everything *came so **easily** to past A.J.*, that I became *spoiled*. As a direct result, this *Relearning* process has been particularly frustrat-ing. *A.J. 2.0* lacks the memory capacity to just look at something, and *file it* into his *future storage*. Now, I **hafta** depend on my computer *Drafts*, my Schedule board and my *Care-givers* to remind me of my *smaller tasks at hand*. This trio of reminders is far less impressive to *the outside world*. : (

But, I've come to ACCEPT its NECESSITY., as I **ONLY** NEED to occasionally im-press MYSELF. :)

I HAFTA give a *SHOUT OUT* to my *Yoda*—Grant Engel—who *spat* these WISE words, as I tried to SPEEDILY FINISH my *writing*, **LIKELY** PREMATURELY:

"Your ambition is admirable, but too much of a good thing can work against you."

As he IS *my Yoda*, Grant could *SENSE* my accident on July 6, 2008:

"PAIN. SUFFERING. I feel. Something terrible has happened. Young (Kaynatma) is in pain. TERRIBLE pain."

My mom—between *INTENSE tears*—stammers out: "Oh, he's done!"

Grant, as Yoda: "NOT if anything to say about it, he has!"

27
MY HINDSIGHT > MY FORESIGHT

S HEART**BROKEN, DISTRAUGHT,** CONFUSED and PISSED as I initially **WAS** after *Ms. Belle* INEXPLICABLY *DUMPED* me, I NOW realize that THAT *UP and DOWN* relationship just better PREPARED me for **MY** (eventual) *EVERLASTING UNION* with a **WOMAN** who ACCEPTS me for who I **AM POST-** *T.B.I.*

28.
AFTER MY *BELLE*

M **Y FORMER FIANCÉE** *broke my heart* when she suddenly, and still inexplicably, dumped my already *wounded ass* on April 6, 2012. Technically, we were engaged! Plus, we were living together! So, by **LAW**, I needed to hire more *Caregivers* for more hours (24 7) on a reworked schedule. *Far LESS* importantly, she cost me *mucho dinero*. So, I was naturally very psychologically *TOPSY TURVY* upon learning of this **SECOND** *catastrophe*.

The ONLY good thing that resulted from her leaving was the beginning of my *writing*. Naturally, I started as very agitated, flustered, miserable and **DIS**quieted. But, over the course of the next ~6+ years of *recovery*, I've tried to *COOL my heated temper*. I KNOW I'm a good person. And, I KNOW she's a good person. I mean, barely nine months after we started dating, her new, young**ER** boyfriend (ME) gets in a HORRIFIC, life-threatening car accident that leaves him horribly mangled and comatose. So, *PROPZ to her* for *sticking WITH her heart* after that. Just *in the LONG*-run, we all handle adversity **differently**: Some of us *rise UP* and *"ATTACK the attack"*(—my *Martial Arts* instructor)., while some of us *shrink BACK* and *move ON* to eas**IER**, LESS challenging *work*. I suppose I **SHOULD've** known that she lacks the *BALLZ*—metaphorically AND literally—to *MAN up* to such a test.

But, joking aside, there **WERE** certainly countless good times. U**N**fortunately, I canNOT remember 'em, and she's no longer here to remind me.

: (

So, I'm *stuck with* our last experience together—which is STILL a questionable story due to my **SHAKY** *memory*. But, as *A.J. 3.0* finally concluded, She HAD to have been an amazing woman, because why ELSE would *ORIGINAL* (and GENIUS) *A.J.* have *stayed WITH* her for so LONG?!

As MUCH as I complained, my former *belle* OVERALL produced more **PRO**s than **CON**s in me. After alotta *DEEP reflections*, I've concluded that She was *everything I WANTED in a FEMALE partner*, **BEFORE I KNEW** exactly **WHAT** I *WANT*. So, as MUCH as it *SCARS my HEART*, I now know EXACTLY the type of woman I DO and do**N'T** *WANT and NEED*.

Upon further, and FINAL, review, I'm concluding that my EX-*belle*'s utter lack of concern for her own ambiguity and ignorance drives me to truly NOT care about her highly questionable mindset.

She had umpteen chances to explain and to try to redeem herself, yet she blew 'em all. I'm just stating the facts.

I *operate* in phases:

Soon after first dating her, I loved that I love**D** (PAST tense) her. Then, I really loved that she love**D** me. Shortly after my accident, I hated that she hated me, for I still love**D** her. Now, she just ignores me. Thus, I love that she hates me and vice versa. (AUDIBLE sigh) She brought my antipathy on herself.

AFTERTHOUGHTS

So, if I were to summarize the preceding three volumes into a common *phrase* for which I try to conduct myself, it'd be:

CALM, COOL and **COLLECTED.**

Mentally, I'm pretty much always **calm**, as still not too much confuses me, and I'm confident in my decisions.

Physically, I like to think that I remain **cool** (metaphorically **and** temperature wise) throughout any and all *ordeals*.

Psychologically, I try to keep a *clear* mind in all circumstances. That way, my *thought processes* remain **collected.**

Plus, I like to *take my time* to *gather/collect all my thoughts.* Sooo, it's a deliberate pun.

Furthermore, I've decided that, since I know **not** when ('tis not "if", 'cuz it's definitely **not** *hypothetical!*) my leg nerves will *reawaken*, nor when my vocal cords will *return*, I'm gonna *settle on* being a habitual writer.

If it's any consolation for my lack of *romantic* **success**, I *hooked up* with this beauty called **loneliness**. And, i convinced her to have a *threesome* with **ineptitude.**

Numbers **relax** me. They put my ever processing brain at ease. Sooo, I randomly calculated how much money at least I'd make by age 75 for **not** resuing that terrible tire company:

~$3,213,028 in 43 years. I stated it's *approximate*, because 1) I can't foretell how long I'll live, 2) I can't foresee all of my expenses, 3) the stock market fluctuates and 4) I don't wanna brag.

Life goal for everyone:

Unfuck yourself.

Personally, I'm trying to regain a large **portion** of the *marvel* I once **had** *before* that accident *dimmed* my *fuckin'* sunshine.

I am, metaphorically, a **diamond** *in the rough*. So, my "sunshine"'s more of a *glistening shimmer*, when *tilted toward a preferable light*.

(→ MORE trigonometry)

I'm a "world SHAKER"
(—'COOL HAND LUKE').

I can't help it!

My life is so complicated and extensive, that I can**not** stop *writing*. So, check out my forthcoming 'Confessions of a Quasi Competent *Traumatic Brain Injury* Victim'.

(It's like an *addendum* to my *Memoirs*. It's more updated.)

Ya know what?! I'll VOLUNTEER to be your *H.A.P.P.I.N.E.S.S.*

(**H**andicapped but **A**thletically **P**rofound and **P**rudent **I**ntellectual **N**eeding **E**xtra **S**uper **S**tandards)

According to an interesting fuckin' article in the November, 2015 issue of the educational journal, *language sciences*, people who *curse/swear* **often** are generally smarter than those who fuckin' don't.

I'm so, so, sssooooo *bright* (pun intended.), that I yearn to try to **again** *illuminate* others' eyes to the vivid *wonders* of what I **can** do.

If *ignorance* *is* **bliss**, then why do we seek knowledge?! Personally, I'd much prefer a *deluge* of trivia to a *dearth* of facts, as characterized by my first 23 years.

Someone (much) wiser than myself once said,

"It is how you rise from a fall that truly defines you as a *man*."

I couldn't agree more, considering I am now an author.

My *Book of* **Life** is not over. I'm just hoping to **end** these *chapters* on a/MY *Traumatic Brain Injury* like YESTERDAY.

In further hindsight, I am still mentally **brilliant**. But, emotionally, I've rather *obtuse*.

This *unawareness* negatively affects my sociability.

Ultimately/*in the looong run, the juice will be well*-worth the *squeeze*!

I *write*, when I'm unhappy. But, I become happy, when I *write*.

It's a very self-therapeutic sequence.

As I *walked* to my bathroom to *stand* and urinate, I realized that I'm **now** here for two reasons: to do math and to inspire folks. And, I'm not *seein'* just any numbers.

I'm like a cold sore, in that you'll never know, when I come back.

"I don't have *delusions* of grandeur. I have an actual *recipe*."

(—'Limitless', which **was** kinda like **my** biography minus the drug stimulant)

I **am** a bit of a unicorn in that I'm somewhat *imaginary* and quasi/faux *indestructible*.

The **right** girl **will** *bring out* the **hero** *in me*.

(Scientific semi-joke:)

I'm *LIVING. I OCCUPY SPACE. I HAVE MASS.*

Ergo, I *MATTER*.

Using my extensive *bioengineering* studies, I'd interrogate y'all:

Wouldn't you agree, that a *strep throat* for a giraffe could be lethal?!

Based on the afore reading, a wise *third party* **concluded**—using mathematical jargon—that

"(My) awesomeness level asymptotically approaches infinity."

My (slightly biased) *theory evaluation*: that's *about* right.

As a potential/semi/*faux*/almost *doctor* and semi/*faux* informal *comedian*, I like to **heal** people with laughter. Math and humor are like leukocytes to me: they're just in my blood. ('cuz my father was a mathematics extraordinaire, and my uncle's a professional comedian.)

'Tis more than a *craving*:

I *yearn* for the most **powerful** *mind influence* around *nostalgia*!

Am I **crazy**, or did I just **blow** *your* **mind**?!

Don't feel sorry for yourself. The *greatest knowledge* comes the *oddest places* i.e. A semi-mute with a *Traumatic Brain Injury*.

Relax! In the words of the famed mathematician John Nash in 'a beautiful mind':

"What's the point of being *crazy*, if you can't have a little fun?"

Alas! Everything that has a **beginning** has an **end**.

(Unless we're discussing the classic film *The Neverending Story* and being *painfully* literal)

Speaking of *"ends"*, my ex-*belle*'s never explaining why she **ended** us legitimizes my (seemingly) obvious **conclusion** that she cannot *handle the fact* that a (younger) *Traumatic Brain Injury* victim is way smarter than she will ever be.

My blatant bitterness demonstrates just how *destructive* she was to my psyche.

As I approached *my 32nd year in my travails aboard Earth*, I stressed to y'all as you see me:

Look past the wear n' tear to see the reservoir of charm *underneath*.

(My party guests *got the message*, as I remained Mr. **Popular**.)

I've constantly *told myself* **that** over the last ~8.48 years to motivate myself to *push through* my tough times.

Not **everyone** will *understand* my *journey*. That's okay. I'm *here* to live **my** life, not to make **everyone** *understand*.

I do *whatever* I can, as *hard* as I can, to accomplish as much as I can, for as *long* as I can. Well done, A.J.!

As I *look back* on my **ups and downs**, I've gotta *treasure* the good times, and *forget about* the bad.

(*forgetting* should **not** be a problem.)

In the *poker game of* **life**, I *played a* **ginormous** *hand*, and I **lost**. I'm tryin' to *ante back in* as a writer.

I realize that I kinda date everything in my *writing*.

(My *T.B.I.* kinda forces me to do so. → I need *ORDER* and *numbers!*)

Thus, I've been rushing both my *editor* and my *illustrator* to finish.

But, I've accepted that my *Memoirs* (and all future books) are my *Participation Certificate in a Youth Soccer League*.

(True, I wasn't all that good (timely) at *WRITING*. But, I finished!) At soccer, I was a *BEAST*: feared and dominant.)

So, no more rushing! We'll finish, when we finish. It's more about just the fact that I'm *working* and *functioning*, than it is about how speedy it's accomplished.

GIFTED folks really struggle with loneliness. They start to feel resentment and anger. Since I'm not a mean spirited person, that acrimony *turns inward* and morphs into intense regret and self-hate.

Whenever I encounter a seemingly *indomitable* task (which is frequently), I intrinsically ask myself,

"How *far* am I gonna *take* my *battles*?"

After successfully *completing* said *task*, i answer:

"The question is not how far. The question is, do you possess the constitution, the depth of faith, to go as FAR is as NEEDED?!"

(—*Il Duce*, 'The Boondock Saints')

SSSHHH! IF people KNOW how smart I really AM, then it'll be much MORE difficult to *CONTROL* 'em with my mind.

Initially, post-accident, I set out to only *better* myself via countless physical workouts and constant mental observations. But, *thanks to* my editor, I now *aim to improve society's own self-analysis*. Do I wanna make *history*? No. That's too bold and too vague. I just wanna make a **difference**.

Pre-injury, I was a fighter who knew how to double as an artist. **Post**-comas, I am a (linguistic) artist who knows the basics of being a fighter.

Propz to my editor for *weathering the storm* that **is** my incessant capitalization, ceaseless **bolding**, unremitting *italicization*, excessive "quotation usage" and repeated synonym use.

Additionally, she helpfully questioned my sophomoric slang.

Further **thanks** go to my editor for *pointing out* how often I apologize for my various *peculiarities*. I must be **proud** of my *eccentricities*.[1]

Kudos to my illustrator/computer technician! He knows just how to calm *T.B.I.* maligned A.J. *Kaynatma*, who likes to refer to himself in the third person, by stating,

"This is not something that getting angry will fix. But patience and cooperation will."

As an incessant optimist, I **assure** y'all that *the best is yet to come*.

(WAIT and *SEE!*)

---

[1] ALSO a mathematical term

Plus, evidently, I have **much** to say!

Though I may have completed *writing* this book, the *Book of My Life* will **never** *close*: I *aim to* continue to *touch* people well after my *days* **end**.

I am drastically and severely *bent* but definitely not **broken**. In a way, my volatile psyche is (like the fantastic film) *unbreakable*.

I'm living proof that *the mind is a* **terrible** *thing to* **waste**.

After my life has ended, and all my accomplishments and adversity have been *weighed*, I cannot help but wonder: will I be remembered? If so, how? As a math virtuoso? As an impatient employer? As a respectful teacher? As a forgetful *handicapee*? As a kind hearted friend?

I *aim to* make myself known as a persistent **battler** and as an unrelenting *obstacle hurdler*.

"Success is not final, failure is not fatal: it is the courage to continue that counts."

(—WINSTON CHURCHILL)

I **was** great (past tense). Now, I am determined to **re**establish my *strength*.

(pause to allow my ginormous ego to catch up.)

The fact that I can admit, teach about and even joke about my painfully debilitating *Traumatic Brain Injury* is courageous and commendable.

The movie *Psycho II* confirmed that, after his rehabilitation, only others' provocation can and will restimulate one's craziness. Ergo, I surround myself with honest, understanding, easy going people.

So, I was sittin' o'er my toilet, just waitin' for my *anus to explode* (true story!), when I got to *thinkin'* **musically** (how odd!):

"Gettin' BETTER"
By A.J. Kaynatma
"Dealin' with a *T.B.I.* can be quite exclusive.
I know too well.
I try so hard, everyday

To gain some respect.
No notable results yet.
After a decade, I'm writin' books as a way to *vent*.
WALK and TALK are my ultimate goals.
Somehow, I did not forget my *Biophysics*,
Which I apply in my workouts.
Get. Gettin' better.
It's gradual progress. It's not obvious to *outsiders*.
Get. Gettin' better.
It's gradual progress. It's not obvious to *outsiders*.
NOT too late to improve.
Just gotta find my legs' groove.
Ev'rything's gotta have ORDER! *Math's* IN *music*.
I'm gettin' better, doubters.
Gettin better. YEAH!
I'm gettin' better, doubters.
Gettin better. YEAH!
Dealin' with a *T.B.I.* can be quite exclusive.
I know too well.
There are plenty o' times I get ridiculously lonely.
Just *suck it up* and *push through*.
Lately, I'm SEEIN' improvements and FEELIN' more!
I won't *give up*.
Now I've gotta be quite a BIT more obvious,
Because you ALL can't see my thoughts.
Get. Gettin' better.
It's gradual progress. It's not obvious to *outsiders*.
Get. Gettin' better.
It's gradual progress. It's not obvious to *outsiders*.
NOT too late to improve.
Just gotta find my legs' groove.
Ev'rything's gotta have ORDER! *Math's* IN *music*.
I'm gettin' better, doubters.
Gettin better. YEAH!
I'm gettin' better, doubters.
Gettin better. YEAH!
I'm gettin' better, doubters.
Gettin better. YEAH!
I'm gettin' better, doubters.
Gettin better. YEAH!
I'm gettin' better, doubters.
Gettin better. YEAH!

I'm gettin' better, doubters.
Gettin better. YEAH!"

My own mother doesn't understand my resilience. She asks me: "why do you have such **perseverance**? Such **determination** despite so many *obstacles*?"

My response: "Because I **choose** to."

This is the end!

(Of my *writing* for this book)

Alas! 'tis also the beginning!

(Of my new life)

P.S. After **aaaaaalllll** I've been through, during my extensive editing, I decided that after my (eventual) death, I'd like to donate **my** brain to science. It'll be a *reeeeeal eye opener*!

P.P.S Since the details and intricacies of just how COMPLICATED and unprecedented my mind really **is** are so extensive, please also read my coming *"Confessions"*.

Even the life-notes of strictly mathematical A.J. Kaynatma are somewhat indeterminable.

(A.J.'s memoirs' length = 314 pages, pi = ~3.141592653589792384 ...)

Printed in Great Britain
by Amazon